The Life of
ELBRIDGE GERRY

With Contemporary Letters to the
Close of the American Revolution

Volume II

BY JAMES T. AUSTIN

DA CAPO PRESS • NEW YORK • 1970

A Da Capo Press Reprint Edition

This Da Capo Press edition of
The Life of Elbridge Gerry
is an unabridged republication of the first edition
published in Boston in 1828 and 1829.

Library of Congress Catalog Card Number 77-99470

SBN 306-71841-3

Published by Da Capo Press
A Division of Plenum Publishing Corporation
227 West 17th Street, New York, N. Y. 10011

Manufactured in the United States of America

THE LIFE

OF

ELBRIDGE GERRY.

With Contemporary Letters.

FROM THE CLOSE OF THE AMERICAN REVOLUTION.

By JAMES T. AUSTIN.

BOSTON :
WELLS AND LILLY—COURT-STREET.

1829.

DISTRICT OF MASSACHUSETTS, TO WIT:

District Clerk's Office.

BE IT REMEMBERED, that on the first day of January, A. D. 1829, in the fifty-third year of the Independence of the United States of America, Wells and Lilly, of the said District, have deposited in this Office the Title of a Book, the Right whereof they claim as Proprietors, in the words following, *to wit :*

" The Life of Elbridge Gerry. With Contemporary Letters. From the close of the American Revolution. By James T. Austin."

In conformity to the Act of the Congress of the United States, entitled " An Act for the encouragement of Learning, by securing the Copies of Maps, Charts and Books, to the Authors and Proprietors of such Copies, during the times therein mentioned ;" and also to an Act, entitled, " An act supplementary to an Act, entitled An Act for the encouragement of Learning, by securing the Copies of Maps, Charts and Books, to the Authors and Proprietors of such Copies during the times therein mentioned ; and extending the Benefits thereof to the Arts of Designing, Engraving, and Etching Historical, and other Prints."

JNO. W. DAVIS,

Clerk of the District of Massachusetts.

ADVERTISEMENT.

THE continuation of the Biography promised in the first volume is now submitted to the public;—sooner indeed than was then intended—but in deference to the opinion of many whom the author did not feel at liberty to disregard.

BOSTON, MASSACHUSETTS,
JANUARY 1, 1829.

CONTENTS.

ERRATA.

Page 21, note, for *cong.* read *conv.*
Page 83, 18th line, for *disunion* read *discussion.*
Page 104, 5th line, dele *the subject of.*
Page 227, 17th line, for 1748 read 1798.
Page 279, 15th line, dele the semicolon after the word *forgotten.*
Page 307, 29th line, for *for* read *from.*
Page 328, 8th line, for *mass* read *Massachusetts.*
Page 399, 6th line, for *show* read *shew.*

THE LIFE

OF

ELBRIDGE GERRY.

————◆————

CHAPTER I.

*State of the country........Convention at Annapolis.........At Philadel-
phia form a constitution of government for the United States........
Details of its progress.*

A FORMER volume has recounted the agency of
this distinguished citizen in the service of his country, from the dawn of the revolution until after the
peace of 1783. It closed at a period when retiring from the scenes of his former labours, he was
entering on new engagements in private life, with
the honours of a well earned popularity, and the
richer treasure of domestic happiness.

The relaxation then allowed him was hardly interrupted by a place in the house of representatives of Massachusetts, to which his fellow towns-
men immediately elected him on his return from
the congress of the United States, as a mark of

their affection and respect.* But the habits of his life were too strongly interwoven with the public interest to render him an indifferent spectator of political affairs, which notwithstanding the cessation of hostilities, were not less alarming than during the most disastrous periods of the war.

The government of the United States had a merely nominal existence in 1786. Foreign powers beheld its weakness almost without disguising their contempt. They seemed to be guided by a belief, that, altho' the relation of the colonies to Great Britain had been nominally dissolved, there was a natural inability in a people to preserve the forms of self-government, and that a period of anarchy would place the spoils of freedom within their reach, or that the new nation would revert to its former dependence, chastened and humbled by the wearisome and useless exertions it had made.

The condition of things at home presented the same gloomy appearance. The authority of congress had fallen from its original dignity. It was manifest that it could not long compress or direct the separate power of the states, whose conflicting interests threatened every day a dissolution of the confederacy. The high personal character, which had once constituted the principal sanction

* Congress having passed a resolve for appointing commissioners to settle with the contractors of the army, the office was conferred on Mr. Gerry, but he declined accepting it.

of its measures, was departing from its councils.
The statesmen of the revolution, dissatisfied with
its imbecility, had mostly retired to other departments; the few who remained were unable to preserve its original energy. Some of them honestly
believed that its vitality could not be prolonged,
and that patriotism might permit it to expire, in
the hope of evoking from its ashes a spirit of higher
capacity and power.

MR. KING TO MR. GERRY.

NEW-YORK, JAN. 7, 1787.

My DEAR SIR,

Congress is not yet organized, and it is uncertain when it will be; the anxiety and dissatisfaction still continues, which has for some time existed, concerning the government of these states.
God only knows what will prove the issue. It is
most certain that things will not long continue in
their present condition if foreseeing the dangers
which hang over us, we do not unite in measures
calculated to establish the public happiness; I am
confident that no man will be able to bear up
against the calamitous events, which will otherwise force themselves into existence.

You have seen the Virginia law for the appointment of delegates to a convention in Philadelphia
in May; Gen. Washington, Mr. Wythe, Randolph,

Madison and others are appointed for this convention. Pennsylvania have appointed Mifflin, the two Morris, Fitzsimmons and three others on the part of that state ; Hamilton, who is a member of the assembly of this state, will exert himself to induce them to send members ; Jay and others are opposed to the measure, not alone because it is unauthorized, but from an opinion that the result will prove inefficacious.

General Washington will not attend, although there will be at the same time and place a general meeting of deputies from all the state societies of the Cincinnati. If Massachusetts should send deputies, for Godsake be careful who are the men ; the times are becoming critical ; a movement of this nature ought to be carefully observed by every member of the community.

I beg you to be assured of the constant friendship of

Your's sincerely,

RUFUS KING.

Hon. Mr. Gerry.

Among the most obvious causes for the embarrassments and distress of the country was the condition of its commerce. In separating from Great Britain, the United States had become with regard to that country a foreign nation, and could not expect an exemption from her navigation laws,

at least without conceding an equivalent, which
there was no general authority to regulate or prof-
fer. The importance of the American trade had
been felt both before and during the war of the
revolution, and it readily presented itself to the
statesmen of the day as an instrument to be used
for the securing of reciprocal advantages with the
commercial countries of Europe. It was therefore
determined to take such measures as would place
this great interest under one central power, who
should direct it for the general good, and a convention for this purpose was projected to assemble
at Annapolis in Maryland. Delegates were accordingly appointed by several states, to convene
there on the first Monday of Sept. 1786; and Massachusetts authorized "Lieut. governour Cushing,
Elbridge Gerry, Francis Dana and Stephen Hig-
ginson to meet such commissioners as might be appointed by other states of the union, for the purpose of considering the trade of the United States,
of examining the relative situation and trade of the
said states, of considering how far an uniform system in their commercial regulations might be necessary to their common interest and permanent
harmony, and of reporting to the United States in
congress assembled such an act relative to this
great object as when agreed to by them, and confirmed by the legislature of every state, will enable the United States in congress assembled effectually to provide for the same."

In this cautious manner was the first step taken
to establish a government of authority over the separate states. But the measure was evidently too
limited and inefficient for the purposes intended.
The commissioners from Massachusetts viewed it
in this light, and severally declined accepting the
appointment, and the delegates of the few states
who assembled at the time designated, did little
more than give currency to a conviction that a
radical change in the organization of the government would be necessary for its safety.

A project was gradually maturing to hold a
general convention in Philadelphia, with extensive powers and ampler duties.   In Massachusetts
a rebellion had broken out against the local government, and the rebels had resorted to arms.
The utmost energy of the civil and an expensive
exertion of military power was required to suppress
it.   The danger of such a state of things, and the
practical illustration of the doctrine, that a government strong enough to execute the laws was demanded for the personal security of the citizens,
turned men's minds more seriously to the duty of
providing such stability as should prevent the lawless repetitions of outrage.   The character of the
state was elevated by the firmness and decision of
its constituted authorities, and an argument deduced from these circumstances for providing the same
useful power for the emergencies of the nation.

MR. KING TO MR. GERRY.

NEW-YORK, FEB. 11, 1787.

MY DEAR FRIEND,

I congratulate you on the favourable situation of the government in the western counties; Lincoln has undoubtedly answered the most sanguine expectations of his friends, and indeed I confess has accomplished, by the aid of warrants, what I did not apprehend could be effected in that cautious manner of proceeding.

The declaration of the existence of a rebellion will do great honour to the government, constitution and Massachusetts. I can already mark good consequences in the opinions, which it authorizes relative to our vigour and spirit. I feel myself a much more important man than I was in the humility of a few days past.

I hope the most extensive and minute attention will now be paid to the eradicating of every seed of insurgency; remember however that punishment to be efficacious should not be extensive; a few and those of the most consequence should be the victims of law. Do you attend the legislature? How will they stand on the plan of a convention at Philadelphia? For a number of reasons, although my sentiments are the same as to the legality of this measure, I think we ought not to oppose, but to coincide with this project. Let

the appointment be numerous, and if possible let
the men have a good knowledge of the constitutions and various interests of the several states,
and of the good and bad qualities of the confederation.

Events are hurrying us to a crisis ; prudent and
sagacious men should be ready to seize the most
favourable circumstances to establish a more perfect and vigorous government.   I hope you will be
at leisure to attend the convention.   Madison is
here. I presume he will be preparing himself for
the convention ; you know he is a delegate for
Virginia ; he professes great expectation as to the
good effects of the measure.

    Farewell,   R. KING.

The articles of confederation, which feeble as
they were, yet formed the only cord of connexion
between the states, did not seem to authorize a
general convention of delegates without the advice
and consent of the United States in congress assembled.   In some parts of the country their approbation was not deemed indispensable, in others
the movements of the local legislatures were retarded by a deference to the only authority, which
had even the semblance of a control over national
affairs.   Popular feeling soon gave a suitable direction to congress, and on 21st February 1787,

they resolved, in pursuance of the provisions of the confederation that a convention of delegates, to be appointed by the several states, be holden at Philadelphia, on the second Monday of that year, " for the sole and express purpose of revising the articles of confederation, and reporting to congress and the several legislatures, such alterations and provisions therein, as shall, when agreed to in congress and confirmed by the states render the federal constitution adequate to the exigencies of the government and the preservation of the union."

This act of congress gave all the legality, which the existing forms of government required to the proposed assembly, and a convention was formed at the time and place appointed in the resolve by delegates from all the states of the union, excepting Rhode Island. Sixty-five persons were elected members of the convention. Of these, fifty-five attended its sessions. Six of them had affixed their signature to the declaration of independence in 1776. Among the others were the most distinguished names on the merit roll of the country, and at their head the illustrious leader of the American armies, who again lent the weight of his high personal character to secure with the fortress of civil institutions, the liberties he had protected through the vicissitudes of war.

The legislature of Massachusetts, on the 10th of March, appointed to the honourable and responsible trust of representing its interests, and the common interest of the union in the convention at Philadelphia, Francis Dana, Elbridge Gerry, Nathaniel Gorham, Rufus King and Caleb Strong. The great importance attached to the duty is demonstrated by the imposing weight of character selected for its performance.

The convention being organized, Edmund Randolph, formerly governour of Virginia, on 29th May, proposed for consideration fifteen resolutions, as the groundwork of a constitution, and Charles Pinckney of South Carolina offered a draught of a national government in sixteen articles. These several propositions were referred to a committee of the whole convention, and formed a text for debate.

The august tribunal to whom this important subject was intrusted, was the first in the history of mankind in which a great and free people had undertaken by their representatives to establish the principles and forms of civil government. Its members brought to the mighty task a rare spirit of patriotism and unimpeached integrity. But their situation was wholly without precedent. Questions presented themselves which philosophy had never attempted to solve, nor experience, that better teacher in politics, been called upon to decide.

The same intelligence and ability of mind and the same honest desire to promote the common good, might from education or habit or local situation reason very differently on topics, which this convention were called to decide. As the condition of affairs, which rendered some modification of the existing government necessary, was traced to one or another set of causes, so unquestionably would be considered the propriety of erecting a new building, or endeavouring to repair the tottering fabric, which had become wholly unsuited to the times.

Among the delegates in convention were many, who had been practically sensible with what limping steps the measures of congress had proceeded in the days of revolution, and how imperfectly its want of authority had been aided by such auxiliary motives as could be brought to bear on the people. They had felt the wastefulness and ruin produced by the negligence or the obstinacy of those, on whom the government were obliged to rely without the power to command. They had beheld the army at one time almost disbanded, because there existed no coercive power to fill its ranks; and famishing and freezing at another, because there was no lawful way of appropriating to its use the resources of the country. They had seen the credit of the country exhausted in war, when yet it was rich in those means on which credit might properly be based; and in peace they had found commerce languishing, industry paralyzed, and the character of the nation degraded, because no concentrated power could direct its natural spirit of enterprise, or arrange with its rivals a fair competition in proportion to its means. These members might naturally enough consider the weakness of the public arm as the cause of general distress, and be expected to place their dependence for future prosperity only on a government strong enough to secure obedience to its will.

On the other side were many among the delegates at Philadelphia, who in the appropriate walks of civil life had first been called to withstand the encroachments of established authority ; who had commenced their labours in the public service by investigating and explaining the rights of the people in opposition to the claims of the government ; who had learned as an axiom in politics, that power, by its own appropriate energy, however obtained, or by whomsoever possessed, will increase and extend and perpetuate itself ; and tracing to this principle all the misery and desolation of the recent war, and all the sufferings and sacrifices, which had been required to bring it to a close, might very reasonably entertain a jealousy of every depositary of political power and rely for the security of public liberty on the inability of invading it.

With too little power in the government, it was obvious that neither independence nor tranquillity could be preserved ; with too much, a battery would be erected hostile to liberty. Where was the exact point in which the advantages of authority could be realized without its dangers, and freedom preserved without the hazard of anarchy? On this great question the records of history were silent; the memorials of former ages were those of licentiousness or despotism. Rulers and people were so constantly in conflict that hostility between them seemed an unavoidable condition of human society.

On such a debateable field it is not surprising that the members of the American convention could at first find no neutral ground. In addition to the difficulties already enumerated others existed in the condition of the country, scarcely less perplexing. The delegates who assembled were representatives of sovereign states, met together in confederacy, each of whose members was equal to either of the others. In its integral character, each state exercised all the powers of an independent political body, and the new sovereignty, if one was to be created, could obtain no other authority than what was shorn from these separate parts. But the equality existing among these parts was that of rights, and not of strength. They differed among themselves in territory, population, wealth, physical and moral resources, and in whatever other means of advancement one people could have over another. If a contribution to the common head was to be made in proportion

to the relative condition of the parts, they would
retain after the existence of the new government,
all their original inequality, and the smaller having
an inferior share of power, could not be expected
very cordially to accede to the plan. If any other
principle was adopted, a sacrifice would be exacted of the larger, in which it was against all the
analogies of human conduct to expect they would
readily concur.

Concession and compromise became therefore
indispensable; but whatever is thus produced,
though it may have the support of all, rarely possesses the approbation of any.

When the common good is to be purchased by
individual sacrifice, he whose former rights are
curtailed finds it often very difficult to realize that
he has received an equivalent in exchange. There
will naturally be a struggle to make the substrac-
tion as little as possible, and a reluctance both in
demanding and yielding, which may destroy the
beneficial purposes of the original design. The
inconvenience of this state of things was fully felt
by the delegates at Philadelphia.

A question of authority early presented itself
for the consideration of the convention, and might
by one form of decision have been fatal to the
hopes of the country. The resolve of the continental congress authorized the assembling of delegates for the sole and express purpose of revising the articles of the confederation and reporting

amendments. The commission to the Massachusetts members, and to all others appointed by a
state legislature under the operation of this act,
expressly or by necessary implication confined
their authority to this exact object. The members from Virginia and some others had been appointed in pursuance of the recommendation made
by the former convention at Annapolis, independent of any resolve of congress, and were not
therefore absolutely bound by its terms. Notwithstanding this difference, was it not the expectation of the whole people that the confederation should be revised merely and not destroyed;
that amendments should be made to the old system and not that a new one should be formed,
and would the adoption of either of the plans proposed conform to the authority of the delegates?

This question, which is not without plausibility
on either side, was of primary importance in an
assembly which could not consistently begin a system of free government in an act of usurpation, or
expect the confidence of the people while they
transgressed their authority. It was seized upon
with masterly skill by some members of the convention who found that the majority were likely
to adopt a system, which they could not approve,
and who hoped by the practice of legislative tactics of this sort to defeat what they could not in
any other way successfully oppose. But the con-

vention was rather a committee to advise, than a senate to decree; they could only recommend, they could not enact; and however limited might have been the request, which their constituents made of them, no harm could be done by submitting to the deliberation and good sense of the community what the authority of the people, and not the acts of the convention must afterwards legalize in order to give it effect.

If the authority conferred by congress or by the several states on the convention at Philadelphia, extended only to the proposing of repairs in the old edifice, it is fortunate they were bold enough to disregard the strict letter of their duty in a fair execution of the spirit of it, and instead of propping up the disjointed and crazy building to commence that splendid architecture, in which safely reposes the liberties of their country. In deciding thus to do, the division was not made by the line, which finally distinguished the different parties. All the members from Massachusetts were in the majority.

When these preliminaries were settled, the way was yet hardly opened for the successful prosecution of the grand design. Another question presented itself not connected with any difficulties of detail. It was, whether the new constitution should establish a federal or a national government; that is to say, whether it should act upon the states as states, or upon the people composing the states in their individual capacity of citizens. This important question was not only to be decided prior to all arrangements about the powers or form of the new government, but it entered so intimately into every part of the system, that it was a constantly recurring cause of dissension and debate.

The propositions of governour Randolph, or as they were commonly called, the Virginia plan, avowedly constituted a national government, but the tone and vigour of the government was to be raised or depressed, not more by the degree of power to be given to it, than the manner in which its power should be deposited. Whenever that part of the Virginia plan was under consideration in which these points were presented, great contrariety of opinion among the members was alarmingly made manifest.

The discussions, which these important and conflicting subjects excited, occupied the convention until the 15th June. During this period the disposition of the members was in a good degree developed, the advantage of concerted action was apparent, and the union thus produced began to establish something like the lines of party. The courteous and conciliatory temper with which the session commenced, though sometimes infringed in the ardour of debate, still maintained its influence among the members, while difficulties in the way of any satisfactory conclusion began to present themselves in a manner, which it was feared compromise could not remove.

In this stage of the convention Mr. Patterson of New Jersey offered a series of resolutions proposing what he considered a plan of government strictly federative, in contradistinction to that already discussed, which was supposed to be wholly national.

These resolutions resulted from the consultations of members dissatisfied with the schemes hitherto debated, and by way of distinction were called the Jersey resolutions. In the forms of proceeding, according to the rules and orders of the house, they were moved as a substitute for the plan of Virginia. The differences between the two were principally the following : The Virginia plan proposed a legislature, to derive its powers from the people, and to consist of two branches. The Jersey resolutions deduced the legislative authority from the states, and vested it in a single body. By the Virginia plan, as it was then drawn out, the legislative authority extended to all national concerns, had a veto on all state laws, and could be directed by the will of the majority. The Jersey resolutions confined this authority to certain enumerated subjects and required in many cases, the concurrence of more than a majority of members. The Virginia plan placed the executive power in a single officer, removable only by impeachment ; the other placed the executive power in a plural number, removable on application of a majority of the states. The Virginia plan provided for inferior judiciary tribunals ; that of New Jersey made no arrangement in this particular.

At this period it is obvious that the convention had made but little progress in the scheme of that splendid edifice, alike bold and beautiful, which they afterwards completed.

The two plans were however sufficiently marked and distinct to bring on again discussions, which well nigh caused the convention to separate. The views and feelings of the members had by this time become pretty well understood among themselves. An observer of no common accuracy and intellectual strength, in an official communication justifying his own final negative, has classed them in three parties, of very different sentiments. One, though a small one, wished to abolish and annihilate all state governments, and to bring forward one general government over this extensive continent, of a monarchical nature, under certain restrictions and limitations. The second party was not for the abolition of the state governments, nor for the introduction of a monarchical government under any form, but they wished to establish such a system as could give their own states undue power and influence in the government over the other states. It is in this second class he intended to include both Mr. Gerry and governour Randolph. If, by undue power and influence, the

learned commentator meant only that power and
influence which wealth, population and territory,
would naturally confer in an association where
these were unequally possessed, the description is
not to be complained of as unfair.

Another party, according to the same writer,
considered by him truly federal and republican,
and nearly equal in number to the other two, were
for proceeding upon terms of federal equality ; they
were for taking the existing system as the basis of
their proceedings, and remedying such defects, or
giving such new powers as experience made necessary. The existing system, it is known, acknowledged the perfect equality of all and every
of the confederated states. From this latter party
emanated the Jersey resolutions.

In the discussions, which followed the introduction of the resolutions from Jersey, col. Hamilton,
from New-York, presented his views in a scheme
altogether different from either, which had come
before the convention. He said he had well
considered the subject, and was convinced that no
amendment of the confederation could answer the
purpose of a good government, so long as state governments *did in any shape exist*, and he had great
doubts whether a national government on the New
Jersey plan could be made effectual. The scheme
of col. Hamilton proposed that the legislature
should consist of two branches, the one to be elected for three years, the other for good behaviour,

the former by the people, the latter by electors chosen by the people. The executive was to consist of a single individual, with the unpretending name of governour, to be elected by electors chosen by electors elected by the people, to hold his office during good behaviour, to have the sole appointment of the chief officers of the departments, and the nomination of all others except ministers to foreign courts. The government of the Union was also to appoint the chief executive magistrate of each of the states, in whom was to be placed an unqualified power of negativing any law about to be passed in the state over which he presided.

The inferior points of his system conformed to the boldness of these prominent parts.*

* Journal of cong. p. 130. Pickering's Review, p. 172. Marshall's biography of Washington, in a note to page 353 of vol. 5, adds, " It has been published by the enemies of Mr. Hamilton, that he was in favour of a president and senate who should hold their office during good behaviour." Whether by enemy or friend the publication was substantially true, unless indeed some equivocation may be played upon the words "in favour," and that it may be conceived he was in fact *not in favour* of his own proposition.

Col. H. himself, in a letter to Col. Pickering in 1803, when the extreme unpopularity of such a proposition was most manifest, and after the overthrow of the political party of which those gentlemen were the chiefs, owing, as it unquestionably was, to their high toned notions of government, availed himself of some such ingenious distinction. He avows making the proposition, which it was well known to him was on record, and would one day be published. " The highest toned propositions, which I made in the convention were for a president, senate and judges, during good behaviour;" but he leaves the reader to infer that

It is probable the three schemes at that time
before the convention, may be considered as au-

his mind had not settled down definitively in approbation of his
own proposals.   " I may add (he says, referring to his project in
convention) that in the course of the discussions in the convention, neither the propositions thrown out for debate, nor even
those voted in the earlier stages of deliberation, were considered
as evidences of a deliberative opinion in the proposer or voter."
That they show the tendency and bias of the proposer's mind
can hardly admit of doubt. But the apology is unavailing. His
proposition was not thrown out for debate. He did not venture
to urge a direct discussion of it ; but that it was no light or ca-
sual suggestion is proved by the dignity of the place and the high
intellectual character of the speaker, and by the strong corrobo-
rative language at other times used by him in the course of discussion. Nor can it be excused on the idea that it was in the
earliest stages of deliberation. The proposition was made on
the 18th day of June, when the general sentiments of the delegates had matured and ripened, and when parties marked by
their settled peculiarities of opinion were already defined. It
was introduced on a great and grave occasion, when the whole
force and strength of each individual was called into exertion,
and at a time when the existence of any constitution might
depend on a single vote. There is a completeness in the
scheme of col. H. which might excuse a man from being considered among his " enemies" if he did publish that the proposer
was in favour of something more than a republican government.

The appointment of a governour to each state by the executive
of the union, and the unqualified veto, which such governour
would have on the state legislatures, would so far change the
relative character of the state governments that a friend of state
sovereignty might be excused for considering them annihilated ;
yet, in his letter above cited, col. H. declares, " I never contemplated the abolition of the state governments."

Col. Hamilton's system was introduced by a speech, in
which he maintained and defended the principles, which led to
such startling and novel results. In a mode of illustration not
exactly in the style of eloquence for which he was afterwards

thorizing the remark of the attorney general of
Maryland before alluded to ; at any rate they presented three forms of government, as distinct from
each other, as the classes into which, according
to his account, the convention were divided.

The plan of colonel Hamilton was never distinctly brought into debate ; that of New Jersey
was, after a sharp contest, on motion of Mr. King,
voted to be inadmissible ; and again the convention seriously betook themselves to the task of
arranging in detail the successive propositions first
submitted from Virginia. In this object, however,
the predominant feelings of the friends of the rejected systems were constantly appearing in their
contrarient efforts to consolidate the national power, or to strengthen the authority of the states, and
to give a more popular form to the projected government. As an example of this may be mentioned the debate on the tenure of the office of
senator. On one side it was moved (by Mr. Read
of Delaware) that it should be during good behaviour. Nine, seven, six and four years were severally proposed ; Mr. Sherman of Connecticut remarked, a bad government is the worse for being

distinguished, he remarked, " I confess that my plan and that
from Virginia, are very remote from the ideas of the people.
Perhaps the Jersey plan is nearer their expectation. But the
people are gradually ripening in their opinions of government—
they begin to be tired of an excess of democracy; and what
even is the Virginia plan but pork still, with a little change of
the sauce."

long. Frequent elections give security and even permanency. In Connecticut we have existed 132 years under an annual government, and as as long as a man behaves himself well, he is never turned out.

Col. Hamilton. We are now forming a republican government. Real liberty is neither found in despotism or the extremes of democracy, but in moderate governments. Those who mean to form a solid republican government, *ought to proceed to the confines of another government.*

Mr. Gerry. It appears to me that the American people have the greatest aversion to monarchy, and the nearer the new government approaches to it, the less chance have we for their approbation.

After this debate the question was carried for five years, and a biennial rotation.

But the utmost strength of the opposing parties was displayed on the question of representation. It was now well understood that neither the federative plan of New Jersey nor the monarchical scheme offered by the delegate from New-York, could be successful, but that the Virginia resolutions must be modified to the acceptance of the convention or its members would separate without coming to any result.

But this again brought into operation all those principles, feelings and attachments, general and local, by which the several parties in the convention were already designated. To preserve under

a national government that federative principle,
which should give each member of the confederacy an equality of power still continued the first
object of the advocates of state rights, which those
who were desirous of a consolidated government,
and those who were willing to preserve the state
sovereignties in their relative importance here
found a common ground, on which their efforts
might be united.

The difficulties on this perplexing subject, and
the fluctuating opinions of the convention are seen
in the progress of the examination, and the different votes of the convention at different times.
Governour Randolph's original draught directed
the members of the first* branch to be chosen by
the people of the states and those of the second
by the first, out of a proper number of persons
nominated by the individual legislatures, but their
relative numbers were not defined by him.   In
the debate on 7th June, this was altered, and it
was resolved that the members of the second branch
should be chosen by the state legislatures.   On
the 11th June, the convention decided that " the
right of suffrage in the first branch of the national legislature ought not to be according to the rule
established in the articles of confederation," (which
gave each state one vote) " but according to

* In the early period of the convention the popular branch
of the legislature was usually called the first: and the senate the
second.   It was subsequently changed.

some equitable ratio of representation," and afterwards that the representation should be in proportion to the whole number of white and other
free citizens of every age, sex and condition,
including those bound to servitude for a term of
years, and three-fifths of all other persons not
comprehended in the foregoing description, except
Indians, not paying taxes in each state." And this
modification was at that time agreed to by all the
states but New Jersey and Delaware. The convention then refused to sustain a motion that in
the second branch of the national legislature each
state should have one vote, but resolved that the
right of suffrage in the second branch ought to be
according to the rule established for the first, which
latter proposition was supported by all the large
states and opposed by all the small ones, excepting only that New-York voted against it.

As yet however nothing definite was settled.
The several propositions of governour Randolph
and the modifications and amendments of the convention were on the 19th June presented by the
committee of the whole to the house in the shape,
which the votes of the committee had given them,
by which it appeared to be the sense of the committee that the equality of the states was not to
be allowed in either branch of the legislature, but
a rule was to be established according to some
equitable ratio of representation, which ratio was
yet to be ascertained. On the question whether

these resolutions should be accepted by the house
they who disapproved the report, "found it necessary" to use the words of the attorney general
of Maryland " to make a warm and decided opposition," to which he himself contributed by speaking "*upwards of three hours*." The report in
favour of inequality in the first branch was sustained, but when the question on a like inequality
in the second branch was taken in the convention, five states were in favour and five against it ;
the vote of the eleventh, which had only two
members on the floor, being lost by division of
opinion between the delegates.

In such a state of disagreement as to this most
important and essential part of the system, the
convention might well be considered as approaching to the termination of their labours, and abandoning to all the storms of anarchy the country,
which they had not ability to preserve. But the
good genius of the nation prevailed. A committee of compromise was appointed, consisting of
one from each state, of which Mr. Gerry was
elected chairman, who reported that happy arrangement, which substantially now forms the constitution of the United States. It was not however accomplished without great difficulty, and
produced new discussions in the committee of a
like temper and earnestness with that, which had
marked the discussions in the house. We met,
says Mr. Martin, and discussed the subject of

difference ; the one side insisted on inequality of suffrage in both branches, the other insisted on equality in both ; each party was tenacious of its sentiments. When it was found that nothing could induce us to yield the inequality in both branches, they at length proposed by way of compromise, if we would accede to their wishes as to the first branch, they would agree to the equal representation in the second. To this it was answered, that there was no merit in the proposal ; it was only consenting, after they had struggled to put both their feet on our necks, to take one of them off, provided we would consent to let them keep the other on, when they knew at the same time, they could not put one foot on our necks, unless we would consent to it, and that by being permitted to keep on that one foot, they would afterwards be able to place the other foot on whenever they pleased.

A majority of the select committee (he continues) at length agreed to a series of propositions by way of compromise, part of which related to the representation in the first branch nearly as the system is now published, and part of them to the second branch, securing in that an equal representation, and reported them as a compromise upon the express terms that they were wholly to be accepted or wholly to be rejected ; upon this compromise a great number of the members so far engaged themselves that if the system was progressed upon agreeably to the terms of compromise they would lend it their names by signing it, and would not actively oppose it, if their states should appear inclined to adopt it. Some however, in which number was myself, who joined in the report, agreed to proceed upon those principles, and see what kind of a system would ultimately be formed upon it, yet reserved to themselves in the most explicit manner the right of finally giving a solemn dissent to the system if it was thought by them inconsistent with the freedom and happiness of their country. This will explain why the members of the convention so generally signed their names to the system ; not because they thoroughly approved or thought it a proper one, but because they thought it better than the system attempted to be forced on them.

This report of the select committee was after long dissension adopted by a majority of the convention, and the system was proceeded in accordingly. Near a fortnight, perhaps more, was spent in the discussion of this business, during which we were on the verge of dissolution, scarce held together by the strength of a hair, though the public papers were announcing our extreme unanimity.

The report produced by the committee of compromise, and accepted by the house, established the relative rank of the several states as they would stand in representation under the forms of the new constitution, a great and difficult subject, but not the only one, which had occasioned an alarming diversity of opinion.

The chairman of that committee, without pledging himself for his vote on the final questions before the convention, laboured to bring about a satisfactory result of this intricate subject, which ought to exculpate him from every suspicion of being hostile to the specific objects of the convention, or of maintaining an irreconcilable animosity to the plan in progress.

At the time when this important committee were endeavouring to reconcile the conflicting sentiments of their colleagues, it is evident he must have been sensible of the advantage of accomplishing the duty assigned him, and that there was a possible, and even highly probable expectation of doing so in the way indicated by the course the convention had pursued.

Factious hostility to any rational form of general government, imputed to those who did not concur in the eventual labours of the delegates, can with no propriety be charged on one who devoted so many anxious hours to the elaborating a practicable scheme as was employed by the members of this efficient committee, in whose power it would have been, at any moment, to have brought the business of the convention to an unsuccessful termination.

The report of this committee, by affording some prospect that one of the most unmanageable points of controversy was not fatally decisive of success, revived the hopes of the assembly, and excited a new spirit of exertion. A draught of the constitution, as it was presented by the resolutions adopted in the progress of discussion, was printed for the exclusive use of the members. After being again revised and amended, a new edition was printed for the same purpose. Both of them, and more essentially the first, differ from the instrument, which received the signature of the members and became the supreme law of the land. In these documents the modifications successively made in the form of the constitution may be traced, some of them serving only to show the slow progress by which the charter of government attained its eventual excellence, and others marking changes of a serious character, which the maturer judgment, or often the temporizing policy of the parties recommended for adoption.

These tracks of the progress of the convention are like old charts of a well known coast, more regarded by the antiquary, who traces out the errors of the first adventurers, than by the navigator who has no interest beyond the most recent discoveries. They will not however escape the researches of a curiosity eager to take every shoal and current in the great sea of political liberty.

The preamble to the first printed copy of the proposed constitution differs from the one finally accepted in omitting to state the objects for which

the constitution is framed.   It is simply, "We,
the people of the states of New-Hampshire, &c.
do ordain, declare and establish the following constitution, for the government of ourselves and our
posterity."

With regard to the executive power are the following provisions :

The executive power of the United States shall
be vested in a single person.   His style shall be
The President of the United States of America,
and his title shall be his Excellency.   He shall
be elected by joint ballot by the legislature.   He
shall hold his office during the term of seven years,
but shall not be elected a second time.

He shall appoint officers in all cases not otherwise provided by this constitution.

He shall be commander in chief of the army
and navy of the United States, and of the militia
of the several states."   The important limitation
now found in the constitution, confining this authority over the militia to their being in actual service, is omitted.

There is no recognition of a vice-president.

With regard to the legislative power there are
the following provisions :

The legislative power shall be vested in a congress, to consist of two separate and distinct bo-
dies of men, a house of representatives and a senate.

All bills for raising or appropriating money, and

for fixing the salaries of the officers of government, shall originate in the house of representatives and shall not be altered or amended by the senate. No money shall be drawn from the treasury, but in pursuance of appropriations that shall originate in the house of representatives.

No tax or duty shall be laid by the legislature on articles exported from any state, nor on the migration or importation of such persons as the several states shall think proper to admit, nor shall such migration or importation be prohibited.

The legislature of the United States shall have authority to establish such uniform qualifications of the members of each house, with regard to property, as to the said legislature shall seem expedient. The members of each house shall be ineligible and incapable of holding any civil office under the authority of the United States, during the time for which they shall respectively be elected, and the members of the senate shall be ineligible to, and incapable of holding any such office for one year afterwards.

The members of each house shall receive compensation for their services, to be ascertained and paid by the state in which they shall be chosen.

Of the senate it is declared,

The senate of the United States shall have power to make treaties, and to appoint ambassadors, and judges of the supreme court.

The senate shall choose its own president, and other officers.

Authority is also given to the senate to constitute a special court, composed of commissioners, to decide conclusively on all controversies between states as to jurisdiction or territory, and all controversies concerning lands claimed under different grants of two or more states.

The judicial power is extended to all other " controversies between two or more states," and " to the trial of impeachment of officers of United States."

The election of a treasurer of the United States is given to the two houses, and is to be made by joint ballot.

The second printed edition of the constitution conforms more nearly to its ultimate provisions. The changes, which had been ordered, are incorporated, and the arrangement and collocation of subjects are methodized and put into more appropriate form.

In addition to some amendments of detail and of provisions, which had probably escaped attention at an earlier review, care is evidently bestowed on the phraseology, and effort made to correct as far as might be the ambiguity of expression.

For instance, this reprint contains the following enactments : " The president shall at stated times receive a fixed compensation for his services, which shall neither be increased nor diminished during the period for which he shall have been elected."

The strict grammatical construction prohibits any alteration in his duties and not his emoluments. It was on motion so altered as to read in conformity to the meaning of the draughtsman. The president shall at stated times receive for his services a compensation, which shall neither be increased nor diminished.

Again, the clause printed as follows : " The migration or importation of such persons as the several states now existing shall think proper to admit, &c." is amended to read, " such persons as any of the states, &c."

Other verbal alterations, the import of which would be apparent only to an exact and critical eye, were made with a freedom, which shows the solicitude of the convention to present in a shape the most unexceptionable, as well the great principles they established as the language in which they should be secured.

The desire of the convention to arrive at such a result, as notwithstanding the intrinsic difficulties of the task should receive the support of all its members, was manifested as well by the closeness of their application* as by the frequent modification of the articles, which from time to time was permitted.

* On the 18th August the convention resolved to meet punctually at 10 o'clock every morning, Sundays excepted, and sit till 4 o'clock P. M., at which time the president should adjourn the convention, and that no motion for adjournment be allowed.

MR. GERRY TO GENERAL WARREN.

PHILADELPHIA, AUG. 13, 1787.

My Dear Sir,

It is out of my power in return for the information you have given me to inform you of our proceedings in convention, but I think they will be
complete in a month or six weeks, perhaps sooner.
Whenever they shall be matured I sincerely hope
they will be such as you and I can approve, and
then they will not be engrafted with principles
of mutability, corruption or despotism, principles
which some, you and I know, would not dislike to
find in our national constitution.   I wish you had
accepted a seat in congress, for the next year will
be important.

Adieu my dear sir.—Make my respects, &c.

Your sincere friend,

E. GERRY.

Hon. J. Warren.

———

On the 17th September 1787, this celebrated
assembly announced to the country the result of
its deliberations.   Thirty-eight members sub-
scribed the plan proposed.   Sixteen signatures are
wanting.   Among the latter in addition to the
subject of this memoir, was governour Randolph
and Mr. Mason of Virginia, Mr. Lansing and chief

justice Yeates of New-York, and Mr. Martin of
Maryland. Mr. Strong* of Massachusetts obtained
leave of absence before the final question was taken, so that the instrument bears the names of
only two members from that state.

It is somewhat remarkable that while governour
Randolph supplied the original materials out of
which the constitution was elaborated, they suffered such changes in their passage through the or-
deal of the convention that he thought proper to
withhold his consent to the plan, which they eventually assumed.

* Afterwards governour of the commonwealth.

CHAPTER II.

THE period, which has elapsed since the convention at Philadelphia terminated its session has allowed ample opportunity for ascertaining the competency of the constitution, which the wisdom of that assembly presented to the American people, for the great purposes it was intended to accomplish. Under the government, which from that time was established, the United States as a nation have acquired rank, wealth and power, which the eye of patriotism in the widest range of its prophetic vision could never have foreseen. The strength of the government for all purposes of national protection, and its inaptitude to any exertion adverse to the most perfect political liberty demonstrate the exact balance of those combined and contrarient principles, which render it formidable where power is to be exercised for general good, and harmless where an undue exertion of authority would endanger the personal security of the citizen.

How much the prosperity of the country is attributable to the constitution of its government, how much has resulted from geographical position, what share has its cause in the intelligence, virtue and enterprise of the people, and how much has resulted from the prudence and ability of the successive administrations of its affairs, cannot now with any exactness be ascertained. The road on which we have travelled, though not without impediments and danger, has conducted us as we know to an elevated and commanding station; what might have been the termination of another path is shut out from all human observation. Enjoying the great national blessings with which Providence has indulged us, we are forbidden to suppose that any other than the course we have taken could have been equally prosperous.

Under the operation of the constitution the country has been eminently happy; and success so far as it has been procured by the instrumentality of the form of government, may be justly claimed by the advocates of that form as proof of their forecast and political skill. It is however to be considered that the constitution reported by the convention, although accepted and ratified by the people, has never been, or for a single year only, the actual frame of government for the nation. Amendments of a character if not essentially to change its original features, yet calculated to soften and remould them, were proposed at the first session of the first congress in New-York, and by the assent of the people became very soon a part of the fundamental law of the country. Between the advocates in the convention for one form or another the question is yet open to discussion whether the existing constitution with all its early amendments is conformable to the principles urged by those, who gave it originally their assent, or restores it to the plan of those, who were induced to withhold from it at first the sanction of their names.

Mr. Gerry, as has been already remarked, was one of a minority in the convention who disapproved some of the principles, which the constitution finally assumed, and having arrived at the conclusion in his own mind that it did not comport with the well being of the country, with regret indeed but without hesitation he refused it the sanction of his name.

This act of refusal, even admitting the validity of the objections, which existed in his own mind, has been charged upon him as impolitic, injudicious and unwise. He had laboured, it was said, with an industry and perseverance in the details of the scheme, which demonstrated a belief in the necessity of some essential change in the existing order of things; it must have been manifest that such change could only be the result of compromise and concession, and no practical statesman would believe that, when such were the means of operation,

all his own favourite objects would be preserved.
The difficulties, too, experienced by him, during
four months of close application to this arduous labour, must have satisfied any man that a new convention would meet only to encounter new difficulties, and that the results, in their present form,
if not the most desirable, were in fact the only
ones, which could ever be obtained.   To a statesman, it was apparent that the alternative was not
between this constitution and a better, but between this and none.

The objections thus urged did not pass without
due consideration, but they seemed to him to put
policy in opposition to principle, and in such case
the habit of his life left him in no doubt on which
side to take his stand.   The question was indeed
momentous.   To recommend to others what the
party himself did not approve ; to become responsible for consequences, the dangers of which were as
firmly believed as if they were visible ; to place
the confiding and industrious people of a great nation under a power, which might crush them by its
weight, or embark them on the stormy ocean of
politics, in a vessel too frail to encounter the perils
of the voyage, was a course of too doubtful integrity to be easily adopted.   It was that indeed
which many honourable members of the convention
were willing to take, for reasons unquestionably
satisfactory to themselves, but in the mind of the
delegate from Massachusetts, compromise had its

limits, and concession its legitimate bounds ; beyond these his ideas of duty forbade him to pass, and poising himself on his own character, he assumed the responsibility of acting on the principles, which his judgment approved.

In communicating to his constituents, the legislature of Massachusetts, the constitution adopted by the convention at Philadelphia, Mr. Gerry announces his own dissent, and maintains his opinions in the following letter.

———

MR. GERRY TO THE SENATE AND HOUSE OF RE-
PRESENTATIVES OF MASSACHUSETTS.

NEW-YORK, OCT. 18, 1787.

GENTLEMEN,

I have the honour to enclose, pursuant to my commission, the constitution proposed by the federal convention. To this system I gave my dissent, and shall submit my objections to the honourable legislature. It was painful for me, on a subject of such national importance, to differ from the respectable members who signed the constitution. But conceiving as I did that the liberties of America were not secured by the system, it was my duty to oppose it.

My principal objections to the plan are, that there is no adequate provision for a representation of the people ; that they have no security for the

right of election; that some of the powers of the
legislature are ambiguous, and others indefinite and
dangerous; that the executive is blended with
and will have an undue influence over the legislature; that the judicial department will be oppressive; that treaties of the highest importance may be formed by the president, with the
advice of two-thirds of a quorum of the senate, and
that the system is without the security of a bill of
rights. These are objections, which are not local,
but apply equally to all the states. As the convention was called for " the sole and express purpose
of revising the articles of confederation, and reporting to congress and the several legislatures, such
alterations and provisions as shall render the federal constitution adequate to the exigencies of government and the preservation of the union." I
did not conceive that these powers extended to the
formation of the plan proposed, but the convention
being of a different opinion, I acquiesced in it,
being fully convinced, that to preserve the union,
an efficient government was indispensably necessary, and that it would be difficult to make proper
amendments to the articles of confederation. The
constitution proposed has few, if any federal features, but is rather a system of national government; nevertheless, in many respects, I think it
has great merit, and by proper amendments may
be adapted to the " exigencies of government and
preservation of liberty." The question on this

plan involves others of the highest importance :
First, Whether there shall be a dissolution of the
federal government. Secondly, Whether the several state governments shall be so altered, as in effect to be dissolved. Thirdly, Whether, in lieu of
the federal and state governments, the national
constitution now proposed shall be substituted without amendment. Never perhaps were a people
called upon to decide a question of greater magnitude. Should the citizens of America adopt the
plan as it now stands, their liberties may be lost ;
or should they reject it altogether, anarchy may
ensue. It is evident therefore that they should
not be precipitate in their decisions ; that the subject should be well understood, lest they should refuse to support the government, after having hastily
accepted it. If those who are in favour of the constitution, as well as those who are against it, should
preserve moderation, their discussions may afford
much information, and finally direct to a happy
issue. It may be urged by some, that an implicit
confidence should be placed in the convention ; but
however respectable the members may be who
signed the constitution, it must be admitted that a
free people are the proper guardians of their rights
and liberties ; that the greatest men may err, and
that their errors are sometimes of the greatest magnitude. Others may suppose that the constitution
may be safely adopted, because therein provision
is made to amend it. But cannot this object be

better attained before a ratification than after it? And should a free people adopt a form of government under conviction that it wants amendment? Some may conceive that, if the plan is not accepted by the people, they will not unite in another: but surely while they have the power to amend, they are not under the necessity of rejecting it. I have been detained here longer than I expected, but shall leave this in a day or two for Massachusetts, and on my arrival shall submit the reasons (if required by the legislature) on which my objections are grounded.

I shall only add, that as the welfare of the union requires a better constitution than the confederation, I shall think it my duty, as a citizen of Massachusetts, to support that, which shall be finally adopted, sincerely hoping it will secure the liberty and happiness of America. I have the honour to be, gentlemen, with the highest respect for the honourable legislature and yourselves, your most obedient and very humble servant,

E. GERRY.

To the Hon. Samuel Adams, Esq. President of the Senate, and the Hon. James Warren, Esq. Speaker of the House of Representatives of Massachusetts.

————

This official letter sets forth the most prominent objections which, at the period of the promulgation of the constitution, that instrument had to encounter. But it is obviously not written in the spirit of a partizan. Popular topics, calculated to excite the passions of the people, and elsewhere used with adroitness, *ad captandum vulgus*, are not enumerated ; the advantages of the new system are too freely admitted for the purposes of an irreconcilable hostility ; and the intention of supporting it, if legally ratified, is the submission of a good citizen to the authority of the laws, and not the evidence of that spirit of rebellion, which would retaliate its own disappointment by indiscriminate confusion.

It may be proper to review the objections, which were thus contemporaneously made to the constitution of the United States by the subject of this memoir, and ascertain, if possible, how far they have received any countenance from time.

Of the truth of the first assertion, no one, it would seem, could now honestly entertain a doubt. The passions, which in that period of controversy obscured the judgment of the community, have been tranquillized, and no longer obscure that proud principle of independence, which adheres, against all the allurements of popular favour, to the performance of duty.

The convention had deliberated under the strictest injunctions of secrecy. Its arguments, opinions or motives could be known only by their results. It enumerated among its members men of the most distinguished talents, the most exalted virtue, and the most extensive influence. The name of its president was a tower of strength. What a convention, thus constituted, proposed to the people, could not want support; what they on their great responsibility recommended, had already the advantage of anticipated success; and the individual, who in a conclave of such men dared trust his own judgment, and risk his character and fame in opposition to their influence, ventured on a perilous duty, which nothing but conscious integrity would attempt, and the most fearless independence enable him to perform.

The objection, which is first presented alleges that there is no adequate security for a representation by the people.

The security, so far as one is provided, is contained in the second section of Art. 1, which establishes a definite representation in the house of representatives, until an enumeration of the inhabitants of the United States, a representation at all times of one from each state, and a subsequent representation, according to a ratio, which is to be determined by congress. There is, therefore, *de facto*, no security except the pleasure of congress, for any representation after the first census, except for one representative for each state; and as the pleasure of congress could be declared only by the concurrent vote of the two branches, in one of which the states were equally represented, and might desire to preserve that equality in the other, or their equal weight in the union, by a diminished number of representatives in the house, the objection is theoretically at least made out, and resolves itself into another form of expression, for guarding the relative rights of the states.

The danger here gravely apprehended, strikes us now as exceedingly fanciful; but, in the excited state of mind, which that perplexing subject, the relative importance of the great and small states in the confederacy, occasioned, was naturally enough to be expected.

The constitution had fixed the minimum of representation. It indicated without requiring an increase. Was not that indication a sufficient security? Would congress, having the right, dare to make the ratio for a second representative so high, as virtually to exclude any state from the privilege of an increased representation? or would the senate venture, against the will of the popular branch, to insist on such an anomaly. In the public sentiment and the ultimate power of the people, was to be found the security sought for. In every form of civil government is somewhere an ultimate power, which is liable to be abused; to guard against the tendency to abuse is the part of wisdom; to prevent its possibility is eminently hopeless.

The intention of the constitution to secure a gradually increasing representation of the people in the house of representatives, within such limits as would not embarrass the despatch of business, is indicated by its successive provisions : that each state shall always have one delegate ; that an enumeration of the people shall take place within three years, and afterwards every ten years ; and that, until the first enumeration, there shall be sixty-five representatives. The security for conforming to this intention would not be more adequate, if its provisions were more precise. The security for the observance of any provision of the constitution, cannot be found in the constitution itself. It is derived from the virtue of the people, and the fidelity of their agents. The constitution is a chart only, by which the vessel should be steered ; whether she keeps her course, mainly depends on the officer at the helm.

The objection, considered in reference to the sentiments and feelings of the time, is entitled to much greater respect than if tried by the standard of present opinion. The first amendment proposed by the congress of the United States was intended to obviate its force, and was ratified by a majority of the states, but the constitutional number of nine did not assent to it, whereby it failed to become part of the frame of government. The want of a more definite arrangement in this particular, has as yet produced no practical evil. Other difficulties have occurred under the article in question, but the apprehension has probably subsided, which classed too small a house of representatives among the practical evils of the American government.

Indeed, if the theory of the early statesmen be true, that power every where has a principle of expansion, a vitality that keeps it constantly growing and extending itself, the result may as well be found in the house of representatives, as in any other depository of this vigorous germ. It is not easy to see why such an assembly may not extend, or endeavour to extend its authority, as well as an individual, in whom by the theory such inclination is a necessary incident to the possession of power. A tendency of this sort has occasionally been imputed to individual members. The first president of the United States interposed his authority in a case of some delicacy, against the pretensions of the whole house. Its weight and influence, as a department of the government, has been regularly increasing from the first operation of the constitution, and the most distant of the evils, which threaten the American people, is want of power or indisposition to exercise it, on the part of their immediate representatives.

The objection that there is no security for the right of election, refers to the 4th section of 1st article, by which the manner of holding elections for senators and representatives is vested in the state legislatures, with a power in congress at any time to make or alter such regulations, except as to the places of choosing senators.

The fair exercise of this power by congress could never be objectionable ; by their abusing it the electors might be put to extreme inconvenience, and the right rendered of no value. This extraordinary power over the legislation of the states, formed every where a formidable argument with the opposition; but it has not, in practice, been the cause of any complaint.

Again it is objected, that the executive is blended with and will have an undue influence over the legislature.

The first branch of the objection is in point of fact true; but the argument so profoundly maintained in the writings of the Federalist, has defended the provision of the constitution in this respect from even theoretical impropriety. The prophecy of the other part has not been fulfilled. On the other hand, the democratic principles of the constitution, which pervade and animate the whole system, but are chiefly placed in the popular branch of the legislative department, have constantly and steadily advanced in strength and importance. If there be danger in disturbing the exact balances, which the constitution has adjusted, it will come from the opposite quarter to that, which was predicted by its early opponents.

The power and the will of the people are irresistible agents in whatever government they are admitted as elements of its composition, and not only exert their functions in that branch which is the place of their appropriate activity, but extend their influence into all the collateral departments, as we find in a garrison town, the air of military life displaying somewhat of its character in the manners of the peaceful citizen ; or in Catholic countries, the peculiarities of the predominant faith controlling the customs and habits of those even who are not within the pale of the church.

In a government like that prescribed by the convention, establishing the grand democratic axioms that the people are the source of authority, and their happiness its sole object, the checks and restraints on the popular will, which were imposed to produce strength, stability and decision, would be found wonderfully well contrived, if they were able to promote for any length of time these salutary objects ; the apprehension of their counteracting the great design of the government was as little to be justified by theory as it has been unfounded in experience. If the hereditary power of the British crown, with a permanent and powerful aristocracy, has not been able at all times to maintain itself against even a partial representation of the people, the alarm surely was needless that any station provided in the American constitution could withstand, much less corrupt and control, the representatives of the people or the states.

That the judicial department will be oppressive was a much more plausible objection, which may yet be, if it has not been unfortunately realized. This was a new power in the confederacy. It is of necessity intrusted to a very small number of men rendered independent of the popular will by the tenor of office, and appointed to their high stations not by means of that connexion, which creates a sympathy with their fellow citizens, but because of their professional distinction under a good administration, or their political zeal and party attachment under a bad one; a course of life, which in the one case renders them in some degree unacquainted with the state of the public mind, or in the other prepares them to disregard it. In the report of the convention too it is to be remembered that the judicial power of the United States extended to cases, in which a state itself might be a defendant, whereby the whole doctrine of a confederacy of sovereign states was annihilated and an association of political corporations substituted in its place.

The latter authority has been limited by an article of amendment ; and the high and honourable character of the judicial department has done much to preserve the confidence of the people ; but cases have arisen alarmingly confirming the fears of the opponents of the constitution, and others cannot but follow, in which great sections of the country may not think the objection was unreasonable.

Indeed when it found that in the exercise of legitimate authority a majority of seven or ten men may set aside the statutes of congress, or of any of the states, which have passed all the forms of their respective constitutions, because in the opinion of this small body they are in violation of the supreme law of the land, it cannot be doubted that the cautious republicans of the convention might well fear that the power would be oppressive.

That other modes of revision in regard to this necessary power had their several inconveniences is no answer to the objection urged against this. The control over the proceedings and decrees of a state legislature and a state judiciary, which subject the debateable proposition of constitutionality to the decision of three or four individuals appointed by the president of the United States, is in theory a most dangerous state of things, and it may be well for the public peace if in after time it be exercised with so much integrity and intelligence, that it shall not justify the fears entertained by opponents to the constitution in the convention of '89.

It is further to be alleged in excuse for the suspicions at the commencement of the constitution in regard to the judicial department, that the theory of representation, which elsewhere pervades the system, is here entirely abandoned. It was impossible in the nature of things and has not been attempted. No restriction is laid on the appointing power, and it would therefore be possible in the literal exercise of the trust committed to the president, that with the consent of the senate a large part of the country should feel that it had no security on the judicial bench. To those, who found in the practicability of abuse a reason for suspecting it, this might have been sufficient to justify opposition, but in yielding to it they did not rely enough on that general public sentiment, which is the very atmosphere of a republican government, and is produced by the intelligence and integrity of the people themselves.

The treaty making power is confessedly one of the strong points of the constitution, which the jealous republicans of the day may be excused for considering with alarm. Its operation has excited much angry feeling and arrayed the citizens in ranks of party as violent as those of battle, but there is nevertheless in the very essence of this government a redeeming principle, which compels all the functionaries to make their habitual homage to the public sentiment, or more properly speaking so to act that the popular sentiment shall support the correctness of their proceedings when it shall dispassionately exercise its judgment. It is this, which supplies the want of a bill of rights and renders harmless whatever other articles might seemingly tend to entrench on the great charter of liberty.

If the amendments proposed by congress at its first session and which now make part of the constitution, were properly adopted, the further objection, made by Mr. Gerry before its ratification, was well founded, viz. that the powers of the legislature were ambiguous, indefinite and dangerous. These amendments propose and establish ten distinct and important limitations. If the powers, which they restrain, would without the amendments have been enjoyed by congress, the constitution would properly have authorized the exercise of authority, which it is plain the people did not intend ; if otherwise, its language was ambiguous. If it were doubtful whether the powers not delegated to the United States nor prohibited to the states, were reserved to the states respectively, or to the people, the constitution was ambiguous in an essential provision; and that it was doubtful must be admitted from the adoption of the amendment ; or if there was no doubt in the case, and the constitution conferred such a national character on the government of the United States that it took in virtue of its sovereignty whatever it was not expressly prohibited from taking, a form of government was adopted so essentially different from that now existing, that the advocates of the present establishment could not consistently approve it.

The indefiniteness and ambiguity of all written constitutions and of all political declarations, and indeed of language in its most perfect form, are constantly witnessed and lamented. They are without doubt inseparable from the nature of the human mind and the limitation of its powers. It is however the good fortune of the people of these states that whatever of this common imbecility exists in their constitution has not yet real-

ized the apprehensions of their friends.   But even
at this moment its exact meaning is not universally admitted.   Its powers are to be settled by a
construction, which extends or compresses them as
one or another of those rules are applied, which
have advocates in different parts of the country.
Hence it was well observed by an eminent member of the convention, on being felicitated on the
appropriate arrangements they had formed, " that
the practicability of the constitution would depend on the construction that should be put on
the powers it conferred."

It is to be remarked that all the objections suggested by Mr. Gerry regarded the tendency of the
constitution to impair the liberties of the people
and the sovereignty of the states, and that it was
on this precise ground that all the opposition it
experienced throughout the United States was
founded.   All the amendments, from whatever
quarter proposed, were calculated to restrain this
supposed bias.   From those who favoured colonel
Hamilton's propositions it met with no obstacle
or opposition.   It is apparent therefore that the
convention had carried the provisions for a strong
government to the utmost extent, which the people would bear.   In Mr. Gerry's view they were
extended further than was consistent with political freedom, and if this question had been submitted to the people it cannot be doubted that
their answer would by a vast majority have been

given in the affirmative.   But a very different proposition was presented.   Shall the constitution be
accepted as it is, or must the country still hold to
the floating fragments of the confederation, which
like a stranded ship, was expected every moment
to fall in pieces.

The chance of another convention, or a more
popular government, or of continuing as a united
people, under existing forms, was equally desperate, and the question therefore to be decided by
the freemen of the United States was in fact not
whether they approved the plan offered them by
the convention, but whether such a government as
it provided was not preferable to the anarchy and
confusion which might follow its rejection.

Rejection indeed was not contemplated by Mr.
Gerry.   He inclined to accept it conditionally,
and seems to have thought that while the people
had " the power to amend they were not under the
necessity of rejecting it."   There is one remark
however, which he submitted to the legislature,
that should have exempted him from the severe
animadversions to which he was subjected, as it
certainly shows that his opposition would be controlled and limited by an intelligent spirit of patriotism.

" As the welfare of the union," he says, " requires a better constitution than the confederation,
I shall think it my duty to support that, which shall

be finally adopted." This liberality of feeling distinguished Mr. Gerry's conduct in the whole business of the convention. From a distinguished member of that body from South Carolina,* the following extract of a letter may be introduced as an offset in some degree for the severe censures with which he was assailed.

"Your sentiments, my friend, respecting the effect politics should have in private life entirely coincide with my own. I felt it a misfortune that I should be compelled by such judgment as God had given me to differ so greatly from a man, whose judgment I so highly venerate, and whose independence and integrity I bore witness to during the whole session. I ardently wished my friend Gerry to think as I did, that the constitution, with all its imperfections, is the only thing that can rescue the states from civil discord and foreign contempt. Reflecting maturely on the little disposition of most of the states to submit to any government, I preferred giving my consent to a trial of the constitution with all its imperfections; that there are parts I do not like, you well know; I ardently wish to draw in public as I ever shall in private life in unison with a person for whom I have so great an esteem as for Mr. Gerry, but I shall not less admire his independent spirit, his disinterested conduct and his private worth be-

* Hon. Peirce Butler.

cause we differ on measures of great public concern."

It is somewhat remarkable that several strong
points of objection to the constitution, which could
not upon any other principle than the unsatisfactory one of a compromise have been acceded to
by Mr. Gerry, and which would certainly in the
eastern states, have been most popular topics of
crimination, find no place in his public letter.
Upon the subject of the ratio of representation in
either branch of the legislature he is wholly silent.
Nothing is urged against the constitution upon the
ground of its admitting the slaves of the southern
states to swell their share of representation, nor
is the insecurity of the state constitutions brought
out very prominently, although in the convention
he had urged this as a reason why the United
States officers should take an oath to support the
constitution of the states, as a provision more necessary than the one under debate, which provided for an oath of allegiance by the state-officers
to the constitution of the United States.

It cannot be that these subjects were without
due weight in his mind, but he had probably come
to the conclusion that however it might be desirable to modify them, no reasonable expectation
could exist of changing them for others more desirable, and believing that the proposed constitution had in many respects great merits he was
willing to urge no objection merely with a view

to victory as a partizan, but to present those only, which might by proper measures be finally obviated.

In the illustrious names, which were put forward as advocates and friends of the new system, many minds found a conclusive evidence in its favour, which they would not have discovered in the instrument itself. The argument *ex auctoritate,* was pressed to its utmost limit, when probably those distinguished individuals were doubtful of its eventual success, and for a cause differing essentially from that of its open assailants, were quite as distrustful of its merits.

That such were the sentiments of colonel Hamilton are disclosed not only by his original proposition, but by his subsequent conduct. In proof of this an anecdote has been recorded by Mr. Jefferson, which he sanctions by the solemn declaration " for the truth I attest the God who made me."

Before the president set out on his southern tour in April 1791, he addressed a letter of the 14th of that month, from mount Vernon to the secretary of state, the treasury and of war, desiring that, if any important case should arise during his absence, they would consult and act on them, and he requested that the vice-president should also be consulted. This was the only occasion on which that officer was ever requested to take part in a cabinet question. Some occasion of consultation arising, I invited those gentlemen (and the attorney general, as well as I remember) to dine with me in order to confer on the subject. After the cloth was removed, and our question argued and dismissed, conversation began on other matters, and by some circumstance was led to the British constitution, on which Mr. Adams observed " purge that constitution of its corruption, and give to its popular branch equality of representation, and it would be the most perfect constitution devised by the wit of man." Hamilton paused and said, " purge it of its corruption, and give to its popular branch equality of representation, and it would become an *impracticable* government : as it stands at present, with all its supposed defects, it is the most perfect government, which ever existed."

The same eminent authority thus describes the feelings of the president of the convention.

" I do believe that general Washington had not a firm confidence in the durability of our government. He was naturally distrustful of men, and inclined to gloomy apprehensions ; and I was ever persuaded that a belief that we must at length end in something like a British constitution had some weight in his adoption of the ceremonies of levees, birth days, pompous meetings with con-

* Mr. Jefferson to Dr. Jones, MS. published in the Boston Patriot, 22d July '28.

gress and other forms of the same character, calculated to prepare us gradually for a change, which
he believed possible, and so let it come on with as
little shock as might be, to the public mind.   These
are my opinions of general Washington, which I
would vouch at the judgment seat of God, having
been formed on an acquaintance of thirty years."

The opinions or doubts, which are thus unhesi-
tatingly attributed by Mr. Jefferson to the most
eminent of American patriots, have derived countenance from his address to the people of the
United States, on declining another election.
There is no where in that address any strong expression of confidence in the permanency of the
constitution.   It is not described as the " palla-
dium of liberty," " the impregnable barrier of freedom," " the great citadel of free institutions," as
in other places it has been distinguished.   On the
contrary, it is mentioned in very cautious terms
as an improvement merely on the past.   " You
have *improved* upon your first essay by the adoption of a constitution of government better calculated than your former for an intimate union, and
for the efficacious management of your common
concerns."

The whole tenor of the address proceeds on an
apprehension that the government does not possess inherently a power of self-preservation, and
that the dangers to which it was exposed might
overturn it.   Hence the impressive admonition

against popular combinations, injudicious alterations, factions, party spirit, and the insidious wiles of foreign influence. Hence too the props, which are to support it; the encouragement of institutions for diffusive education and the cultivation of public manners, good faith in foreign intercourse and a spirit that should be neutral, as well as a political neutrality, during foreign wars; and hence too that prophetic apprehension that all these would not prevent the downward path of the republic.

" In offering you, my countrymen," is his sincere and affectionate language, " these counsels of an old and affectionate friend, I dare not hope they will make the strong and lasting impression I could wish, that they will control the usual current of the passions, or prevent our nation from running the course, which has marked the destiny of nations."

What course and what destiny ? The course which has led from liberty to despotism, the course of anarchy, revolution and civil war. The destiny that subjected Rome to the Cæsars, and every where but in this new world had exiled all principles of public liberty.

It is not from this to be inferred, that these statesmen had an abstract preference for monarchical or even strong government. Not at all. The just deduction is that they considered a popular government as an experiment, as a hazardous and unpromising experiment, and to be made successful only by the strength of the infusion of those higher principles which it contained.

The report of the convention was no sooner known to the people than it divided them into two opposite and irritable factions. Before the complicated provisions of this new government could be explained, and certainly before the reasons could be understood, by which they were opposed or defended, it was manifest that it had its friends and its enemies, who were assuming towards each other the temper and manners of organized and hostile parties.

Its adoption depended on its being ratified by nine states, and the voice of each state was to be expressed by a convention elected by the citizens of the state expressly and solely for that purpose. To influence public opinion, and to obtain a major vote in these state conventions, was the great object of rivalry.

It cannot be doubted that, for some time after its promulgation, the constitution had for its opponents a great majority of the people of the United States. The novelty of its provisions, the change they made in relation of the states, and the uncertainty always attending any new operations, in which wealth and numbers are concerned, were sufficient of themselves to array against it a formidable force ; but this force was, in almost every section of the country, led on by men the most known and distinguished in the past history of the nation ; by men in whose intelligence, integrity and patriotism, implicit confidence had been reposed in the days of revolution and war. Comparatively a new set of men were the fathers of the constitution, who had yet to acquire that glory, upon which its opponents were already permitted to recline.

Enthusiasm proportioned to the interests depending, and ardent as the character of those who took the lead on the great question before the people, excited the advocates of the constitution to immense efforts to secure the ratification they desired, while its opponents, though not wanting in their duty as watchmen of the public rights, seem to have contented themselves with such exertion as their public station required. The press indeed displayed the conflicting opinions of the parties in every possible form, while earnestness and perseverance seemed to indicate a consciousness that effort would secure the prize. Something of the boldness of the prevailing temper may be learned from judge Dana's letter to Mr. Gerry, dated at Newport, Rhode Island, where he was temporarily residing for the benefit of his health, and dated only a few days before the convention separated.

" This state (Rhode Island) will not choose delegates to the convention, nor order on their delegates to congress. I hope they will not, as their neglect will give grounds to strike it out of the union, and divide its territory between their neighbours. Thus, extend Connecticut down to the Narraganset shore, and running up north through Pawtuxet river to our south line, so as to leave Providence, Newport, and all the islands, to Massachusetts, which, as it would give the commercial part of the state to Massachusetts, would best accord with the spirit and genius of our people, while the residue would perfectly coincide with that of Connecticut. According to my best observation, such a division of this state would meet the best approbation of the commercial part of it, though they are afraid to take any open measures in the present state of things, to bring it about. Their interest must dictate such a measure ; they never can be secure under the present form of government, but will always labour under the greatest mischief any people can suffer, that of being ruled by the most ignorant and unprincipled of their fellow citizens. *This state is too insignificant to have a place on an equal footing with any of the others in the Union,* unless it be Delaware. Therefore a bold politician would seize upon the occasion their abominable antifederal conduct presents, for annihilating them as a separate member of the union."

This must have seemed strange language to the advocates of state rights.

In the discussions and debate upon the ratification of the constitution, its friends had a manifest advantage, independent of the merits of the instrument, in the state of the question before the people.

They had to justify and maintain an examina-
ble, defined, written law, of whose evils and ineffi-
cacy nothing could be known, but in the way of
conjecture or alarm. The confederation had almost
expired by its own weakness, and no other had
been prepared to take its place, but the one they
were urging the people to accept. Between that
and the uncertain, undefined and conjectural arrangement, which either in a better or a worse
form, might hereafter be proposed, if indeed the
anarchy, into which the whole community was re-
solving itself, would allow any other to be proposed, the choice could not be doubtful. It was
not necessary for them to defend the new constitution as a perfect, or even an unobjectionable
form of government; their case was made out, if
the people could be satisfied that the new government was better than none, and that whatever
amendments it required might be safely trusted to
the operation of time.

The report of the convention having been laid
before congress, it was by that body, on 28th
September 1787, " Resolved, that it be transmitted
to the several legislatures, in order to be submitted
to a convention of delegates, chosen in each state
by the people thereof, in conformity to the resolves
of the convention, made and provided in that case."

In obedience to this resolve, delegates on the
part of Massachusetts met in convention at Boston,
on the ninth day of January 1788. Mr. Gerry,

who had a short time previous to the election removed from his native town of Marblehead, and
established his residence in the village of Cambridge, the seat of Harvard University, was not returned a member of the convention, either because
his recent inhabitancy did not make him eligible,
or more probably because his opinions, in regard
to the constitution, were not in conformity to those
of his new neighbours.

The convention of Massachusetts consisted of
three hundred and sixty members, among whom
were many of the most distinguished and honourable citizens of the state. It was understood at the
commencement of the session, from the opinions
expressed by the members, or the known sentiment in the towns from which they were delegates, that a majority were opposed to a ratification, but it was soon discovered that, whatever might be the force of numbers, that of talents,
ability and power in debate, was most triumphantly
with the advocates of the new constitution. A
host of talented young men, destined at a future
day to lead in the legislation or jurisprudence of
the state, had seats in this assembly, and brought
to the interesting discussion of great political questions those rare intellectual endowments by which
the state, in all its departments, has since most
eminently profited. Professional men were mostly
in favour of the new government ; educated men
and men of property, with many exceptions indeed,

favoured its adoption; and in the collisions and
conflict of opinion, the plain, unlettered common
sense of its opponents were no match for the practised eloquence, the logic, and the learning of its
friends.

Governour Hancock, who was supposed unfriendly to the constitution, was chosen president of the
convention, but ill health detained him from its
meetings, by means of which all the influence, of
the acting president, judge William Cushing, was
in possession of its advocates. Mr. Samuel Adams
was in a good measure neutral. To supply the
defect arising from want of political experience
and character, the majority invited Mr. Gerry to
take a seat in the convention, for the purpose of
giving such information as should from time to
time be required of him. As each of his colleagues
in the convention of Philadelphia was a member
of that of Massachusetts, the invitation had the
invidious character of a compliment to Mr. Gerry,
and a reflection upon their integrity or judgment.

In the mean time, no management was omitted
by the other side to secure in numbers the superiority they possessed in talent. The efforts
within doors were seconded by every possible exertion abroad.

The newspapers teemed with essays in every
variety of form, and what argument was unable to
effect, satire, lampoon and scurrility were exhausted to accomplish. Some arts were resorted to,

which were supposed to be justified by the greatness of the object. Personal addresses, not unmixed with threats, were made to some of the members, and a marked distinction in private intercourse was observed towards the " irreclaimable malignants," and those who might be persuaded to change their opinions. A report was soon circulated, that the constitution would be adopted ; and as a consequence a vessel was put on the stocks at one of the northern ship yards, that it might appear that the very ·first prospect of a new government would encourage ship building, commerce, and consequently agriculture, while in truth the money necessary for the purpose was obtained by voluntary assessment, rather to secure the constitution, than to make a voyage.

Encouraged by the change of some few in the assembly, it was thought politic to get rid of Mr. Gerry, whose known opinion and high personal character gave a confidence to the opponents of the constitution, which it would be difficult to destroy.

The awkwardness of his situation rendered this no troublesome task. To make the matter more sure, and more aggravating, the giving of the blow was assigned to a friend, long and intimately associated with him in the trying scenes of national embarrassment.

In withdrawing from the convention, Mr. Gerry

addressed a letter to the presiding officer, the following extracts from which sufficiently explain
the cause.

EXTRACT FROM MR. GERRY'S LETTER TO VICE-PRESIDENT CUSHING.

After having on Saturday morning stated an answer to the question proposed the preceding evening, I perceived that your honourable body were
considering a paragraph, which respected an equal
representation of the states in the Senate, and
one of my honourable colleagues observed that this
was agreed to by a committee consisting of a
member from each state, and that I was one of
the number. This was a partial narrative of facts
which I conceived, placed my conduct in an unfavourable point of light, probably without any such
intention on the part of my colleague.

I was thus reduced to the disagreeable alternative of addressing a letter to your honour, for cor-
recting this error, or of sustaining the injuries resulting from its unfavourable impression, not in
the least suspecting that when I had committed
myself to the convention, without the right of
speaking in my own defence, any gentleman would
take an undue advantage, from being a member of
the house, to continue the misrepresentation by
suppressing every attempt on my part to state the
facts. I accordingly informed your honour that I

was preparing a letter, to throw light on the subject, and at my request, you was so obliging as to
make this communication to the house. My sole
object was to state the matter as it respected my
conduct; but I soon perceived that it was misunderstood by the Hon. Judge Dana, who rose with
an appearance of party virulence that I did not
expect, and followed one misrepresentation with
another, by impressing the house with the idea
that I was entering upon their debates. I requested leave repeatedly, to explain the matter, but he
became more vehement, and I was subjected to
strictures from several parts of the house until it
adjourned, without even being permitted to declare
that I disdained such an intention, and did not
merit such unworthy treatment."

The discussions in convention still proceeded;
the learning of the law, the sacredness of the
pulpit, and the worldly wisdom of the mercantile
profession were successively put in requisition, and
delighted, and instructed, and overwhelmed an ad-
miring multitude; but the leaders of the constitution party were afraid to trust the question to a
final vote.

There yet remained a stern mass of opposition,
which although argued down and silenced in a
great degree, was not disheartened nor converted.

A new measure was devised, on the success of
which great confidence was reposed. The governour had held his own opinions in reserve; both

parties chose to claim his vote.   In this doubtful
state of things, each was anxious to secure his influence, while they, who were not his friends, attributed his absence not so much to disease, which
was the assigned cause, as to a desire of knowing
which side should be taken for popularity.

Although the leading advocates of the constitution were not the personal friends of his excellency, some, over whom they exercised great influence, were supposed to be much in his confidence ; and if by their means he could be brought
to give his name to the constitution, it was thought
that there would no longer be any doubt of the
result.

A select few of the advocates for the constitution waited upon the governour in his sick chamber ; they congratulated him that upon his vote,
and those it would draw with it, depended the
greatest question, which could ever agitate the
country.   They represented to him the glory he
would acquire in the adopting of so momentous a
matter by his own personal exertion, and the popularity to be gained, by accomplishing this object
in a manner that must be universally acceptable.

The desire of securing a better form of government than the existing confederation, was known
to him extensively to prevail, and while the benefits of the proposed constitution rendered it in
many respects desirable, the objections, which had
been made to it, had been fully and anxiously

considered. They were disposed to take that middle course, which consulting and uniting the judgment of the most able and upright men on both sides, could not fail to meet general approbation. With this view, they had prepared a series of amendments, which had been the result of most anxious deliberation. These could not indeed be incorporated into the constitution by the vote of a state, but they could accompany the ratification as the wish and expectation of this important member of the confederacy, and be by that measure finally secured. They tendered to his excellency the honour of proposing them in convention. The reputation of having devised this middle course, the credit of announcing it, the imperishable glory of its success, they had deemed it respectful to offer to him, that to the fame of having given his official sanction to the declaration of his country's independence, might be added that of securing for it a permanent constitution of government.

The charm was irresistible. Wrapped in his flannels, Hancock in a day or two took the chair of the convention, and a scene ensued more in the character of a dramatic representation, than of that serious and important business, which was the occasion of the assembly.

In a speech, wise and plausible enough in itself, but sufficiently ludicrous to those behind the scenes, the governour and president announced the anxiety of his mind, his doubts, his wishes, his conciliatory plan, his recommendation to adopt the constitution without qualification, and to propose for future amendment such alterations as respect for the opinions of the dissatisfied, or a careful regard for public liberty rendered prudent and advisable.

The accession of such a man as Hancock, to the party of the advocates for accepting the constitution, was not without great effect. His high character and consideration in the community, the reserve, which circumstances had seemed to impose upon him, the calmness with which he came into the assembly, the effort, which in defiance of disease, he again made in the cause of his country, the moderation of his councils, which appeared to take a fortunate middle course between the violence of opposing factions, had a most imposing effect on the convention, and seemed already to secure an anticipated triumph. The measure itself was discreet and judicious, and the subtlety of its accomplishment was wholly concealed from those on whose mind it was intended to operate. Encouragement now dawned on the advocates of the constitution, but the favour of the leading oppositionists was not conciliated, and the final question was too important to be submitted to any possible chance.

It had been the policy of the constitution party to operate in conversation and at private interviews, as well as in open debate on those of the opposite side, whom by any means of persuasion it had been thought possible to change. An aged and reverend gentleman, conspicuous for the firmness of his opposition and the plain sincerity of his character, was by that tacit understanding, which regulated the affairs of this assembly, placed under the surveillance of a distinguished member of the legal profession. In the course of the session, the influence of this honest clergyman had greatly strengthened the confidence of his neighbours and friends, and the plainness and directness of his objections, and his terse and comprehensive mode of expression, disturbed the efforts of more rhetorical, and perhaps more logical declaimers.

It was the good fortune of the gentleman above mentioned, to convert him from an opponent into a favourer of the constitution, so that notwithstanding his previous sentiments, his vote on the question of ratification was promised in the affirmative.

But his vote secured was only one point gained, and the ingenious commander was desirous of turning the artillery he had captured on the ranks in which it had formerly been borne. For this purpose, the reverend gentleman was urged to speak in convention, and give evidence of his new faith. " I cannot," said he, " obtain the floor ; the young men are so ardent and quick of motion, that they almost always precede me." " But I can," was the reply of the individual who had been instrumental in the change of his political creed. " Do you rise when the convention opens in the morning; I will do the same; if the president allows me the floor I will surrender it to you."

On the following day, the good old gentleman rose to speak. Half a dozen voices from each side of the house, addressed the chair at the same moment; but the presiding officer gave the individual referred to the privilege of opening the debate. " Sir," said he, addressing the president, " I have some remarks to submit to the convention, but I see a venerable gentleman opposite to me, desirous of speaking, who though differing from me in some opinions, I am always accustomed to listen to with profound respect. I beg leave to waive my right in his favour."

The change in the mind of the reverend proselyte was then first made known to the convention, and produced in the ranks of his former associates, an unaffected alarm, insomuch that one of their number, disregarding the decorum of debate, could not refrain from a strong exclamation of surprise, in the language of the Psalmist, " Help Lord, for the godly man faileth."

The question was at length taken, on a ratification of the constitution by the convention of Massachusetts, and passed in the affirmative, by a majority of nineteen out of three hundred and fifty-five members who voted.

CHAPTER III.

THE triumph of the constitution party in Massachusetts was celebrated with all the pageantry
of conquest. No victory of the revolution was announced with greater enthusiasm, and on no occasion was the exultation of success more offensively
displayed. The vanquished in battle had been
treated with greater kindness than those in debate.
Instead of the courteous demeanour, which the gallant conqueror of a foreign foe deems it honourable to assume, there was a display of that super-
cilious superiority, which marks the triumphs of a
servile war. The state of parties, neither in the
convention nor among the people, could have justified this extravagant rejoicing, had it not been considered the most effective measure to swell the
actual strength of the majority, and to extend the
influence of Massachusetts into states whose conventions were yet to assemble. Doubtful of the
real state of public opinion, the constitution party
determined to assume its control, and to secure

by apparent acclamation, what had been carried with exceeding difficulty through the forms of debate.

The measure was a wise one. Men naturally love the side of power. The appearance of superior strength overawes opposition, and gathers to its standard that vast mass of the community, who always belong to the party of the strongest. The constitution was about to become the law of the land, and the ambitious, who were desirous of its honours, the interested, who might solicit the employments it would confer, and the discontented, whom any change must benefit, added the force of their numbers and their influence to those intelligent patriots, who were the supporters of its provisions, from a belief of their inherent propriety.

The great exultation at the time, the formation of political parties with reference to the question decided, and the superiority, which subsequent success seems to have stamped on the judgment of the advocates of the constitution, have transferred the honour of the event to those whose management was in truth successful rather than their cause.

A general sentiment prevailed that a new form of government was necessary for the existence of the American republic ; and as general an opinion that the constitution, as it came from the convention at Philadelphia, would not answer the purposes intended. But the real question presented to the people, was whether the proposed constitution

should be accepted as it was, with the hope of obtaining after it went into operation, such amendments as were desirable, according to the provision for that purpose contained in the fifth article,
or whether the ratification should be delayed until
the amendments were first incorporated.

It is certainly true, that this was a most important practical difference, and might well excite much
of the controversy, which ensued, but as in all the
leading states amendments were in fact recommended, and the most important of them were as
speedily as practicable incorporated into the constitution according to the forms of law, two inferences are deducible : 1st, That those members of
the convention at Philadelphia who declined signing the constitution, were sustained in their refusal by a large majority of the immediate representatives of the people : 2ndly, That the amazing success of this great experiment on the practicability
of free institutions, is not to be ascribed solely to
the provisions of the constitution, as at first proposed, but to its actual condition after these important alterations were made in it : and it is not
a little surprising, that notwithstanding the constitution, if it must have remained as it was first
promulgated, would have been rejected by an immense vote,* and that the indispensable necessi-

---

* An unqualified ratification was given by Delaware, Pennsylvania, New-Jersey, Connecticut, Georgia, Maryland, and after
the new government had gone into operation, by North Carolina.
                                                        Amend-

ty of important amendments was admitted in the
state conventions, and that those amendments
were in truth afterwards incorporated, they whose
great object was accomplished by the adoption of
these amendments, should have been considered
and treated as the vanquished party, and that those
who were willing to accept of a government in a
form to which the people would not consent, should
have been considered, and should have considered themselves as victors on this great political
arena.

The discussions, which were held in the several
conventions, and by the instrumentality of the
press, did not indeed limit the subject of difference
to the point above supposed. The occasion was
one, which enlisted the pride of men, and made
them competitors rather for victory than for truth.
Exaggeration, misrepresentation and mistake, were

Amendments were proposed by the conventions of Massachusetts, South Carolina, New-Hampshire, Virginia and New-York.
Rhode Island ratified the constitution in June 1790, proposing
amendments. The ratification of Pennsylvania was made on 12th
December succeeding the convention, and was charged at the
time with being urged with unfair precipitancy. It occasioned some disgraceful riots, and other marks of popular tumult.
This is the only large state, which accepted the constitution with
out limitation. The commentaries and declaration of rights by
other states, which do not form part of the constitution itself,
have nevertheless exercised an important influence in the construction of the powers, which that instrument confers, and form
a contemporaneous exposition of its articles, entitled to great
respect.

the natural consequences. Among much profound
learning, in which the science of civil government
was elaborately and thoroughly explained, and
which will serve while men continue free, indelibly
to mark the line between liberty and licentiousness, and to define what force is required for the
purposes of government, without danger to personal
freedom, there was mingled whatever could inflame the passions and exasperate the feelings of
the community. They who favoured the new
system, concealed or diminished its objectionable
provisions, and defended such as were of doubtful
utility; the other side, in retaliation, magnified its
supposed evils, and sounded an alarm for public
liberty probably beyond their fears.

The year 1788 was passed by the statesmen of
the United States under all the agitation and excitement, which attends the disunion of great questions of political interest, and with the anxiety that
awaits the progress of an important and uncertain
event.

Not satisfied with having accomplished their
purposes in Massachusetts, the majority, as now
they must be termed, seemed to consider it requisite for their complete triumph to run down the reputation of all, by whom they had been obstructed.

Past political services, and the character of those
revolutionary patriots, which should have been considered the property of the nation, were of no avail
in the all absorbing interest of the present divi-

sions, and it was apparent that a new party was to be formed, whose title to the confidence of the people was to rest on the zeal or ability with which they had smoothed the way for the adoption of the new constitution.

MR. GERRY TO GENERAL WARREN.

CAMBRIDGE, JUNE 28, 1788.

MY DEAR SIR,

I wish you would so order your arrangements as to favour us with a part of your time, although the alarm of our being together might be such as to station sentries at Charlestown bridge, and the fortifications for the defence of the federalists in Boston.

It is diverting to hear the manner in which these people amuse themselves at our expense. They suggest that I shall not be able to keep this place ; and should it be true, I tell them I hope to find purchasers out of Boston. Others say I am much affected by political events, and disposed to grow melancholy, and so long as this is attended with a *mens conscia recti*, they may think as they please ; for melancholy is like madness, which has a pleasure none but madmen know.

The convention of New-York will, I am well informed, annex a bill of rights to a conditional ratification, which will remove all our objections, and it is believed Virginia will do the same. Patrick Henry has been brilliant in that convention, and very severe on ———— who is reprobated for his duplicity and versatility. I know not what judgment to form with respect to the final event, but trust in Providence for protection from the thraldom, which may be apprehended, unless the new constitution shall be modified and amended. Do not let ———— be deterred from visiting us, for fear that she and ———— may be again distinguished in Boston by the appellation of the anti-federal ladies.

Your's in great friendship,

E. GERRY.

————

Notwithstanding the light and playful spirit of this letter, Mr. Gerry felt severely the revulsion of public opinion, and the loss of that bright popularity, the sunshine and full splendour of which had hitherto shone upon his political path.

In another letter, alluding to the same topic, he remarks: " The vigilant enemies of free government have been long in the execution of their plan to hunt down all who remain attached to revolution principles ; they have attacked us in detail and have deprived you, Mr. S. Adams and myself in a great measure of that public confidence to which a faithful attachment to the public interest entitles

us, and they are now aiming to throw Mr. Hancock out of the saddle, who, with all his foibles,
is yet attached to the whig cause. There seems
to be a disposition in the dominant party to establish a nobility of opinion, under whose control
in a short time, will be placed the government of
the union and the states, and whose insufferable
arrogance marks out for degradation all who will
not submit to their authority. It is beginning to
be fashionable to consider the opponents of the
constitution as embodying themselves with the
lower classes of the people, and that one forfeits
all title to the respect of a gentleman, unless he is
one of the privileged order. Is this, my friend, to
be the operation of the free government, which all
our labours in the revolution have tended to produce ?"

The state of affairs at this period was excessive-
ly galling to honourable men, who next to the
conscientious discharge of duty derived their best
reward from the approbation of the people, and
now saw all the high objects of their laudable ambition broken at a blow, But such was the angry
temper of the public mind, or rather such the state
to which an interested part of the community was
disposed to excite it, that not only they who had
decidedly opposed the constitution, but those even
who had not been conspicuously zealous in its defence, were exposed to the pitiless pelting of the
storm, and devoted to obloquy and disgrace.

Divided as the people were, on the question of acceptance, it is no mark of their stability, that those who were called to pronounce the conscientious decision of their judgment should lose their favour by placing themselves in opposition ; and certainly less to the credit of their justice, that even an error of judgment on this debateable proposition should cancel the debt of gratitude, which the whole revolution had accumulated. But other ages show the insecurity of popular favour, and other periods of our own history are not deficient in lessons, which teach its unsubstantial and evanescent existence.

The boldness of the party, which had not long before been even a weak minority, in assuming a control of public feeling, and fearlessly and rashly assailing the long tried and well favoured servants of the people, whose claim on the affections of their fellow citizens might have given currency even to a bad cause, would be much more the subject of surprise, if its success had not transfixed our astonishment.

Such however, was the rapid change of public sentiment that the constitution party, which at the elections for the convention had, in many places, not dared to avow themselves, was now a most imposing and resistless majority, and flushed with all the pride of unexpected success, were little disposed to regard the feelings, the services, or the character of their defeated adversaries. Indeed,

in the intemperance of the time, the constitution
question superseded almost every where, all other
considerations. The few days of service in the
state convention were esteemed of more importance than whole campaigns in the field; and he
who had only his services in the cabinet of the
revolution, as his credentials to public favour, was
almost sure to be superseded by the greater popularity of more recent favourites.

Thus in the election for members of congress,
at the commencement of the new government, Mr.
Fisher Ames, then only known as a young debater
of talents, prevailed over the immortal father of
the revolution, Samuel Adams. General Warren,
whose public character has been displayed in correspondence with the subject of this memoir, and
who had long enjoyed the esteem, and received the
honours of his native state, was unsuccessful in
Plymouth; and so many others divided the votes
with Mr. Gerry, who was a candidate in Middlesex, that no choice was made on that first theatre
of American independence.

The election of senators under the new government was equally decisive of the temper of the
times. For many years Mr. Gerry had enjoyed
the most implicit confidence of the general court;
no mark of their highest esteem had ever been withheld from him; and on every occasion in which
his name was presented for their ballots, it had received nearly an unanimous vote. Now indeed

the case was changed; so changed that his friends were unwilling to expose him to the mortification of defeat, by proposing him, according to their first design, as a candidate for the senate of the United States.*

The result showed their prudence. Mr. Strong was chosen by both branches, without opposition. But the friends of amendments proposed as his colleague, Dr. Charles Jarvis, personally a great favourite with the people, who though he voted for the constitution in the convention, was known to consider with great respect, the objections that had been made to it, and to be as solicitous as Mr. Gerry, to secure the alterations, which had been proposed. The house of representatives at three successive ballots gave him a majority of votes; but the senate nonconcurred in the appointment, and each time returned a different candidate. The choice finally settled on honourable Tristram Dalton, who had declared in the state convention his perfect satisfaction with the constitution as it stood, without any preference for the amendments proposed.

By a most fortunate selection of a distinguishing name, the advocates for the constitution, who were

---

* More liberal sentiments prevailed in Virginia, where Richard Henry Lee, the mover of the declaration of independence, and a strenuous opponent of the constitution was elected to the senate of the United States against James Madison, its most powerful advocate.

fast forming and organizing themselves into a distinct party in the state, assumed the appellation of federalists; yet inasmuch as the chief objection to the new government consisted in its not being a federal, but a national system, this patronymic might more justly have been claimed by the opposite side. The term however was popular, and the popular party seized it, and under its influence have justified the remark of a judicious observer of affairs, that they who make ballads and songs for the people have commonly more influence than those who make the laws.

A second ballot was ordered for Middlesex, and not only the personal friends of Mr. Gerry, but that political party, to which he might now be said to belong, insisted on again placing his name before the public. The zeal of the one excited the exertions of the other, and efforts were made by both, corresponding to the importance of the contest. The competitor of Mr. Gerry on the first trial had been Mr. Nathaniel Gorham, a gentleman of character and property, whose family had long been residents in the county. He had himself presided as chairman of the committee of the whole, in the convention at Philadelphia, and was distinguished as an advocate for the constitution in the convention of Massachusetts. At the second trial the votes were divided among several competitors. On this occasion the public press opened its batteries of detraction, as if to prove the utter insecurity of reputation, when faction is desirous of destroying it.

To judge by some of the journals of that day, it would be thought that the " antifederal" candidate for Middlesex had neither experience, talents, or public character; that he was some obscure, or not trustworthy individual, who for the first time had entered upon public life in the convention, and grossly mistaking, or willfully counteracting, or from personal interest desirous of defeating the public sentiment, was properly to end his labours with the scene in which they had commenced.

Disgusted with the virulence of the enemies by whom he was assailed, and averse from reengaging in the routine of legislative duty, in which he had all his life been employed, Mr. Gerry addressed the following letter to the electors of Middlesex :

Friends and Fellow Citizens :

It appearing from your suffrages that I am one of your candidates for a federal representative, give me leave for this evidence of your confidence, to express my warmest acknowledgments, but at the same time to request that such of you as may again be disposed to honour me with your votes, will turn your attention to some other candidate ; for although I have been long honoured with the confidence of my countrymen, and am conscious that a regard to their political happiness has been the sole motive of my conduct, yet circumstanced as I am, an election would by no means be agreeable.

Since however my name is again, without any effort or inclination of my own, brought into public view, I embrace this opportunity to explain that conduct, for which I have been treated with so much invective and abuse.

When the question on the constitution was put in the federal convention, conceiving myself to be in a land of liberty, where the privilege of deliberating and voting with freedom would be firmly supported, I voted against the constitution, because in my opinion, it was in many respects defective.

Had my opinion been founded in error, it would have been only an error of judgment. But five states having ratified the constitution, in the fullest expectation of amendments, and two having rejected it, no one can, I think, deny that my opinion has been confirmed by a majority of the union. An attempt has been made by means of invective, to impair or destroy the privilege mentioned; a privilege, which no good citizen will ever permit to die in his hands, and which the good sense of the community will protect as one of the pillars of a free state.

Some have endeavoured to represent me as an enemy to the constitution; than which nothing is more remote from truth. Since the commencement of the revolution, I have been ever solicitous for an efficient federal government, conceiving that without it we must be a divided and unhappy people. A government too democratical, I have deprecated; but wished for one that should possess power sufficient for the welfare of the union, and at the same time be so balanced as to secure the governed from the rapacity and domination of lawless and insolent ambition. To an unconditional ratification I was therefore opposed, because thereby every necessary amendment would be precarious. But as the system is adopted, I am clearly of opinion that every citizen of the ratifying states is in duty bound to support it, and that an opposition to a due administration of it would not only be unjustifiable, but highly criminal.

Amendments every citizen has a right to urge without exciting a spirit of persecution, which is unnecessary in a good cause, and never gains proselytes in a bad one. Every friend of a vigorous government must, as I conceive, be desirous of such amendments as will remove the just apprehensions of the people, and secure their confidence and affection. To defeat amendments of this description, must be in effect to defeat the constitution itself. When the question on amendments shall have received a constitutional decision, I shall cheerfully acquiesce, and in any event, shall be happy to promote the interests of the respectable county of Middlesex, of this commonwealth, and of the United States.

The part, which I have had to act, and the uncandid treatment, which I have received in this
matter will, I trust, justify me in being thus explicit, for I am conscious that every part of my political conduct has had for its object, the public
welfare.

  I am, with the highest respect,
     Your humble servant,
        E. GERRY.

Whether this declaration was intended to aid,
or prevent his election, his friends would not withdraw his name, and notwithstanding a powerful
competition, they succeeded in electing him on
the second ballot, by a small majority.

In his letter of acceptance to the governour, he
says, " I am deeply impressed with this honourable testimony of the electors of Middlesex, after I
had repeatedly informed them of my declining the
appointment. This however has placed me in a
situation, which of all others I wished to avoid ;
being thereby reduced to the disagreeable alternative of disappointing my fellow citizens, who have
conferred on me their suffrages, or of filling a place,
which the most cogent reasons had urged me to
decline. Under these circumstances, in the critical state of public affairs, I have preferred the latter, being determined to sacrifice every personal
consideration, to the acceptance of the office ;
that desirous as I am of the establishment of a

federal government, no act of mine may have the least appearance of impeding it."

The sincerity of his views is made more apparent by a letter to his confidential friend.

———

MR. GERRY TO GENERAL WARREN.

CAMBRIDGE, FEBRUARY 15, 1789.

My Dear Sir,

I suspect you will consider me as manifesting a disposition to change my principles, or of a want of resolution to adhere to them, when I tell you it is probable I shall go to congress. Indeed if this be your opinion, you will alter it when I assure you of all political events in which I have been interested, my election I consider as most unfortunate to myself. I had not, during its pendency, the most remote idea of acceptance, but thought of it with horror.

I now think the measure one of all others that threatens destruction to my peace, interest and welfare, and yet such has been the torrent of abuse against me, that no person here will listen to my declining; my best friends say they shall be sacrificed by my refusal, and that I myself shall be considered as an obstinate opposer of the government, which is an opinion that has recently been much circulated.

Should I decline then, I am to be considered as

a non-juror in Great Britain, or an Irish Catholic, and sooner than so live, I would quit the continent. In accepting, I see nothing but two years of extreme disagreeables. To gratify my friends, and to avoid the consequences menaced, I have selected a certain positive evil; whether it be the least of the two, I am yet to learn.

In another letter to the same gentleman, after having taken his seat in congress, he thus writes: " I cannot accept your compliments, for I assure you my situation here is a very awkward one. I foresaw that it would be impossible for me to feel easy in a branch of the federal legislature where I had few or no connexions or friends. Whatever the state of my case may be upon republican principles, I cannot separate it in my mind from an idea of degradation, when I reflect that the flower of my life has been spent in the arduous business of the revolution, and see a preference given to those who have endured very few of its toils; but we both know that republics were never remarkable for the constancy of their attachment, and therefore private life is the place in which we are most to look for happiness, especially when the road to political honours lies through the mazes of intrigue, servility and corruption. I have had so much to do with legislation, that I feel an aversion to any further occupation of that kind, and am satisfied that retirement would most contribute to my own and my family's happiness, therefore I fear not any

mortification from my enemies; but from my friends
I do indeed experience it, by their urging me to
places, which are neither pleasant, lucrative nor
honourable. Their measures put me in trammels;
had I declined, it would have been said and believed
that I was a determined enemy to the federal government, and my friends would have been reproached for supporting a man, who would not attend congress to procure the amendments he had warmly insisted upon. Indeed I should have been obliged to
leave the state, to seek a more agreeable residence,
which could only have been done by the sacrifice
of much property; I have therefore been obliged,
by accepting this place, to submit to a temporary
mortification to counteract the malignity of inveterate foes.

"I cannot but smile at the art or folly, for I
know not which is the true cause, of those who
represent me as being *elated* at my appointment,
when the acceptance is indeed forced upon me by
circumstances, which operate as a great injustice
to myself. As to the new government, I am and
always was a federalist, but not in their sense of
the term. I feel bound in honour to support a
system that has been ratified by a majority of my
fellow citizens; to oppose it would be to sow the
seeds of civil war, and to lay a foundation for military tyranny. I shall be a spectator merely, until
I can form some adequate idea of men and measures."

CHAPTER IV.

First Congress of United States........Parties therein....Speech on amendments to the Constitution........The public creditors........Employments of private life........Origin of the Democratic party........ Commentary on the account given by the biographer of Washington.........French revolution.........British treaty.........Chosen to the Electoral College of Massachusetts........Votes for Mr. Adams........ Correspondence with Mr. Jefferson on the election........With a lady.

THE government of the United States, under the federal constitution, was organized at New-York in April 1789. There was a charm of novelty in its arrangements well calculated to aid its intrinsic merits, and secure a propitious popularity.

Congress however like the nation itself, was composed of men, who in the national or state conventions, or in the primary assemblies of the people, had taken opposite views of the new frame of government, and formed different estimates of its worth. Principles, which were brought into the earlier discussion of its character, had lost none of their force, and passions, which collision excited, if they had in some degree subsided, were certainly not extinguished. Honest men of all parties were disposed to give the new system a fair setting off, and to provide all reasonable equipments for its long and profitable voyage. Opposition was unorganized. Indeed as the constitution was the supreme law of the land, they who objected to its ratification, now that their original objections were unavailing, professed to treat it with the respect due to sovereign authority.

The political elements collected in the first congress, notwithstanding these appearances, could not easily assimilate ; and their natural repulsion was increased by artificial excitements. They by whose efforts the government had been called into being, felt themselves its natural guardians, and were unwilling to share their honours with less fortunate companions ; while the other class, who considered their oath of fidelity as security for allegiance, resented as derogatory and offensive every attempt at discrimination. It was soon apparent that lines of division would be drawn, not easily to be effaced.

The state elections had given to the federalists*

* In the course of an early debate, Mr. Gerry took occasion to remark that he did not like the term national, in a resolution then before the house. However correct it was abstractly considered, it had acquired in the debates on the constitution, a technical meaning, and was used to designate a consolidation, and not a confederacy of the states. The term federal too, he said, properly belonged to those, who really desiring a federal union, had felt it a duty to oppose one, which in their view had few fedral principles, and it was improper that the friends of amending the system should be called antifederalists, inasmuch as they eminently were the advocates of a federal government. As the question had been presented to the people, it was between those who were then for ratifying the constitution, and those who would have delayed it, or between ratifiers and anti-ratifiers. These then should have been their denominations, which by abbreviation might entitle them to the appellatives rats, and anti-rats.

decided superiority in numbers, and an imposing weight of character. Ambition, not easily excluded from an assembly of statesmen, secured for them the arrangements and confederacy of a political party. Power was in their hands, and its natural tendency to self-confidence and pride was not diminished by the mode of acquiring it.

Stern republicans, who had resisted the existing form from a jealous apprehension of its consequences, found in thus realizing their fears, new cause of respect for their judgment, and none for relinquishing opinions, which experience seemed to them gradually to confirm. Other incidents strengthened these convictions. There appeared to one class of the community too much conformity in the external form of the new government to the pageantry of European courts, in levees, audiences and addresses, not suited to the plain habits of an unostentatious democracy. Efforts to confer high titles on its great functionaries,* to make a discrimination in the rank and emoluments of the two branches of the legislature ; to fix compensation for services beyond the standard of like duties in the states, and above all, the latitude of construction, which there was a supposed inclination to give to the language of the constitution, early filled many minds with serious apprehensions.

* The president to be called his *highness*. So at first voted in the senate. Some newspapers proposed that the members of the house of representatives should be called honourable ; senators to be addressed as right honourable.

The exercise of government patronage was a further, and as it always has been, an irritating subject of dissatisfaction and uneasiness. The friends of amendments, now generally and most unwisely held up in the light of an opposition according to English precedent, began to apprehend that if they were not marked by a stern principle of exclusion from participating in the honours of public employment, they were beheld with suspicion and slight regard.

The composition of the cabinet and appointments to which the personal knowledge of the president extended, were not included in their dissatisfaction, but beyond that line the unfriendly influence of a government party was thought to be visible.

Indeed the personal character of the president was fortunately for the country a rock, on which the whole community rested. Implicit confidence was placed in his patriotism and ability ; and his alternate gratification and reproof of the leaders of each party, restrained the tumult of the waves, which at that early period threatened to sweep from before them the then unsettled fabric of freedom.

It was perhaps pardonable to believe that men, who opposed the constitution, would embarrass the government. But there were measures of such novel and intricate character incident to the establishment of a federative empire, that a more

candid consideration of the motives of the public
agents is now due to their fame. A desire to secure
such amendments to the national charter as had
been deemed necessary by the states, was indeed
the anxious wish of those statesmen with whom
Mr. Gerry had acted. To motives derived from a
conviction of their intrinsic importance, were added without doubt those, which addressed themselves to their pride of opinion and their character
before the people; but even the question of amendments they were willing to postpone to the more
urgent subjects, which the organization of a new
government pressed on their notice.

Mr. Gerry, who unquestionably spoke the sentiments of this class, gave ample evidence of their
disposition to aid in good faith those measures of
general interest for which the government was instituted, and of the reluctance with which they
would be driven into opposition by illiberality or
harshness.

" I am of opinion," he said in debate, " that we
should despatch the important subjects now on the
table, and reserve the great questions concerning
the form of the constitution, to a period of tranquillity and leisure. It is indeed a momentous
subject, and very near my heart, and I shall be
glad to set about it as speedily as possible ; but I
would not stay the operations of government on
that account. I think our political ship should be
first got under way, and that she be not suffered

to lay by the wharf, until she beats off her rudder, or runs a wreck on shore. I wish an early day may be assigned for the consideration of amendments, to prevent the necessity, which the states may feel themselves under of calling a new convention. If I am not one of those fascinated admirers of the system who consider it all perfection, I am not so blind nor so uncandid, that I cannot see, or will not acknowledge it has beauties. It partakes of humanity; there is blended in it virtue and vice, excellence and error. If it be referred to a new convention, we risk some of its best properties. My opinion was openly given, that it ought not to have been ratified without amendments, but as the matter now stands, I am firmly of opinion that the salvation of America depends on the establishment of this government, whether amended or not. If this constitution, which is now ratified, be not supported, I despair of ever having a government for these United States."

The sentiments thus expressed, were those to which candid men could take no exception. They were the honest sentiments of a class of the community, which if not then an actual majority, was numerous and respectable enough not wantonly to have been assalied. It tended nothing to unanimity, that such men found themselves looked upon with suspicion, and their professions listened to with an incredulity that was little else than an imputation upon them of stratagem and fraud.

The feelings, which this state of things excited, were not calmed or conciliated by the measures proposed and adopted by congress. There was a radical difference of principle among the members, as great, as could be found on the subject of the subject of the constitution itself, in the propositions of Mr. Pendleton and the scheme of Colonel Hamilton. Notwithstanding this fact, which would sooner or later produce more open discordance, Mr. Gerry and his political friends lent with good faith the aid of their abilities and experience to the measures of the government. In the commercial and financial departments, where previous application had given him great facility and acquaintance, he was early put in requisition, and in forming the first tariff and tonnage bills, he laboured with great industry and perseverance. Information, which is now easily acquired through regular channels, and is systematized by the assistance of clerks, was then obtained by the exertion of individual members. The vast mass of documents, which went into the composition of these first bills of revenue, were collected, arranged and consolidated, by his personal labour.*

With zeal for an efficient and energetic administration, and a sincere desire to cooperate in establishing it, his views and those of his friends

* The voluminous correspondence and the immense statistical abstracts among his papers, is authority for the remark in the text.

were in many respects so different from the majority of congress, that they could not escape the imputation of conducting a concerted opposition.

"It is my rule," said he in a private letter, "to support such measures as I think good or harmless, and to oppose those, from whatever quarter they come, which are in my opinion of a different character; but when the project is ripened into a law, I feel bound to respect it, however its passage may have been procured. But this does not satisfy a certain class of men, who have very pompous notions of government, and seem disposed to make those powers, which were objectionable in the theory of government, felt and feared in the practice of it. There is a strong disposition to make the administration exclusive, and if there was not more resistance in the character of the president than there is in the provisions of the constitution, such would be most decidedly the case. A fair competition among honourable men gives alarm. There are those who wish to increase the value of their chances, by diminishing the number of rivals, and to hold nearly one half the community in a state of alienage, so that they may be no more trusted than the partizans of the pretender. Even this would be less intolerable, if they were willing to take the credit of their design, but while they are themselves the origin and cause of opposition, by a superciliousness, which belongs to the better sort, they contrive to represent the true friends of the people as promoters of strife and division. All this is painful to us as citizens of a country, which has suffered so much for freedom, and exceedingly unpleasant to those who are called into its councils. The judiciary bill will surprise you. It now stands so that we are to have a court with original jurisdiction in cases affecting life, liberty and property, without an appeal, and composed of judges not removable except by conviction on impeachment. But you will consider me as a great antifederalist, and to preserve your good opinion I will not enter into a further explanation of matters depending. They may be changed in their progress, and I suppose come out perfectly federal, which I know you will think perfection itself."

Mr. Gerry undervalued his influence in this first congress of the United States. True indeed, the spirit of party had its residence there, and the general character of a statesman was not a sufficient badge of honour, without wearing the colours under which he was enrolled. It was true also that the rank, in which Mr. Gerry was usually found, was not the party of the strongest, and that the general supervision and direction of affairs, to which he had been for many years accustomed, had passed to other hands ; but on subjects of difficulty and importance, it was impossible that he should not be listened to with attention and respect. In the discussions, which agitated that assembly, in all matters connected with finance, on

the proposed discrimination between the public creditors, on funding the indents of the state treasu-
ries, and the assumption of the state debts, he expressed very largely his opinions, and was most
generally in the majority of the house.

In the protracted debate upon the first report
of the secretary of the treasury, Mr. Gerry entered very fully in defence of some of its propositions, which might have afforded a popular theme
for opposition, if there had been a settled design
to embarrass the operations of the government.

After defending the power of congress to assume and pay the state debts, he enquires, Who
are the holders of state certificates? Some of the
state creditors, he replies, were officers and soldiers of the late army. The first army of the
United States was raised, armed and clothed by
the states. The officers and soldiers have as
strong a claim on the justice of the country, as
those who were enlisted at the close of the war;
a greater indeed, as they came forward in those
dark moments, when to the dangers of ordinary
warfare, were superadded the penalties of rebellion. These men acknowledge no difference in
their rights because they were enlisted by state
instead of continental authority; for they were
adopted by congress, formed into one army, fought
the same battles, and shared the same hardships.

Another part of the state creditors, are men,
who furnished supplies for the union, during the

late war. Can any one, who recollects the circumstance, imagine a difference between them and continental creditors, except that they came forward in our extremest need, when the more distant authority of congress was inadequate to the occasion. Part of the state debts were continental debts assumed by the state on the earnest recommendation of congress; other parts were occasioned by the states having undertaken expeditions against the common enemy for the general good, or having paid to their citizens interest on the continental debt.

It is said the proposed assumption will raise the importance of the union and depress the states. If I thought so I should oppose it, because the constitutional balance between the states and the union, ought to be preserved. I view the constitutions of the united and individual states, as forming a great political machine, in which the small wheels are as essential as the large ones, and if either are deranged, the movement will be imperfect; but I humbly conceive a contrary policy will have the effect predicted. Suppose congress refuse to assume the state debts; they will make, as they are able, provision for their own creditors, but it is doubtful if each of the states can make a similar arrangement, and if they fail, the discrimination will most materially impair their respectability. The United States creditors will naturally magnify the honesty, integrity and ability

of the general government, and hold in contempt
and derision, the injustice or poverty of the local
authorities.   A clamour might be raised against the
state governments, made more general by the contrast between them and the nation, and the pecuniary interests of a large class of citizens, operat-
ing to their injury, may have a prejudicial effect
on their permanency or their strength.

The national government may incline to oppress
the states, and I ask whether they would not be
better able to resist this attack if they had no
creditors to provide for.   The common maxim is,
out of debt, out of danger, but the opposite argument reverses it, and in my opinion, very un-
soundly.

A discrimination will establish two contending
parties.   They who look to the union for their
payments will be desirous of extending its power
of taxation, revenues, resources and credit.   They
who look for their payments to the states, will be
prone to diminish the continental power, for the
purpose of enlarging the funds from which they
are to derive their reward.   This discord will defeat the operation of both.

It has been suggested that the state debts may
not have been fairly liquidated.   I should think
from personal observation there was no ground for
this fear. The creditors of Massachusetts have had
their accounts adjusted quite as strictly as those

of the federal government. Other states have acted in the same manner.

It is said we are unacquainted with the ability of the union, and therefore it is improper to pledge the public faith for the payment of a debt, which may possibly exceed its means. I do not now, and never did, despair of the ability of the United States to pay their debts. Our finances are indeed deranged, but we are taking measures to extricate ourselves from the evil of such a situation, and should not be deterred from ascertaining the amount we owe, from present inability to pay it. By the secretary's report, we can now pay two thirds the interest. With increasing resources and a gradual diminution of the interest, we may eventually discharge the whole. But let me not be misunderstood. I would not pledge the government to what it could not perform. I would not subject it to any engagement, which it might not be able to make good. But the acknowledgment of our obligation is one thing, the mode of discharging it, another. The best interest of the creditors as well as the nation, is to make such arrangement as by securing the actual performance of what is just, will so modify the means as not to make it inconveniently onerous. The secretary's report goes on the ground of admitting the force of all the public contracts. He allows no preference as to continental creditors, among whom, if their claims could be examined, would be found weightier causes of difference than exist between the classes, whose rights are severally referable to the states or the nation. There is the same principle to prevent discrimination in either case. Indeed by the constitution, the efficient means of revenue are conveyed to the federal government. The states are almost wholly without them, and it cannot be reasonable that they should give up the resources for paying the interest on their debts, unless those debts are assumed by the nation. If indeed sir, with limited resources and a heavy debt, the states are to commence the operations of the new confederacy, the smaller will soon be crushed ; the larger will be scarce able to get along. Their independence is but nominal; their sovereignty must exist but in name, and a consolidated government take the place of the system, which such a measure would destroy.

With the second congress of the United States, Mr. Gerry terminated his services in the legislature. He had declined reiterated and importunate solicitations to be a candidate for reelection, and retired to his farm and family at Cambridge. Many reasons produced a disinclination to be longer concerned in political affairs. The citizens of the United States were fast forming themselves into fierce and irreconcilable parties, and it was the policy of the dominant power, to identify the op-

position with hostility to the constitution itself.
That hostility on the part of Mr. Gerry had passed away, and not only in conformity with his early
declaration, that he would submit to the will of
the majority, but because the recent amendments
had essentially changed its character, he was disposed to give it a fair trial and an honest support.

There was, however, in the early measures of
congress, much to excite the apprehension of so
jealous a republican, always alive to the dangers
of political power, and habitually regardful of public liberty ; and without participating in that spirit
of party, which rallied its members on all occasions, under their several banners, he was too frequently found opposing the measures of the majority, to be classed among their friends.   On the
other hand, when the movements of the administration met the approbation of his judgment, he
was not deterred from lending them his support,
although the occasion might be one, which the opposition had selected as favourable for a combined
attack.   The integrity and independence, or if
any one so chooses to call it, the singularity of
mind, which would not submit to be bound by the
shackles of party, would not give to either side a
security for his vote, and would obviously in the
end deprive him of the favour of both.

But his most intimate personal friends were
chiefly among those, whose attachments combined
them with the government.   Against these he

could not very frequently take a stand without dissatisfaction to them, nor be on their side without violence to himself. Nor was the state of affairs in congress calculated to gratify his ambition or reward the long labours of experience. He who had been one of the chief leaders and directors of the administration, when the whole authority of government was confided to the delegates of the states, could find little pleasure in being one of the lower branch of a deliberative assembly, where the charge of arranging and directing the great movements of the political machinery, was in other hands. A new generation of statesmen had arisen since the declaration of independence, whose active spirit, under the peculiar condition of things, elevated them over those earlier patriots, by whom the resistance of the colonies had been first promoted.

Motives equally strong were also derived from his personal concerns. A young and numerous family claimed that attention, which their mother's infirm health could but partially bestow, and threw on him the responsibility of forming their principles, superintending their education, and preparing them for the duties of society.

As a father, he found a field for his labours, upon which he entered with all the zeal and more than all the pleasure, which the patriot and statesman had experienced in different pursuits. Peculiarly kind and affectionate in his disposition, the culture of the infant mind had an irresistible charm for him, while his benevolent feelings and affable manners endeared him to the young objects of his regard.

Perhaps no individual of any profession or employment, certainly none whose temper had been so often tried in the angry tempests of political discussion, was more thoroughly mild, placid and placable. If experience had not shown how inflexible were his purposes, and how perseveringly he pursued them in the great concerns of public duty, if the firmness with which he maintained his sentiments, or the untiring efforts, by which they were inculcated, had not been repeatedly displayed in critical situations of political life, it might have been supposed that the softer elements of human nature were too intimately mingled in his character, to enable him to maintain the rank he obtained among statesmen ; while on the other hand those, who were acquainted with the mild and gentle spirit, which displayed itself at home, and witnessed the conciliatory temperament, which rendered him the favourite and friend of the youthful circle, might well have been surprised at the vigorous efforts and the immovable firmness of his public conduct. This delineation of his private character, is very different from the picture presented by political adversaries, who saw him only when considerations of public duty imposed their irresistible weight upon his mind. In the angry collisions of a later period, and in the personal resentments growing out of an unfortunate state of affairs, there were many, who believed what the press seemed desirous of establishing, that the leader of the republican party had the ascerbity of temper, the ferocity and vindictiveness, which belonged to the Brissots and Dantons, to whom they chose to resemble him, and that the government of Massachusetts was wanting at one period in nothing but power to have resembled itself to the most busy period of the revolutionary guillotine. Such is the distorting atmosphere of party, and the credulity, which under its excitement, receives the most monstrous fictions for truth.

Mr. Gerry passed the succeeding four years in the superintendence of his farm, and the cultivation of those young plants of a more endearing description, which providence had intrusted to his care. Efforts were made in vain to draw him into various situations of a public character. The citizens of Middlesex, elected him in May 1793, to the senate of the commonwealth, but he declined the honour of a seat in that body, and would not permit himself to be named as a candidate either for the council or the house of representatives, as he was repeatedly solicited to do by his friends.*

* A very flattering effort was made to draw him back to public life, which profitable and honourable as it was, he had the resolution to withstand. The commissioners under the sixth

Even the correspondence, which he had hitherto extensively carried on, seems during this interval to have been in some degree relinquished. All the energy of mind, which for so many years had been devoted to his country, were confined to the little territory under his control, and the young republic of which he was the natural head.

Of this period of tranquillity and peace he often afterwards spoke with unmingled satisfaction, and was inclined to consider it as the happiest passage of a long life. His residence was near the seat of the university at Cambridge. Few young men resorted to that institution without desiring the privilege of his acquaintance. The hospitality of his mansion and the urbanity of his manners, domesticated the most respectable of them in his family circle. Strangers, whom curiosity or interest led to that centre of literary attraction, were received in a manner suited to the rank he had held in the public councils,

article of the treaty of London, consisting of two Americans and two Englishmen, assembled in Philadelphia in May 1797, and an attempt was to be made to choose the fifth, which would complete the board, by mutual consent. The government of the United States were very desirous he should be an American, and deeming it probable if some highly respectable and well known character was nominated, the British would accept him, they were anxious to propose Mr. Gerry. The business would have conformed in some degree with his accustomed habits of mind, and in other respects would have been both agreeable and lucrative, but he declined permitting his name to be submitted to the board.

although the hospitality of a generous disposition, made an inconvenient inroad on his property.

Like most of those, who had been actively concerned in the direction of the revolution, Mr. Gerry had retired from the service of the country with no other emolument than the honours it conferred. The fluctuation of affairs, which had required a constant watchfulness over private concerns, and incessant public employment, which obstructed it, prevented not merely the increase, but almost the preservation of those means, which the early patriots had carried into the contest. Fortunes had been realized indeed in the changes of the times, but the Deity who presided over the distribution of wealth, seemed to consider that the statesmen and soldiers of the country had reward enough in the glory they acquired, and that opulence was to be conferred as a compensation for the want of other titles of respect.

" It is necessary for me," said Mr. Gerry in a letter of this date, " to become a farmer, and to endeavour to preserve those resources, which political engagements have allowed me little opportunity, and I might say, less inclination to improve."

During these four years of domestic seclusion, those dissensions, the germ of which was starting when Mr. Gerry retired from congress, had struck their roots deep and firm, and extended over the entire continent. It was impossible that he could either have been careless of the progress of events, or indifferent to their consequences. His temporary removal from the sphere of operations, made him, unquestionably, a calmer observer, and probably a less heated partizan, than those who were more actively engaged in the labours of the field, so that on his return to public life he was unwilling to sacrifice private friendship and the habits and attachments of former years to the stern Moloch of the day; yet his principles always assimilated, and his conduct soon identified him with the great democratic party of the United States.

This party, which for nearly the whole duration of the existing government, embraced a vast majority of the American people, has in some parts of the country, and particularly in the native state of Mr. Gerry, been for nearly an equal period wholly deprived of political power. While its members in some sections have enjoyed all the honours of the people, they have in others been treated almost as outlaws, with the humiliation, which attaches to an inferior and degraded caste.

The political class to whom the subject of this memoir most intimately belonged, have found among their other misfortunes, that their motives were misunderstood, their principles misstated, and their conduct defamed. The leading historian of the country, whose own great talents suited so well the subject most interesting to Americans, which he selected for his theme, has by a series of sarcastic and derogating animadversions, contributed to propagate the favourite opinion of their adversaries, that this disturbing power in the state was a fermenting mass of faction, ignorance and disappointment. The lion, says the fable, was not the sculptor of the piece.

Before the formation of the constitution, the distresses, which had been occasioned by the operations of the war, had amassed themselves in a degree, which in many places deranged the whole economy of life. Debts had accumulated, specie vanished, and the enforcement of creditor rights often dissolved the only sources from which remuneration could proceed. Time was necessary for the reaction of public energies. There were found, as a consequence of this state of things, two classes of men, one of whom insisted on the strict execution of the letter of the bond, the other were willing to delay for a convenient period, the exertion of judicial power, upon the principle, that as the war had in many cases wholly destroyed the claims of the creditor, by annihilating his debtor's property, and sometimes his life, so in all it had produced a good reason for lenity and delay.

To this incident it has pleased the biographer before alluded to, to trace the commencement of political parties, and omitting even the plausible reasons, by which the one defended its opinions, to trace the origin of the democracy of the country through a systematic hostility to the constitution, up to a nefarious disregard of personal obligations, and a contemptuous indifference to the validity of private contracts, the demands of justice, and the security of law ; and as in this division of the community, the affluent would naturally be on one side, andmen of more moderate circumstances on the other, so the former are, by necessary inference, identified with the honour, the virtue, and the character, which are attached to a good government, and the latter with those demoralizing habits, which spring up among men, whom revolution could not impoverish, nor rebellion destroy.

Neither hostility to the constitution, nor opposition to the government can fairly be traced to this source.   On these latter points men were divided who acted together on the first.   The condition of things before the convention at Philadelphia, was not one, which can identify the opposition to their projected system with any preconcerted design of subverting it ;   and dissatisfaction with the constitution, as it came from the hands of its framers, is improperly charged to be a motive for subsequent opposition to the government.   No individual did more to secure the success of the administration than the first secretary of state, who is well known to have been displeased with the original principles of the constitution.   No one did more to establish the great

democratic party of the United States than he who
was the projector and defender of the constitution
in the convention, and its leading advocate before
the people.   The instances alluded to are not cases
of individual exception ; they are examples followed by vast multitudes, and refute the imputation that the administration commenced under the
auspices of wealth and integrity, and was beaten
down by poverty and fraud.

If the origin of the great democratic party is to
be traced to a period antecedent to that in which
it was formed, it may be sought in those highly
enlightened and honourable sentiments, in which
the revolution was commenced and accomplished.
The chivalrous leaders of those perilous times
persuaded themselves that the happiness of the
people was the only legitimate object of government ; that the means of the people were not to
be exacted without their consent, nor was their
consent to be expected for an useless or wasteful
expenditure.   The British government, by viola-
ting these principles, raised that storm, which
swept away their authority ; the new government
was objectionable as it failed to secure them, and
the administration reprehensible by its similar
tendencies.

For the correctness of the facts, or the accuracy of the deductions, which combined this party
together it is not necessary to contend, but it is

proper to demand for them higher motives than sordid cupidity or profligate injustice.

The class of men who, anterior to the commencement of hostilities, had so freely discussed the tendencies of political power towards despotic exertion, and who had, with pertinacity and courage, contended for the rights of the people in all controversies between the colonies and the empire, may have extended their analogies too far in applying them to a government elected by the citizens over which it was placed. Be it so. It is a question of fact, which posterity may settle against them, and still leave their honour unquestioned and their integrity unimpeached.

The intimation that poverty and faction first opposed the constitution, and then the administration of the government erected under it, was made to receive countenance by the fact, that the wealth, which the government created, readily enlisted on its side.

The new constitution went into operation, when the debt of the revolution had depreciated to an eighth of its nominal value. This had passed, in a great degree, from meritorious creditors, who had expended their property or their blood to acquire it, into the hands of speculation and traffic. In many instances the funds, concealed when patriotism required them to be expended, were lavished in the acquisition of those certificates, which the country had issued in evidence, as well of its justice as its poverty.

A vast proportion of the whole debt of the nation had changed hands. The duty of providing for its payment was universally admitted. The right of discrimination between the original owners and their assignees, though long and ably maintained, was of doubtful character, and the faith of the nation, which finally redeemed all its promises with interest, raised into existence an army of pensioners, who were ready, with the common feelings of household troops, to prove their devotion by the excesses of their zeal.

The accumulation of fortune, thus suddenly produced, aided the administration, not only by its actual strength, but by that appearance of respectability, which opulence never fails to confer.

Causes intrinsic and immovable, for the formation of the great parties of the country, may also be traced, without disparagement to either, in an original difference of opinion concerning the arrangement of political power. The opposite and counteracting forces of the states and the nation, it was admitted on all hands, were necessary to preserve the relative proportions of the whole and the parts, as the centripetal and centrifugal forces maintain the balance of the solar system. But the principle was more easily admitted than applied. What the proportion should be was not ascertained. A desire improperly to increase or weaken these forces, was ascribed by each party, with sincerity no doubt, to its opponent, as premeditated wrong.

The plan of col. Hamilton, for the distribution and continuance of the powers of government, had more real than ostensible friends. They, who considered it as the beau ideal of a good constitution, would endeavour to render the actual condition of the existing one as conformable to its principles as its established forms would allow ; while others, who saw the prerogatives of authority advanced further than, in their opinion, the safety of public liberty permitted, would on all questions calculated to increase them take the side of opposition.

In every written law involving extensive concerns and matters of detail, much is unavoidably to be settled by construction. To ascertain which of two meanings is the intention of the enacting power, forms no small part of the common business of the judiciary department ; and the most curious facility of language has never yet presented a series of propositions, whose exact meaning was universally admitted. There is certainly no exception to the common ambiguity of language in the constitution of the United States. Hence a cause of great difference of opinion. By one class of statesmen it was considered wise to expand its powers by construction, and in all those cases, which admitted of two modes of interpretation, to adopt that, which should strengthen the principles of power. The opposite course reconciled itself more easily with the views of another class. The motives, which led to results thus deduced were impeached instead of being traced, as they ought to have been, to that formation of mind, education and character, which might vindicate their integrity. Hence the favourers of a strong government, who chose to consider themselves federalists, were designated as aristocrats and supporters of oligarchy ; the friends of a more popular system, who claimed the appellation of republicans, were represented as democrats, demagogues, and hypocritical courtiers of the people.

The connexion between the dignity of office and the intelligence, which deserved it, was ingeniously claimed by the dominant party, and not only the daily press, but works of more permanent authority, have countenanced this suggestion, and a sneer of contempt at the absurdity of argument or the frivolity of fear, which disturbed the party in opposition, is but ill disguised by the affected impartiality of history.

In a bill proposed at the first congress, organizing a department of the treasury, a clause was inserted, making it the duty of the secretary to digest and report plans for the improvement and management of the revenue, and the support of public credit. It was opposed under an apprehension of the extension it would give to ministerial influence, its imitation of the British parliament, and as a precedent, which would be extended to countenance the personal introduction of these ministers on the floor of the house. Upon

the discussion of the bill, says the biographer of
Washington, Mr. Gerry remarked, that "he had
no objection to obtaining information, but he could
not help observing the great degree of importance
gentlemen were giving to this and the other executive officers.   If the doctrine of having prime
and great ministers of state were once well established, he did not doubt he should soon see them
distinguished by green or red ribbon insignia of
court favour and patronage."

It might be well twenty years after the danger
had passed, to ridicule the means by which it was
defeated, by way of proof that there never was any
cause of alarm.   But if members of the cabinet
had been admitted on the floor of congress to
explain, and of course enforce their schemes of
finance and policy ; if the secretary of the treasury might personally have opened his budget, and
the secretary of state his schemes of foreign or
domestic relations, the executive power would
have acquired an increased momentum, at the expense of the representative rights of the people.
The effort shows the views of the different members of congress, not merely on the details of this
particular subject, but on principles so fundamental as naturally to separate them like the different elements of the material world.

In the importance and novelty of the measures
brought into discussion, both in the halls of congress and in the assemblies of the people, difficul-

ties enough presented themselves to vindicate the
judgment of any one from reproach, on whichever
side he was found.   Ignorance only would be self-
confident or rash.   It is not unlikely indeed, that
a desire of participating in the enjoyment of power influenced the champions of the day, and that
the spoils of victory might have been among the
inducements to the contest ; but what candour is
there in ascribing more honourable motives to
those who fought to preserve their authority, than
to their competitors, who were striving to obtain
it ?   On both sides were men of high principles,
ardent patriotism, great experience and rare intellectual capacity.   At the head of the government was a tower of strength, which they of the
adverse faction wanted.   The federalists claimed
him as their leader.   But Washington was above
the atmosphere of party.   He belonged to his
country, to the cause of civil liberty, to posterity,
mankind.   He alone by the force of that sound
judgment, which on so many occasions had contributed to the safety of the state, could maintain
a dignified neutrality in the midst of the wasting
warfare that was raging around him.   If in the
asperity of remark on the administration, an arrow
of obloquy was aimed at the chief magistrate, it
rung harmlessly on the shield of public opinion.
Whatever in the councils of the nation satisfied
the opposing party, was with affectionate regard
ascribed to his personal virtues ; other measures

were traced to the influence of the counsellors who surrounded him.

In the first arrangement of his cabinet, the generous confidence of the president had collected a fair representation of the different opinions, which agitated the country.   Circumstances in which he had no agency, produced a resignation of some members, and its composition essentially changed.

The weight and influence of the government became essentially federal, and this advantage of position they, who possessed it, were naturally desirous to preserve.

While in the domestic concerns of the country so many disturbing forces intervened to prevent the regular gravitation of the system, the French revolution burst on the astonished world, like a comet, that from its horrid hair shook pestilence and war.

For a people who were endeavouring to throw off the yoke of oppression, there was naturally excited, in those who had successfully performed the hazardous experiment, a strong and operative sympathy.   Gratitude for the services of that nation, was a motive of unmeasured force.   The early friends of the American republic were in hostility with its ancient and still suspected enemy.   They presented a spectacle, in which freedom and the popular will were arrayed against the authority of long established power.   When the American administration, with an intelligence

and caution suited to the circumstances of a growing but unsettled empire, took the position of
neutrality and repressed the exuberance of feelings honourable indeed but unsafe and unwise, it
produced a sullenness of temper and a sentiment of
distrust, as if they too were joining in a conspiracy
of kings, and avowing the common affinity by
which government, no matter what is its form,
places itself by the side of government in any contest for popular rights.

But neutrality was too obviously suited to the
interests of the United States to be demolished by
the escalade of opposition ; and that generous enthusiasm, which at its first excitement would have
rushed into battle, was succeeded by more sober
judgment and calmer feelings, the best advocates
of peace.

The executive opened a negotiation with the
British government, and the treaty, which resulted from it, unchained the fierce spirit of hostility and separated the community into irreconcilable factions. Passion and those personal and
private motives, by which the elements of party
are blown into a blaze, operated with all their
force, and they, who had other motives for resentment, saw in this measure that fatal error,
which properly managed would unsettle the power of their rivals. The treaty itself and the manner of its being negotiated, presented points of
extreme difficulty, justifying almost any view of it,

which the statesmen of the day found themselves disposed to take.

It is not to the present purpose to detail the arguments, which with a power of intellect as honourable to the intelligence, as indicative of the strong feelings of the American people, were urged on the question of ratifying the treaty negotiated by Mr. Jay. It is necessary only to allude to the motives of the party, by whom its rejection was enforced. In vindication of their judgment, may be cited the authority of its friends.

"The enlightened negotiator," says Mr. Hamilton, "not unconscious that some parts of the treaty were less well arranged than was to be desired, had himself hesitated to sign it. When the treaty arrived, it was not without full deliberation and some hesitation that I resolved to support it." In the senate its ratification was recommended by a mere constitutional majority. In the house of representatives, on a question introduced to test the opinion of that body, there was a vote of thirty-seven in its favour to sixty-two against it.

The president doubted what to do, and balancing in his mind the objections and advantages, with great delay and anxious reflection, finally assented to a conditional acceptance.

Of the commercial advantages of the treaty of London, many undoubtedly ventured an opinion who were incompetent to decide. But its political character was on a level with every capacity. It

was supposed to be the first step, and a very conclusive one, in taking sides between the two great
belligerents, and with a bold spirit of opposition
to the sentiments and feelings of the people, to
have selected the wrong one.

In the character and objects and governments
of the hostile nations, were traced a resemblance
to the character and sentiments of conflicting parties in the United States, and the aristocratic and
monarchical tendencies of the constitution, gradually expanding in the progress of administration,
were here it was alleged fully blown out and developed ; and by a natural association, the government that was but in name republican, would be
found on the side of kings in a crusade against
liberty and the rights of man.

These ungenerous imputations on the one side,
were met with corresponding severity on the
other.

To such violence were the angry feelings of the
community excited, that when the brutality and
ignorance of the French democrats were stripping
society of its forms of decency and order, subverting the institutions of religion, and confounding
all distinctions of education, morality and wealth,
the same appellation, with a view of expressing
a similarity of temper, was ordinarily bestowed
on the opposition party to the federal government, until the name of a democrat became as
odious as that of a witch or a tory ; and when

the jacobins of Paris, the ferocious murderers of age and infancy and innocence, were dripping with human blood, and celebrating their infernal orgies round the guillotine, like cannibals at a feast, their name was in the common language of the day affixed to a numerical half of the American people, with a design to have them considered as instigated by like horrible perversity.   Less causes than these, have in other ages raised the standard of civil war, and less moderation and patience than marked the insulted party of the opposition, might have repeated in the fair fields of our country the scenes of Hexam or Bosworth.

The progress of events abroad, and the arts by which each of the two American parties were identified with a foreign policy, had a tendency to strengthen the administration and weaken its assailants.   The French revolution was not found to be that desirable and rational march of liberty, which had at first claimed the sympathies of the actors in our own.   The anarchy, which it encouraged, the subversion of law, order and government which it threatened, and often times accomplished, the vast force, which it concentrated, and the little justice or humanity, which directed it, alienated the affections, which it took no care to conciliate, and its frightful excesses made the several administrators of its power, objects of fear, horror and surprise.

During the storm, which was thus shaking to

its centre the government and very existence of
the American confederacy, Mr. Gerry was in the
retirement of his farm and his family, watching
its progress with anxiety and solicitude, but not
exposed to any undue share of its evils.   The excitement and irritation, which personal conflict
necessarily produces, it was thus his good fortune
to escape, and with more calmness and deliberation to observe the movements of contending parties.   On most questions of domestic policy he was
entirely in unison with his former associates.

Of the foreign politics of the country he had
in some respects a different opinion.   The dangerous operation of the English government, on the
feelings, manners and principles of the country,
he realized with all the force, which had been
ascribed to them, and was particularly fearful
of increasing a connexion, which should give to
its influence the authority, which was denied to
its power.   The resources and the profligacy of
the French nation were in his mind causes of
alarm, that should suggest a course of prudence
and policy calculated to preserve the neutral and
favourable position of the United States.   The admiration, which their early efforts had excited, had
yielded to astonishment at their singular success,
and horror at the want of principle by which their
power was directed.   Partiality for French politics,
or a sympathy for French principles, then so commonly charged on his party, whether true or false

with regard to them collectively, was wholly unfounded in its application to him.

While such conflicting interests and jarring opinions agitated the people of the United States,
they were called upon to select a successor to the
only man, whose ascendency over the public mind
could control the licentiousness of faction, by commanding universal confidence and esteem.   Great
and radical differences on the essential principles
of government gave to this contest all the zeal,
which sincerity and judgment could bring into
the field.   With these the fiercest passions were
enlisted, and ambition, pride, the love of power
and desire of retaliation, the lordly feelings, which
delight in maintaining an ascendency, and the
proud spirit that revolts at it, arrayed themselves
under opposing banners, with a parade little short
of military triumph.

Mr. Gerry, without being previously consulted
by his fellow citizens, was called into the electoral
college of Massachusetts, and gave his vote for
Mr. Adams.   It occasioned the following correspondence.

MR. GERRY TO MR. JEFFERSON.

CAMBRIDGE, MARCH 27, 1797.

My Dear Sir,

Permit me, with great sincerity, to congratulate
you on your appointment to the office of vice pre-

sident of the United States.   It was, in my mind,
a very desirable object, and a wish, which I ardently expressed at the meeting of the electors ; but
as we were unanimously of opinion that Mr.
Adams' pretensions to the chair were best, it was
impossible to give you any votes, without annulling
an equal number for him ; otherwise you would certainly have had mine, and I have reason to think several others for vice president.   The constitution,
as it respects these elections, makes a lottery of
them, and is I think imperfect.   There was probably a plan laid, by coupling Mr. Pinckney with Mr.
Adams, to secure so many votes in this list for the
former, as with those for him in other lists, would
bring him into the chair ; but this was fortunately
seen through and defeated : and I flatter myself that
the elections will eventually have a happy effect on
the public mind, by the accommodating disposition
of the president and vice president, their mutual
friendship for each other and the pursuit of a general system of moderation, exploding foreign influence of every kind, in every department of government.   Being unconnected with parties, whose
extremes I confess have been disagreeable to me,
and have detached me from politics, I am a retired spectator, enjoying nevertheless the uncontrolled right of judging for myself, and of expressing independently to my friends, my ideas of the
measures springing from public and of the artifices
from private views.   Thus circumstanced, give me

leave to express my apprehensions, that the consequence of this election will be repeated stratagems to weaken or destroy the confidence of the president and vice president in each other, from an assurance, that if it continues to the end of the president's administration, the vice president will be his successor ; and perhaps from a dread of your political influence. Indeed I think such an operation has already commenced, and that you will discover it ; but your mutual good sense will see through the project and defeat it. Wishing you to possess a full share of the public confidence, which I am sure you always merited, and with it much private happiness,

I remain

Your sincere friend,

E. GERRY.

MR. JEFFERSON TO MR. GERRY.

PHILADELPHIA, MAY 13, 1797.

MY DEAR FRIEND,

Your favour of the 27th of March did not reach me till April 21st, when I was within a few days of setting out for this place, and I put off acknowledging it till I should come here. I entirely commend your dispositions towards Mr. Adams, knowing his worth as intimately, and esteeming it as much as any one, and acknowledging the preference of his claims, if any I could have had, to the high office conferred on him. But in truth I had neither claims nor wishes on the subject; though I know it will be difficult to obtain belief of this. When I retired from this place and the office of secretary of state, it was in the firmest contemplation of never more returning here. There had indeed been suggestions in the public papers, that I was looking towards a succession to the president's chair ; but feeling a consciousness of their falsehood, and observing that the suggestions came from hostile quarters, I considered them as intended merely to excite public odium against me. I never in my life exchanged a word with any person on the subject, till I found my name brought forward generally, in competition with that of Mr. Adams. Those with whom I then communicated could say, if it were necessary, whether I met the call with desire, or even with a ready acquiescence ; and whether, from the moment of my first acquiescence, I did not devoutly pray that the very thing might happen that has happened. The second office of this government is honourable and easy, the first is but a splendid misery. You express apprehensions that stratagems will be used to produce a misunderstanding between the president and myself. Though not a word having this tendency has ever been hazarded to me by any one, yet I consider as a certainty that nothing will be left untried to alienate him from me. These machinations will

proceed from the Hamiltonians by whom he is surrounded, and who are only a little less hostile to
him than to me.   It cannot but damp the pleasure
of cordiality when we suspect that it is suspected.
I cannot help fearing that it is impossible for Mr.
Adams to believe that the state of my mind is
what it really is ; that he may think I view him
as an obstacle in my way.   I have no supernatu-
ral power to impress truth on the mind of another,
nor he any to discover that the estimate, which he
may form on a just view of the human mind as
generally constituted, may not be just in its application to a special constitution.   This may be
a source of private uneasiness to us ; I honestly
confess that it is so to me at this time ; but neither
of us are capable of letting it have effect on our
public duties.   Those who may endeavour to separate us, are probably excited by the fear that I
might have influence on the executive councils.
But when they shall know that I consider my office
as constitutionally confined to legislative functions,
and that I could not take any part whatever in executive consultations, even were it proposed, their
fears may perhaps subside, and their object be
found not worth a machination.   I do sincerely
wish with you, that we could take our stand on a
ground perfectly neutral and independent towards
all nations.   It has been my constant object
through public life ; and with respect to the Eng-

lish and French particularly, I have too often
expressed to the former my wishes and made to
them propositions, verbally and in writing, officially and privately, to official and private characters,
for them to doubt of my views, if they could be
content with equality. Of this they are in possession of several written and formal proofs, in my
own hand writing. But they have wished a monopoly of commerce and influence with us, and they
have in fact obtained it. When we take notice
that theirs is the workshop to which we go for
all we want ; that with them centre, either immediately or ultimately, all the labour of our hands
and lands ; that to them belongs, either openly or
secretly, the great mass of our navigation ; that
even the factorage of their affairs here is kept to
themselves by factitious citizenships ; that these
foreign and false citizens now constitute the great
body of what are called *our merchants,* fill our sea-
ports, are planted in every little town and district
of the interior country, sway every thing in the
former place by their own votes and those of their
dependents, in the latter by their insinuations and
the influence of their ledgers ; that they are advancing fast to a monopoly of our banks and public funds, and thereby placing our public finances
under their control ; that they have in their alliance
the most influential characters, in and out of office.
When they have shown that by all these bearings
on the different branches of the government, they

can force it to proceed in any direction they dictate, and bend the interests of this country entirely to the will of another ; when all this, I say is
attended to, it is impossible for us to say we stand
on independent grounds, impossible for a free mind
not to see and to groan under the bondage in which
it is bound. If any thing after this could excite
surprise, it would be, that they have been able
so far to throw dust into the eyes of our own citizens, as to fix on those who wish merely to recover self-government, the charge of subserving
one foreign influence, because they resist submission
to another. But they possess our printing presses,
a powerful engine in their government of us. At
this very moment they would have drawn us into
war on the side of England, had it not been for the
failure of her bank. Such was their open and loud
cry and that of their gazettes till this event. After
plunging us in all the broils of the European nations, there would remain but one act to close our
tragedy, that is, to break up our union : and even
this they have ventured seriously and solemnly
to propose, and maintain by argument, in a Connecticut paper. I have been happy however in
believing, from the stifling of this effort, that that
dose was found too strong, and excited as much
repugnance there as it did horror in other parts of
our country, and that whatever follies we may be
led into as to foreign nations, we shall never give
up our union, the last anchor of our hope, and that

alone, which is to prevent this heavenly country from becoming an arena of gladiators. Much as I abhor war, and view it as the greatest scourge of mankind, and axiously as I wish to keep out of the broils of Europe, I would yet go with my brethren into these rather than separate from them. But I hope we shall keep clear of them, notwithstanding our present thraldom, and that time may be given us to reflect on the awful crisis we have passed through, and to find some means of shielding ourselves in future from foreign influence, commercial, political, or in whatever other form it may be attempted. I can scarcely withhold myself from joining in the wish of Silas Deane, that there were an ocean of fire between us and the old world. A perfect confidence that you are as much attached to peace and union as myself, that you equally prize independence of all nations and the blessings of self-government, has induced me freely to unbosom myself to you, and let you see the light in which I have viewed what has been passing among us from the beginning of this war. And I shall be happy at all times in an intercommunication of sentiments with you, believing that the dispositions of the different parts of our country have been considerably misrepresented and misunderstood in each part as to the other, and that nothing but good can result from an exchange of opinions and information between those whose circumstances and morals admit no doubt of the integrity of their views. I remain with constant and sincere esteem, dear sir,

> Your affectionate friend and servant,
> Th. Jefferson.

The design alluded to by Mr. Gerry, has since been distinctly avowed by the leader of the party,* and the declaration made by Mr. Jefferson, that the projectors of the scheme under the pretence of friendship for Mr. Adams, were only less hostile to the one than the other, was within a short time placed wholly beyond dispute.†

In answer to a letter of congratulation, the following was received from a lady, who in the elevated sphere she was called to fill, displayed all that dignity and elegance, which entitles her to the admiration and respect of the community, as her private virtues and amiable character secured the affection of her domestic circle, and the esteem of her friends.

---

* "It is true that the faithful execution of this plan would have given Mr. Pinckney a somewhat better chance than Mr. Adams, nor shall it be concealed that an issue favourable to the former would not have been disagreeable to me, as indeed I declared at the time, in the circles of my confidential friends."— *Letter from A. Hamilton on the public conduct, &c. of J. Adams,* page 17.

† Ibid. page 18.

MRS. ADAMS TO MR. GERRY.

QUINCY, DECEMBER 31, 1796.

DEAR SIR,

Your obliging favour of December 28th, I received by the hand of Dr. Welch. I thank you sir, for your congratulations, which receive their value from the sincerity with which I believe them fraught. The elevated station in which the suffrages of our country have placed our friend, is encompassed with so many dangers and difficulties, that it appears to me a slippery precipice, surrounded on all sides with rocks, shoals and quicksands. There is not any man, in whom again can be united, such an assemblage of fortunate circumstances, to combine all hearts in his favour, and every voice in unison, as has been the singular lot of the president of the United States. Yet even he, with the full tide of favour and affection, has tasted the bitter cup of calumny and abuse, an imported cup, a foreign mixture, a poison so subtle as to have infected even native Americans. What must a successor expect, who has near half the country opposed to his election? as well as all the friends of the rival candidates mortified at their defeat.

You sir, have been too long conversant in public life, and full well know " the pangs and heart aches" to which it is subject, not personally to mix commiseration with your congratulations.

At my time of life, the desire and wish to shine in public is wholly extinguished.

Retirement to Peacefield, the name which Mr. Adams has given to his farm, is much more eligible to me, particularly as my health has severely suffered by my residence at Philadelphia. But personally I shall consider myself as the small dust of the balance, when compared to the interests of a nation. To preserve peace, to support order, and continue to the country that system of government under which it has become prosperous and happy, the sacrifice of an individual life, important only to its near connexions, ought not to be taken into consideration.

I fully agree with you in sentiment as it respects the election of Mr. Jefferson. I have long known him, and entertain for him a personal friendship, and though I cannot accord with him in some of his politics, I do not believe him culpable to the extent he has been represented. Placed at the head of the senate, I trust his conduct will be wise and prudent. I hope it will be a means of softening the animosity of party, and of cementing and strengthening the bond of union.

There never was any public or private animosity between Mr. Adams and Mr. Jefferson. Upon the subject of Paine's Rights of Man, there was a disagreement in sentiment. Mr. Jefferson " does not look quite through the deeds of men." Time has fully disclosed whose opinion was well founded.

The gentleman you alluded to as an active agent

in the election, has no doubt his views and designs. There are some characters more supple than others, more easily wrought upon, more accommodating, more complying. Such a person might be considered as the ostensible engine, which a master hand could work. To what other motive can be ascribed the machiavelian policy of placing at the head of the government, a gentleman not particularly distinguished for any important services to his country, and scarcely heard of beyond the state, which gave him birth, until sent upon a public embassy.

" Corruption wins not more than honesty." I feel sir, when addressing you, the confidence of an old friend, and that an apology is unnecessary for the freedom of communication.

Be pleased to present my compliments to Mrs. Gerry. It would give me pleasure to receive a friendly visit from her and from you.

I am, dear sir,

      With sentiments of respect and esteem,

        Your friend and humble servant,

             ABIGAIL ADAMS.

CHAPTER V.

THE election of Mr. Adams was a signal triumph to the federal party. It gave them, for at least four years, the command of the government, the influence of place and patronage, and the vantage ground of their opponents, which they lost no time to improve.

The executive chief was not it is true, selected by their voluntary preference. Men of leading influence among them entertained serious doubts of his fitness for the station, but " to preserve the harmony of their party, they thought it better to indulge their hopes than listen to their fears."*

Those of them, who were desirous of an undue share of influence, who from behind the throne would be greater than the throne itself, anticipated from the character of Mr. Adams insurmountable obstacles to their schemes of personal ambition. The experience of the president in the service of his country at home and abroad, through all the troubles of the revolution, and since the

* Hamilton's letter, page 16.

organization of its government, and the natural temperament of his mind justly proud of its resources, and confident in its strength, were not likely to devolve on the aspiring spirits, who surrounded him, the attributes of office, while he himself should hold a barren sceptre in his hand. The attempt to render him a mere automaton under their control, and the resistance, which his integrity and pride roused in opposition, soon produced that disunion in his cabinet, which mainly contributed to its fall.

The views of the president were however essentially those of the federal party, as they related to measures of domestic policy or foreign intercourse ; and the spirit of his first communication to congress, was well calculated to elevate the confidence of his friends, and to diminish the influence of his opponents.

It spoke of the disposition of France to alienate the people of the United States from their government ; a charge, the belief of which caused higher resentment than almost any other on the long catalogue of wrongs, and it gave point to the accusation, by something more than an intimation, that a conduct so demoralizing had already been encouraged by a party at home. The energy, with which the speech incited the citizens of the United States to convince France they were " not a degraded people humiliated under a colonial spirit of fear and sense of inferiority, fitted to be the miserable instruments of foreign influence, and regardless of national honour, character and interest," implied an accusation against all that class of the community, who by recommending a policy different from his own, had tended to produce the disgraceful condition at which he spurned.

The popular language of the day described the republican party as a French party, and the speech of the president was calculated to fix upon them the seal of reproach. It left a sting, which high and honourable men could not but resent. It was contrived, at some expense indeed, to bring to the aid of the executive those principles of loyalty and attachment to their political institutions of which the Americans are proud, by describing the opposers of the administration as miserable instruments of foreign influence, regardless of national honour, character and interest.

In the existing state of things, the first effort of sound policy was to restore the amicable relations between the United States and France, or if that was impossible, to bring to the standard of the administration a strong accession of force from the opposing ranks, by making the impossibility apparent.

The president therefore avowed his design of instituting a " fresh attempt at negotiation, and his intention to promote and accelerate an accommodation on terms compatible with the rights, duties, interests and honour of the nation."

In this declaration of the president subsequent events proved he was sincere. If the language of his coadjutors be taken for true, it is not now to be doubted that the same integrity of intention influenced their councils. But the great republican party, while they hailed every effort with acclamation, which might tend to preserve the blessings of peace, yet with the jealousy, which belonged to such times, doubted whether the parade of negotiation was any thing more than an artful effort to reconcile the nation to the alternative of war.

By this great section of the community it was believed, that the past intercourse of the countries was not carried on in good faith by the American ministers; and that the show of negotiation was artfully contrived to demonstrate its inefficiency, with a view to enlist the public sentiment in measures, which must necessarily follow the failure of an amicable settlement. They imputed to their rivals a desire, as old as the constitution, to convert the government into something stronger than a mere representative republic, and as the first step in this drama, to draw a closer connexion with England, whose government and forms of administration, and whose principles of civil policy were more accordant with their own. They imputed to them a desire of producing such a state of public affairs as would place at the command of the executive an imposing military force, an in-

creased revenue, a vast official patronage, and
a coercive power over the personal liberty of
its citizens.   Public opinion it was certain must
be elevated by the occurring of a crisis, to facilitate the progress of such operations, and the
failure of a negotiation, which would necessarily
produce a formal war, would be the consummation
of their hopes.

Not only did the republican party hold opinions
diametrically opposite to these grand schemes, but
the great body of the federalists it was known
needed only to discover them, to overwhelm them
with reprobation.   The plan belonged to the elevated few, who could expect to succeed in it only
by those master strokes of policy, for which if
their inclination suited, they were not deficient in
ability.

This conspiracy against the public liberty, imputed to the leaders of the dominant party and
proclaimed by their opponents like the prophecies
of Cassandra to incredulous ears, has since been
wonderfully countenanced by the disclosures, which
the then president has made ;* and it may be
now taken for true, that it was a combination of
a comparatively small circle of influential men,
against the sense of the nation, and that these
were even less guided by motives of personal ambition and desire of authority, than by a zeal for
their country's welfare, which in their opinion

* President Adams' letters, No. 2, p. 66.

could be preserved from dissolution in its weakness, only by the tonics of their philosophy. The fact that such a plan existed in the cabinet, explains many of the measures, which form the history of those interesting times.

In pursuance of the president's declaration, he instituted a commission to the French republic, and as a pledge of his own sincerity, he proposed to place among its members some distinguished individual of the party, whose course of policy commanded the confidence of the opposition. In a private interview with Mr. Jefferson, the appointment was offered to him, but declined. The interior of the cabinet is so well drawn by Mr. Adams, that it may be best described in his own words.*

"From Mr. Jefferson I went to one of the heads of departments, whom Mr. Washington had appointed, and I had no thoughts of removing. Indeed I had then no objection to any of the secretaries. I asked him what he thought of sending Mr. Madison to France, with or without others? Is it determined to send to France at all? Determined? Nothing is determined till it is executed, smiling. But why not?—I thought it deserved consideration.—So it does; but suppose it determined, what do you think of sending Mr. Madison? Is it determined to send Mr. Madison? No; but it deserves consideration. Sending Mr. Madison will make dire work among the passions of our parties in congress, and out of doors, through the states! Are we forever to be overawed and directed by party passions? All this conversation on my part was with the most perfect civility, good humour, and indeed familiarity; but I found it excited a profound gloom and solemn countenance in my companion, which

* *Correspondence of the late president Adams,* p. 63.

after some time broke out in " Mr. President, we are willing to resign." Nothing could have been more unexpected to me than this observation. Nothing was further from my thoughts than to give any pain or uneasiness. I had said nothing that could possibly displease, except pronouncing the name of Madison. I restrained my surprise, however, and only said, I hope nobody will resign : I am satisfied with all the public officers.

Upon further enquiries of the other heads of departments, and of other persons, I found that party passions had so deep and extensive roots, that I seriously doubted whether the senate would not negative Mr. Madison if I should name him. Rather than expose him to a negative, or a doubtful contest in the senate, I concluded to omit him. If I had nominated Madison, I should have nominated Hamilton with him. The former, I knew, was much esteemed in France ; the latter was rather an object of jealousy. But I thought the French would tolerate one for the sake of the other. And I thought too that the manners of the one would soon wear off the prejudices against him, and probably make him a greater favourite than the other. But having given up Madison, I ought to give up Hamilton too. Who then should I name ? I mentioned Mr. Dana and Mr. Gerry to the heads of departments and to many leading members in both houses. They all preferred Mr. Dana. But it was evident enough to me, that neither Dana nor Gerry was their man. Dana was appointed, but refused. I then called the heads of departments together, and proposed Mr. Gerry. All the five voices unanimously were against him. Such inveterate prejudice shocked me. I said nothing, but was determined I would not be the slave of it. I knew the man infinitely better than all of them. He was nominated and approved, and finally saved the peace of the nation ; for he alone discovered and furnished the evidence that X. Y. and Z. were employed by Talleyrand ; and he alone brought home the direct, formal and official assurances upon which the subsequent commission proceeded, and peace was made."

The secretary of state has denied this statement of the president. He says, " I have before stated, that when Mr. Adams first proposed Mr. Gerry for one of the envoys, the heads of departments objected, and that Mr. Adams gave way and substituted chief justice Dana, of Massachusetts, but on his declining, Mr. Adams recurred to Mr. Gerry, and in a manner to preclude any further opposition.   As to senators, I am perfectly persuaded I never spoke to any one of them.   We had entire confidence in general Pinckney and general Marshall, and only wished to save them from being embarrassed with a difficult and troublesome associate, and such to their extreme vexation and delay, Mr. Gerry proved to be."*

A difficult and troublesome associate any one would be, whose views either of the foreign or domestic relations of his country differed from a majority of his colleagues.   At the moment when Mr. Gerry's name was proposed to the cabinet, he held a rank in the councils of the country above that, which had then been attained by either of his colleagues, and the apprehension, if it truly existed on the mind of the secretary, that he would be a difficult and troublesome associate, must have arisen from his belief that it would be difficult to bend the integrity of his mind from the principles he espoused, and troublesome to carry negotiation to the point, which the secretary desired, when a party to its progress had different views of the interest of his country.

But the clamour, which the cabinet made against

* Pick. Review, p. 137.

the president's nomination, was more than compensated by the confidence, which it gave to the republican party.

From all quarters letters poured in upon Mr. Gerry urging his acceptance, and placing the responsibility of a refusal on such grounds as left him without the possibility of declining.

From the mass of these solicitous epistles, the following, from the great leader and champion of his party, is selected as well for the powerful reasons, which it enumerates, as for the influence, which it had in producing the acceptance, which it urged.

MR. JEFFERSON TO MR. GERRY.

PHILADELPHIA, JUNE 21, 1797.

MY DEAR FRIEND,

It was with infinite joy to me that you were yesterday announced to the senate as envoy extraordinary, jointly with general Pinckney and Mr. Marshall, to the French republic. It gave me certain assurance that there would be a preponderance in the mission sincerely disposed to be at peace with the French government and nation. Peace is undoubtedly at present the first object of our nation. Interest and honour are also national considerations; but interest, duly weighed, is in favour of peace, even at the expense of spoliations past and future; and honour cannot now be an

object. The insults and injuries committed on us
by both the belligerent parties from the beginning
of 1793 to this day, and still continuing by both,
cannot now be wiped off by engaging in war with
one of them. As there is great reason to expect
this is the last campaign in Europe, it would certainly be better for us to rub through this year
as we have done through the four preceding ones,
and hope that on the restoration of peace we may
be able to establish some plan for our foreign connexions more likely to secure our peace, interest
and honour in future. Our countrymen have divided themselves by such strong affections to the
French and the English, that nothing will secure
us internally, but a divorce from both nations ; and
this must be the object of every real American,
and its attainment is practicable without much
self-denial ; but for this, peace is necessary. Be
assured of this, my dear sir, that if we engage in
a war during our present passions and our present
weakness in some quarters, that our union runs
the greatest risk of not coming out of that war in
the shape in which it enters it. My reliance for
our preservation is in your acceptance of this mission. I know the tender circumstances, which
will oppose themselves to it ; but its duration will
be short, and its reward long. You have it in your
power by accepting and determining the character
of the mission, to secure the present peace and
eternal union of your country. If you decline, on
motives of private pain, a substitute may be named

who has enlisted his passions in the present contest, and by the preponderance of his vote in the
mission, may entail on us calamities, your share
in which and your feelings will outweigh whatever pain or temporary absence from your family
could give you. The sacrifice will be short, the
remorse would be never ending. Let me then
my dear sir, conjure your acceptance, and that
you will by this act seal the mission with the confidence of all parties. Your nomination has given
a spring to hope, which was dead before. I leave
this place in three days, and therefore shall not
here have the pleasure of learning your determination, but it will reach me in my retirement and
enrich the tranquillity of that scene. It will add
to the proofs, which have convinced me that the
man who loves his country on its own account,
and not merely for its trappings of interest or
power, can never be divorced from it; can never
refuse to come forward when he finds that she is
engaged in dangers, which he has the means of
warding off. Make then an effort, my friend, to
renounce your domestic comforts for a few months,
and reflect that to be a good husband and a good
father, at this moment you must be also a good
citizen.

With sincere wishes for your acceptance and
success, I am with unalterable esteem, dear sir,

Your affectionate friend and servant,

TH. JEFFERSON.

Mr. Gerry.

To the above may be added one from a gentleman who, well known to be of the federal party,
was not considered of the conclave who formed
the majority of the cabinet.

—

MR. OTIS TO MR. GERRY.

PHILADELPHIA, JUNE 22, 1797.

DEAR SIR,

It was with peculiar pleasure that I this day
certified the advice and consent of the senate to
your appointment, to be envoy extraordinary to
the republic of France, by a large and respectable
majority.   I hope, however dear and amiable your
family and the great pleasures of domestic retirement, you will once more step forward to the aid
of your country, whose independence and happiness you have contributed, by great and unremit-
ted exertion, to achieve, against every consideration that may suggest itself to your mind.   You
will go under peculiar advantages, in perfect confidence of both the great parties into which our
country is unhappily divided, and from long experience, acquainted with its general interests.

Selfish considerations do not preponderate in
your mind ; if however, you can serve your health,
which I am persuaded a sea voyage at this season
would do, and your country at the same time, both
pursuits are laudable.   In the name of your many
good friends, and in conformity to my own incli-

nations to see you again in public life, I repeat my
solicitations that you would make an effort and
gratify as well as serve your country.

My best respects to Mrs. Gerry, and tell her I
expect her aid in doing away every objection that
may present itself to your acceptance of an honourable appointment, in this very critical state of
our public affairs.

With assurances of my best wishes and respects,
        I have the honour to be, sir,
            Your most humble servant,
                        SAM'L A. OTIS.

The Hon. Elbridge Gerry.

———

Nothing could have been more unexpected to
Mr. Gerry than the appointment, which thus required him to enter again into public service. The
condition of his private affairs and the peculiar
situation of his family presented almost insuper-
able obstacles to the task assigned him. Yielding
however to the inducements, which Mr. Jefferson
had powerfully arrayed, at a sacrifice of personal
feeling, which it would be difficult to describe, and
an abandonment of private interest, which never
afterwards was repaired, Mr. Gerry embarked for
Europe on the 9th August, 1797.

The American envoys arrived at Paris at a period peculiarly inauspicious to their views.* They

———

* The state of society was not exactly that, which an American would have preferred. In a familiar letter to one of his fa-

found the republic elated by conquests, and triumphing as well in its policy as its arms. The military strength of Europe, which originally threatened the destruction of the new nation, was scattered and overthrown. " The conspiracy of kings," to destroy the principles of liberty was annihilated, and her victorious troops released from the discouraging duty of defending her own territories, had engaged in a war of conquest, whose glory surpassed the proudest periods of her power.

Spain, Portugal, Holland had successively yielded to her arms. Italy was conquered. Rome submitted its pontifical pride to her dictation. Germany, by the treaty of Campo Formio, was under her control. Vienna and Venice had seen her flag wave in triumph on their walls. A million bayonets, directed by military genius as original as astonishing, were ready to extend her conquests to the limits of the world.

Nor were the interior affairs of the republic calculated to encourage in her government a less haughty spirit or a less offensive demeanour.

mily, Mr. Gerry says, " The morning after my arrival I was waited on by the musicians of the executive, and the succeeding morning by a deputation of Poissards or fishwomen for presents. Major Rutledge was kind enough to negotiate for me, by which means I avoided the kind caresses of the ladies, and an interview with the gentlemen. They expected fifteen or twenty guineas, which each of us, according to custom was obliged to give them. When the ladies get sight of a minisier, as they did of my colleagues, they smother them with their delicate kisses ! So much for the *dignity* of the corps diplomatique. *MS. letter, 9th October* 1797.

The power of the directory had just been confirmed by the revolution of 18th Fructidor [4th
Sept. 1797] and an authority, nominally that of the
people, but in truth of the army, had escaped from
the danger of dissolution by the boldness of its
councils, and perpetuated itself by disregarding the
constitution to which it owed its existence.

The executive directory had overcome its enemies, and amid excesses of all kinds contrived to
retain the favour of the people. It now wielded
the military force of the nation, and felt all the
pride and importance, which could be derived from
this vast array of influence and power.

A second negotiation with England, conducted
with lord Malmsbury by the ministers of the directory, had been broken off, having exhibited the
obstinacy and the haughtiness of the parties rather
than any sincere desire for peace. To the French
nation therefore only one enemy remained, and
upon that enemy the force and the indignation of
the whole population was about to be concentred.

" Although," say the directory, " so much has
been done, so many kings conquered, so many
people set free, and the republic itself established
by the valour of its armies, yet the country expected one more sacrifice, since that enemy, who
had been the original cause of all the horrors and
miseries they had suffered, both from foreign and
civil war, remained to be crushed. The safety of

the republic is endangered whilst the English government exists.*

Bonaparte, after concluding a treaty with the emperor, so astonishingly favourable to France, that it has been supposed to have added an entire fifth to her ample military means, was himself ready to take command of the force, which the haughtiness of the republic destined to achieve the last of its labours. The success of this effort, which was to complete the conquest of the world, was not more the subject of national exertion than popular enthusiasm. The feelings of the community were excited by past success to a species of madness in this great effort of aggrandizement, and with an ardour characteristic of the country, already anticipated their complete success.

It was true indeed, that the naval strength of the mistress of the ocean gave some opposition to efforts, which must be made within her reach, and that the resources at her command were well arranged to protract the period of her overthrow ; but however these incidents might affect the rulers of France, they had apparently little force on the minds of the people, and seemed principally operative in accumulating such magnificence of force as would look down opposition.

The popular belief was that England was on the point of revolution; that oppressed by a ruinous

* Proclamation of the Directory, Nov. 1797.

debt, and borne down by unequalled taxation, the nation was already more than half conquered, and that the appearance of a formidable force, under which the disaffected could rally without fear, would almost without a blow complete the triumph of the invaders.

If the difficulties of the extravagant enterprise were better known to the directory and its generals, somewhat of a similar delusion prevailed over even the soundness of their judgment. That a powerful internal opposition existed in Great Britain was beyond doubt ; how far it would aid an invading enemy was a matter of speculation. Deluded by their success on the continent, and calculating on their arts as well as arms, the government of France did not permit themselves to doubt, that when the flag of the republic should be fairly planted on the British shore, it would be hailed as the standard of liberty, a signal for the demolition of the monarchy and the dissolution of the government.

With feelings of ancient hostility and rivalship were mingled something of resentment and indignation at the obstacles, which delayed their anticipated triumph. They looked to the destruction of this last enemy as an event certainly to happen, but protracted by circumstances vexatious indeed but not formidable, which while they delayed the gratification, served only to sharpen the eager spirit of revenge.

It could not facilitate the objects of the American embassy, that the principal cause of complaint against the nation it represented, was an imputed attachment to the great enemy of the republic, with whom it had recently by treaty drawn closer the ties of alliance and friendship, and that an identity of principles and interest had grown up between them, which it was the policy of the republic to discredit and condemn.

In the character of the individuals composing the French government, the American ambassadors found no cause for greater satisfaction. The recent revolution had deposed Carnot and Barthelemi. To Barras, Reubel and Lepaux were added Neufchateau and Merlin, the latter more than suspected of having a direct interest in the captures made by French privateers on the American commerce. None of them were distinguished for talent or respected for public services. They collectively supported their little less than imperial station, by a courage that nothing could intimidate, and a ready disposition to disregard for personal aggrandizement any restraints, which honour or justice would ordinarily have power to impose.

As secretary for foreign affairs, Talleyrand, now known as well for the versatility and greatness of his genius as for the profligacy of his character and the successful hypocrisy of his life, contrived to exercise an almost unlimited authority, without being able to obtain confidence ; suiting himself exactly to the exigencies of the government by the powers of his intellect and the flexibility of his principles.

At such a period of triumph, of confidence and hope, before men who limited their ambition neither by precedent nor virtue, the envoys of the American government presented themselves at Paris. They came, it was well known, to complain, to remonstrate, to demand redress. They came to unfold the unfriendly disposition of the French government towards the only people who had established free institutions upon popular principles, and had demonstrated the practicability of the system, which the French nation professed to support; and they came to add to their representation of wrongs they were suffering, their grief at the inconsistency of a policy, which alienated from the only republic in Europe the only other republic in the world. They came too, with the character and the feelings of the representatives of a free people, proud of the independence of their country, undismayed by the general overthrow of kings and the revolution of empires, to urge before the gigantic victors of Europe the rights of justice in the language of equality.

It might have been foreseen that such an embassy would be received with coldness, and subjected to such inconveniences as the course of diplomacy can readily present; but it was hardly to have been anticipated that an extraordinary and important delegation of unusual dignity of character, as well in the forms by which it was instituted as by the number and respectability of the individuals composing it, would have been obliged to remain six months in the capital of a nation, nominally at peace with their country, not merely unaccredited but exposed to personal and official mortifications of the most humiliating kind; and finally to return, not only without affecting the object of their mission, but without the common courtesy of an official discussion of it.

To aggravate the evils incident to so painful a situation, an unfortunate and serious misunderstanding, the common accident of joint missions, arose between the envoys themselves, the blame of which, although the high and honourable distinctions subsequently bestowed by their country on the individuals concerned, may be considered as exculpating each of them successively, fell at the time principally upon one.

To place the conduct of the envoys in a proper light, the history of the mission will be distinctly stated and such remarks will be added as are due to the individual, whose share in it gives occasion to its being mentioned in this place.

A brief retrospect of events, previous to this extraordinary mission to France, is necessary to a correct estimate of American policy.

The commencement of the French revolution found the American people ardently and universally interested in its success. Grateful for the aid accorded to them in their own struggle, they joyfully beheld the blessings of freedom dawning upon France. Proud of their own liberty, it was natural for them to believe that no political society could admit of more desirable advantages. In their feelings for the prosperity of republican France there was an enthusiasm proportioned to the sublimity of the scene it presented.

A chivalrous and gallant people had for ages been bound in the fetters of despotism. They now broke their chains and were free. The first impulse to this noble act was derived from America. They who had been to the rest of the civilized world a model of intellectual character and learning and taste, envied for their wealth, power and renown, whose glory for ten centuries had thrown its dazzling rays over the history of mankind, and whose arts and arms had divided the empire of the world, condescended to receive from this young nation the most valuable jewel within their ancient domain. America had borrowed from France her power and wealth to establish the foundations of her empire, but she repaid the vast obligation with more than an equivalent, in giving to France the principles of civil liberty, and instructing her in the knowledge that freedom was the first requisite for public happiness.

Pride, sympathy, gratitude, principle, all combined to make the French revolution not merely popular in the United States, but ardently and enthusiastically supported by the American people. For a long period after its commencement there was probably nothing short of their own independence for which they felt a more zealous concern. The interest, which was excited for the prosperity of their ancient allies was increased by those still unsettled feelings of animosity, which survived towards their former foe.   There were resentments not allayed, recollections of past injuries not effaced, mournful memorials of the calamities of war every where to be seen through the country, which enlisted their inclinations as strongly against one party as more generous sentiments excited them in favour of the other, and led them to see in the measures of the English government against France, only that enmity to freedom, which had been manifested toward themselves.

The first check to that exaggerated gratitude, which was rapidly hurrying the United States into war, was the proclamation of neutrality issued by president Washington on the 22d day of April 1793.

That cautious and intelligent statesman, and the profound councillors of his cabinet, well knew that the primary duty of the American people was to preserve their own yet unsettled institutions. They knew the United States were in no condition for another war.   A government yet untried by experience, and depending for its permanency on the success of its first operations, would most unwisely hazard the chances of a new contest. The elastic spirit of a young people, it was seen, was beginning to throw off the evils of their recent condition, to refill their exhausted treasury, to diminish their public debt, to revive their decayed commerce, and to reanimate their natural enterprise. For these desirable objects a few years of peace were indispensable, and the first measure of that wisdom, which then guided the affairs of the nation, was to counteract the inclinations of the people, until their calmer judgment applauded the restraint.

Peace with both the belligerents and the advantage of a neutral attitude, which could profit by their sacrifices, became the pole star of the American government, and however difficult the navigation, however dangerous the adverse winds and counter currents of the voyage, it was by this direction that policy commanded them to steer.

The vast objects, which the United States had to accomplish, the immense, and but that they have been realized, the incredible advantages of a neutral character, were not more obvious to her government than, it was seen by the belligerents respectively, would be to them an opposite course. Against the machinations and violence of both of them, and the prejudice and passion of their own citizens, this desirable position was to be maintained by the American government.

Circumstances of exceeding delicacy and difficulty were constantly occurring, which might lead
immediately to war.   The rulers of France early
conceived an opinion that there was a necessary opposition between the people and their government ; or at least that this was universally
true except only in France.   The course of their
policy as well as arms alarmed many of the most
intelligent of the American patriots, and the
predictions and warnings, which Edmund Burke
sounded in Europe, found among the reflecting
statesmen in the western hemisphere many res-
ponsive hearts.

The mission of Mr. Genet, the whole of whose
extravagant diplomacy in this country might be
recounted in proof, alarmed still more the apprehensions of impartial men, who saw that a popular
attachment to his country and its cause superseded
the regard that should have been paid to the one
which he visited, and that on questions of national
jurisdiction, about which intelligent men could not
differ, a strong feeling often carried by acclamation his opinions against those of the government.

While the conduct of the minister of France
evidently displayed a determination to appeal from
the government to the people of the United States,
and seduce their affections into a war, which their
judgment would not sanction, a measure of his
country gave some appearance of interest to the
object of his wishes.   The ports of the French

colonies were thrown open to American commerce, and the "hasty credulity" of mercantile enterprise, lost no time to improve the gainful opportunity. Whether the motive for this act was to secure a commerce to their own subjects in neutral bottoms, which their scanty marine could not carry on, or more artfully to draw the enemies cruisers on the rich freights that would be presented to their cupidity, and thus contrast an admiration for their own generosity with indignation at their enemies rapacity ; or whether it was in truth the evidence of that friendly spirit, which republics should feel for each other, was at the time a subject of discussion, but it was at singular variance with an order of the national convention, which allowed French ships to bring in for adjudication such neutral vessels as were loaded in whole or in part, either with provisions destined for enemy ports, or merchandise belonging to enemies.

Threats that were unexecuted, whether from inability or good will, had much less effect on the public mind than a liberality, which could be understood, and in contrast with the colonial system of other nations the free trade to French colonies was highly appreciated. The denunciations of their decrees were hardly felt, but the mercantile advantages, in those instances which escaped the hostility of their enemy, were fully possessed. While therefore influential and leading men in and

out of the government of the United States began
to find in the revolution, as it was proceeding in
France, principles destructive of liberty and law,
private property, personal security and moral conduct, the general feeling of the public mind
cemented still stronger the original attachment,
and by dividing more distinctly its admirers and
its enemies increased that internal hostility, which
threatened the peace of the nation.

So long as the measures of France tended even
against the exertions of intelligent men, to bring
the two countries into a connexion of a more intimate character, her great enemy, regardless of
national law or the obligations of the existing
treaty, was accumulating subjects of complaint,
and indemnifying herself for the loss of popular
favour by extensive devastations on the commerce
of the United States.

An order of council, which when intrusted to
her powerful navy was no dead letter in the statute book, authorized British cruisers to stop all
vessels loaded wholly or in part with provisions,
bound to any port in France or occupied by the
armies of France.   This insane attempt to starve
a whole people, which with as much insult as injustice, was justified by cited aphorisms from political writers, was enforced by the indiscriminate
destruction of neutral property, which it swept as
with a whirlwind from the ocean.   Nor did even
the profligacy of the pretence, which was given for

it, secure credit to the grounds upon which it was defended. In America it was believed to be part of a plan for the subversion of free governments, and to have been started at a time when partial successes and the strength of the coalition gave some expectation that France would be overthrown. The vexatious practice of impressment added new fuel to the flame of popular animosity. The detention of the western posts in direct violation of the treaty of 1783, though justified as a retaliation for deficiencies on the part of the United States in the execution of the same compact, was regarded as a voluntary addition to the miseries of an Indian war, which it was supposed to encourage if not excite, while the whole system of the English navigation laws was complained of as intentionally severe and ruinous to the commerce of the United States.

Other instances of injustice and wrong in the conduct of the belligerents seemed to demonstrate that in their efforts for mutual injury, no sentiment of justice was felt for neutral rights; and while each, by every possible art, was endeavouring to force the United States into a war with the other, the taunting intimation of one of them was in train to be realized, that a nation, which would not fight for honour would be obliged to contend for existence.

But high and chivalrous principles better suited the spirit of the people than the condition of the country. They were adapted to an athletic and robust nation rather than one whose strength was yet in the gristle. If the policy of peace must be abandoned it would be well in selecting an enemy to make sure of a friend.

On the selection of that friend the people of the United States were greatly divided, while the strength of the popular feeling was not exactly re-echoed by the public functionaries. The French government, amid all its acts of injustice and injury, affected to speak with the United States as friends. In the glowing language, which marked their official despatches, they say, " An analogy of political principles; the natural relations of commerce and industry; the efforts and immense sacrifices of both nations in the defence of liberty and equality; the blood, which they have spilled together ; their avowed hatred for despots ; the moderation of their political views ; the disinterestedness of their councils ; and especially the success of the vows they have made in presence of the Supreme Being to be free or die, all combine to render indestructible the connexions, which they have formed."

" Doubt it not citizens, we shall finally destroy the combination of tyrants ; you, by the picture of prosperity, which in your vast countries has succeeded to a bloody struggle of eight years ; we by that enthusiasm, which glows in the breast of every Frenchman. Astonished nations, too long the dupes of perfidious kings, nobles and priests, will eventually recover their rights, and the human race will owe to the American and French nations their regeneration and a lasting peace."

It was this very " analogy of political principles," so captivating to the nation at large, that alarmed the minds of the administration and induced them to put obstacles in the way of a more intimate fraternization. The British government, on the contrary, which " wounds by its pride and offends by its haughtiness,"* while the objects it was contending for were more congenial to national security, so far from affecting in its diplomatic intercourse to secure popular favour, allowed eighteen months to expire without deigning to give an answer to an elaborate and profound argument made by the American secretary of state† in complaint of the conduct and principles of the government of Great Britain towards the United States.

As a last effort to prevent a war, into which circumstances were rapidly hurrying the country, a special mission, on 16th April 1794, was instituted to the court of St. James, and intrusted to a citizen eminently distinguished in the annals of the country, and then holding the high office of chief justice of the United States. At the request

---

* Marshall, vol. v. p. 481.

† American state papers, Mr. Jefferson to Mr. Hammond, 29th May 1792. Mr. Hammond to Mr. Randolph, 21st February 1794.

of the French government Mr. Morris was recalled from the republic and the diplomatic intercourse confided to Mr. Monroe.

The alarm, which the unexpected nomination of
Mr. Jay produced on one half of the population of
the United States, was in some degree quieted by
the appointment that followed to the government
of France. The duties and objects of the first
were not distinctly known, but the selection of the
other was received by the party of the republicans
as evidence of the president's impartiality ; and as
each of those ministers was known to carry to the
court, to which he was sent, sentiments that were
not likely to obstruct an amicable arrangement,
there was a calm over the public mind, a prelude to
the storms that were soon to confound it, when
the results of these missions should be announced.

Mr. Jay, as is well known, concluded the treaty
of London, which on its ratification terminated all
existing causes of controversy with Great Britain,
and arranged a new system of commercial intercourse. Mr. Monroe was recalled by the president, not without some marks of dissatisfaction,
which his candid disclosures easily dispelled.*

The negotiation of any treaty with England,
would no doubt have increased the difficulties of
pacification with France. But in regard to this
she complained that her faith had been abused by

* Monroe's View, &c.

misrepresentations and concealment, and her rights
violated by sacrifices and concessions.

The instructions under which Mr. Monroe acted were drawn in conformity to his well known
political principles, in which no member of the
senate had given more evidence of sincerity or
zeal.   He was instructed to declare " that the president had been an early and decided friend of
the French republic ; that whatever reason there
may have been under our ignorance of facts and
policy to suspend an opinion upon some of its important transactions, yet that he was immutable in
his wishes for its accomplishment, incapable of
assenting to the right of any foreign prince to
meddle with its interior arrangement, and persuaded that success would attend its efforts."   He
was directed to let it be seen " that in case of war
with any nation on earth, we shall consider France
as our first and natural ally, to dwell upon the
sense we entertain of their past services and their
more recent interposition in our behalf with the
Dey of Algiers," and alluding to Mr. Jay's mission to England, he was instructed to declare the
motives of that mission to be to obtain immediate
restitution for our plundered property and restitution of the [western] posts.

The sentiments of the executive thus communicated to Mr. Monroe, were repeated in stronger
language by the two houses of Congress.   The
revolution was emphatically declared to be the

cause of liberty, "under that standard whenever it shall be displayed, the affections of the United States will always rally ; the successes of those who stand forth as her avengers will be gloried in by the United States, and will be felt as the successes of themselves and the other friends of humanity. Yes—representatives of our ally, your communication has been addressed to those who take a deep interest in the prosperity and happiness of the French Republic."

With such instructions from one department of the government, and a knowledge of such sentiments in the other, Mr. Monroe presented himself to the rulers of France. His reception was brilliant and flattering, and the conduct, which he pursued, and the language, which he used, was too faithful to his own principles to raise a doubt that all this profusion of attachment covered any thing deceptive.

The condition of things in France was not without uneasiness. The treaty between the two republics had been violated. The commerce of the United States was harassed and plundered. The minister, whom Mr. Monroe succeeded, was not only without the confidence of the government, but an object of particular jealousy and suspicion. The popular favour towards the United States was diminishing by means of reports brought by officers of the fleet of unfriendly treatment in American ports, and a suspicion was entertained that the mission of Mr. Jay was intended to pave the way for an abandonment of the one people and an alliance with the other.

By declarations, the authority for which were found in his instructions, and with a zeal, which had been announced to him as the motive for his selection to the embassy,* the American minister succeeded in putting affairs in good order, and began to accommodate arrangements to his satisfaction, when the treaty negotiated with England was communicated to the directory, and produced as was to have been supposed resentment and indignation.

The fact that a commercial treaty had been negotiated with their rival, that some of its features were in themselves objectionable and injurious, that no overtures had been made to France for the same objects, that not only entire secrecy had been observed as to the pendency of the negotiation, but that the objects and powers of the minister had been misrepresented or concealed, produced on the haughty victors of a thousand enemies, not less the feelings of indignation than the less tolerable expression of disgust and contempt.

While the cause of the United States thus lost its popularity in the eye of the government

---

* Mr. Monroe was informed that he was selected " on account of his known political character and principles." In the Senate of the United States he had moved to suspend the fourth article of the treaty of peace with Great Britain, of 1783.

of France, with singular adroitness it saw fit to
discriminate between the administration and its
minister, whom it exonerated from the suspicion even of intentional deception.   Falling in
with the declarations of the party in the United
States to which he belonged, and adopting the
language of its public journals, the directory chose
to consider the American minister as much deceived as themselves.   Craftily pursuing their design to separate the people from the government,
they affected to believe that this treaty was another evidence of the combination of rulers against
the defenders of the rights of man.

The sensibility of the French government was
not realized by that of the United States.   Believing as they declared, that an independent nation might conduct its diplomacy without the advice or permission of other powers, and that in the
treaty with England they had exercised only their
unquestionable rights, they did not admit that
France had any just cause of complaint ; and having secured by it so much of their cardinal policy
as preserved peace with one of the belligerents,
an attempt was to be made to complete the desirable object by a new effort with the other.

Mr. Monroe was recalled, and Charles C. Pinckney of South Carolina, appointed to succeed him.

If the causes for Mr. Monroe's selection were
complimentary to France or useful to his own
country, the want of similar qualifications in his

successor, denoted either a diminution of that civility or an opinion that it did not produce its expected consequences. In the domestic parties of the country these gentlemen were under different banners.

Mr. Monroe's departure from the French capital was as brilliant as his reception. An audience of leave was accorded to him, and in answer to his address the most flattering testimonials of respect was bestowed upon him by the president director. Unfortunately the speech of Barras on that occasion, and the commentary made on it by the executive of the United States, gave new occasion for umbrage and increased the difficulties in the way of amicable accommodation.*

* *Speech of the president director Barras.*

" By presenting to day the letters of recall to the executive directory, you gave to Europe a very strange spectacle.

France rich in her liberty, surrounded by a train of victories, strong in the esteem of her allies, will not abase herself by calculating the consequences of the condescension of the American government to the suggestions of her former tyrants. Moreover the French republic hopes that the successors of Columbus, Raleigh and Penn, always proud of liberty, will never forget that they owe it to France. They will weigh in their wisdom the magnanimous benevolence of the French people with the crafty caresses of certain perfidious persons who meditate bringing them back to their former slavery. Assure the good American people sir, that like them we adore liberty, that they will always have our esteem, and that they will find in the French people republican generosity, which knows how to grant peace as it does to cause its sovereignty to be respected. As for you, Mr. minister plenipotentiary, you have combatted for principles. You have

The recall of Mr. Monroe was followed by the refusal of the directory to receive Mr. Pinckney, and a declaration "that they would no longer recognise or receive a minister plenipotentiary from the United States, until after the reparation of the grievances demanded of the American government, which the French republic has a right to expect."

In the preceding November, the French minister in the United States announced the termination of his functions, and in an address nominally to the secretary of state, but in reality to the peo-

known the true interests of your country. Depart with our regret. In you we give up a representative to America, and retain the remembrance of the citizen whose personal qualities did honour to that title."

Speech of president Adams.

" With this conduct of the French government, it will be proper to take into view the public audience given to the late minister of the United States on his taking leave of the executive directory. The speech of the president discloses sentiments more alarming than the refusal of a minister because more dangerous to our independence and union, and at the same time studiously marked with indignities towards the government of the United States. It evinces a disposition to separate the people of the United States from the government; to persuade them that they have different affections, principles and interests, from those of their fellow citizens whom they themselves have chosen to manage their common concerns, and thus to produce divisions fatal to our peace. Such attempts ought to be repelled with a decision that shall convince France and the world that we are not a degraded people, humiliated under a colonial spirit of fear and sense of inferiority, fitted to be the miserable instruments of foreign influence, and regardless of national honour, character and interest."

ple, encouraged the idea, which seemed to be the leading principle of his country's policy, that the functionaries of the American government and the party who supported them entertained principles and feelings hostile to the French cause, and were desirous, notwithstanding all their pretensions to the contrary, to involve the two nations in war.

The irritable state of feeling, which existed between the countries, the belief, which a large party in the United States honestly professed, that in the conduct of affairs with the French republic the government of the United States had been unwise and insincere, and the use, which that nation made of this division of opinion to embarrass the American government, were if no other causes existed, formidable obstacles to a continuance of peace. But the collisions of interest or force had accumulated a vast mass of serious complaint.

On the part of France it was alleged that the treaty of Paris was infringed because prizes made by French vessels of war were not allowed to be adjudicated upon in American ports by the consular agents of the republic.

That English vessels of war, which had made prizes on the republic or its citizens were not excluded from the ports of the United States, as by the 17th article of the same treaty they should have been.

That the consular convention had become illusory from the obstacles thrown in the way of its execution by the American government.

That an attack had been made by a British vessel of war on a public vessel of France within the waters of the United States with intention to seize the person and papers of the French minister to the United States, supposed to have been on board, and that this gross invasion of the sovereignty of the United States so injurious to France had been passed over with impunity.

But all other causes of complaint lost their importance in comparison with those, which were connected with the late treaty of London.

" The United States," said the French minister, " besides having departed from the principles of the armed neutrality during the war for their independence, have given to England to the detriment of their first allies, the most striking marks of an unbounded condescension by abandoning the limit given to contraband by the law of nations, by their treaties with all other nations, and even by those of England, with a greater part of the maritime powers. Is it not evidently estraying from the principles of neutrality to sacrifice exclusively to that power the objects proper for the equipment and construction of vessels? They have gone further. They have consented to extend the denomination of contraband even to provisions."*

* Such answers as the American government could give to these complaints were ably stated in the letters of Mr. Monroe to the French minister. The administration by recalling him intimated to the American people that the displeasure of France

On the other side of this account current of in-justice and wrong, the Americans presented the frightful system of hostility, which under one or another decree of the national convention let loose on their defenceless commerce the whole French marine, and the profligacy and notorious corruption of their judicial tribunals, which consummated by chicanery and fraud what rapacity and piracy even had subdued.

A distressing embargo had been laid on their property and seamen at Bordeaux.

Bills and other evidence of debt, given by the colonial government in the West Indies, were unpaid and merchandise taken for public use was appropriated without compensation.

To all this was added the alleged attempt to sow distrust and division between the government and people, and to destroy by their arts what escaped the power of their arms.

In a review of these discouraging circumstances, Mr. Adams determined " to institute a fresh attempt at negotiation;" certain if it succeeded, to secure a most favourable position for his country, and confident if it failed through the obstinacy or

was owing less to the existence of good cause than to his neglect in not making satisfactory explanations. The publication of his correspondence restored him to the favour of his country, by completely disapproving the suggestion, and the secretary of state did not escape the odium of that intentional duplicity, which charged on an agent of the government the consequences justly attributable to the government itself.

wilfulness of France, to draw to his standard that great body of his fellow citizens, who though opprobriously stigmatized in his cabinet, he well knew to be Americans at heart.

It was probably beyond the range of intelligence or ingenuity to carry on negotiations with each belligerent in a manner that would subserve the real interests of the United States, without giving plausible if not substantial cause of complaint to one or both. The executive might indeed have selected its ally and bid its will avouch it, but policy adopted a different language.

> ————— Yet I must not
> For certain friends that are both his and mine,
> Whose loves I may not drop.

When therefore the determination was settled to make the first experiment with Great Britain, the delicacy of the relation to France became every day more attenuated.

The departure of Mr. Jay for the court of St. James was a public act, which as it could not be concealed, it was obviously politic to announce with the appearance of candour, but the very communication of this fact gave new cause for disagreement. The French minister, Mr. Fauchet, insisted that he was told the mission contemplated only an adjustment of our (American) complaints, excluding all commercial arrangements. The secretary denied that he said more than to assure him, " Mr. Jay was instructed not to weaken our engagements with France."

It is not now necessary to discuss the question whether a commercial treaty with England would not *ipso facto* weaken our engagements with France; nor whether the stipulations in the treaty of London could be executed without such consequence; or however these might be, whether when a minister had been directed to negotiate a commercial treaty, the admitted language of the secretary was any thing else than equivocation, to conceal the real design.

The intimacy of the connexion between France and the United States, if weakened by recent causes of complaint, treaties and popular feeling still supposed to exist; and it therefore required, in the opinion of the former, as evidence of the sincerity of the latter, that a frank and full disclosure of its intentions should be made ; and some countenance is undesignedly given to this expectation by the fact, that before the conclusion of the treaty a communication of some kind was made to the French minister, and before its ratification the treaty was submitted to him for his commentaries and opinion.

France thereupon complains, " It was a little matter only to allow the English to avail themselves of the advantages of our treaty, it was necessary to assure these to them by the means of a contract, which might serve at once as a reply to the claims of France and as peremptory motives for refusals, the true motive of which it was requisite incessantly to disguise to her under specious pretexts. Such was the object of Mr. Jay's mission to London, such was the object of a negotiation enveloped from its origin in the shadow of mystery and covered with the veil of dissimulation."*

The American answer maintains that the right to form these treaties has been so universally asserted and admitted that it seems to be the inseparable attribute of sovereignty, to be questioned only by those who question the right of a nation to govern itself, and to be ceded only by those who are prepared to cede their independence.

The complaint as to what should not be done in a specific case is thus answered by an allegation of abstract right. Hence the replication of the French minister in very strong terms. "When the agents of the republic complained of this mysterious conduct, they were answered by an appeal to the independence of the United States, solemnly sanctioned in the treaties of 1778—a strange manner of contesting a grievance, the reality of which was demonstrated by the dissimulation, to which recourse was had—an insidious subterfuge, which substitutes for the true point of the question a general principle, which the republic can-

* Mons. Adet to secretary of state.

not be supposed to dispute, and which destroys by aid of a sophism that intimate confidence, which ought to exist between two allies, and which above all ought to exist between the French republic and the United States."

Again the French government complained of the abusive language of certain public journals of the United States, and were answered with the abstract propositions that " the genius of the constitution and the opinion of the people of the United States cannot be overruled by those who administer the government," and " that among those deemed most sacred is the liberty of the press."

Now the real subject of complaint was not that the administration did not put down these offensive journals by force of law, but that they were known to encourage them by personal patronage, and thus under colour of a professed inability to control the public press, aided and abetted its conductors in disseminating opinions injurious to the cause of France.

The French minister further commenting on the insincerity of the American government, alleges that it was thought proper to send to the French republic persons whose opinions and connexions are too well known to hope from them dispositions sincerely conciliatory, and contrasts that conduct with the eagerness to send to London ministers well known for sentiments corresponding with the object of their mission.

Stripped of the thin veil, which diplomatic forms throw on this subject, the French minister asserts, " The people of the United States are divided into two great parties, differing in their views of the correct policy of the country. One of these is desirous of a more intimate union with England, the other with France. In negotiations with the former power the compliment of selecting negotiators from the party, which deemed its duty to the United States to consist in friendship with England, was paid to her, and the consequence was successful negotiation. No such compliment is paid to France and no such consequence can ensue."

The Americans could only reaffirm their conciliatory temper without denying the facts, from which a different conclusion had been drawn.

CHAPTER VI.

History of the joint mission of Messrs. Pinckney, Marshall and Gerry, to the French republic.......Messrs. Marshall and Pinckney leave France.......Mr. Gerry remains.......His conduct.

THE American envoys met in Paris on the 4th October 1797, and the next day announced their arrival to the minister of foreign affairs, assuring him that the United States were desirous of terminating all differences between themselves and the French republic, and of restoring that harmony and good understanding, and that commercial and friendly intercourse, which from the commencement of their political existence until lately had happily subsisted ; and that the president had appointed them jointly and severally envoys extraordinary and ministers plenipotentiary to the French republic, for the purpose of accomplishing these great objects. They requested an opportunity to present their letter of credence, and assured him of their ardent desire for the speedy restoration of harmony and friendship between the two republics.

On the 8th the envoys had an interview with the minister of foreign relations. The letter of credence was delivered and cards of hospitality received. They were informed that " the directory had directed the minister to make a report relative to the situation of the United States with regard to France, which would be finished in a few days, when he would let them know what steps were to follow."

In a day or two the private and confidential secretary of the minister intimated to the private secretary of one of the envoys, that the directory were exasperated at some parts of the president's speech at the opening of the last session of congress, and would require an explanation; that the envoys would probably not have a public audience until their negotiation was finished, that persons might be appointed to treat with them, who would report to the minister, and he would have the direction, though not actually the conducting of the negotiations.

This communication, circuitous and informal enough, paved the way for subsequent measures equally singular and extraordinary.

A gentleman of respectability privately informed general Pinckney, that another person whom he could introduce, would suggest a plan for accommodation at the instance of Mons. Talleyrand, which if proposed to him by the American envoys, would undoubtedly facilitate negotiations.

After much unofficial parade and affectation of secrecy, the envoys, who found no authorized and ostensible agent of the republic to discourse with, were introduced to these anonymous personages.

The substance of the propositions thereupon submitted to them was, that the envoys should propose to give a softening turn to some parts of the
president's speech, should advance under cover of
a masked loan some millions of dollars for the
French treasury, and in addition to this substantial part of the treaty, should " address themselves
to the private gratification of certain high officers
of government, by compliance with diplomatic
usage," which being interpreted was understood
to mean, supply a fund of fifty thousand pounds
sterling for distribution to prominent individuals.

To induce the envoys as of their own accord to
make these propositions, the haughty temper and irritable feeling of the directory towards the United
States were adverted to, and the friendly exertion
of Mons. Talleyrand under such a stimulus, was
promised in their behalf; an exertion, which his
late successful diplomacy with the emperor, it was
said, enabled him to make with advantage.   The
power of France was displayed in all its greatness.
A war in the north against England was preparing.   On the coast an army of one hundred and
fifty thousand men, directed by the genius of Bonaparte, would invade England, and overturn its
government; or if not adequate to this result, the
alarm spread through the nation, and the enormous
expenses consequent upon it would as certainly
effect its ruin, unless prevented by an humiliating
peace.

In such an event, which was more than merely probable, what, it was asked, would be the difference in the situation of the United States, if they were at peace or war with France?

In the former case the commerce of the world would flow into their channels, relieved from the exactions of England; in the latter the fate of Venice might forewarn them of their own. It was urged that in the present condition of France, vast advantages would result to the United States from delay, which was in effect to gain their cause, and that policy required they should make any arrangement not absolutely extravagant.

A more direct attempt was made on the fears of the envoys. Perhaps you think, they were told, that in returning and exposing to your countrymen the unreasonableness of the demands of this government you will unite them in resistance. You are mistaken. You ought to know that the diplomatic skill of France and the means she possesses in your country, are sufficient to enable her with the French party in America, to throw the blame, which will attend the rupture of the negotiations, on the federalists as you term yourselves; on the British faction as that class of your citizens are termed by France. You may assure yourselves this will be done.

Such was the language of these unaccredited and nameless individuals, who either with or without authority found their way to the drawing room and the breakfast table of the American envoys; and they having no other individuals with whom to discuss the relations of the two countries, condescended to hear them.

The answer of the envoys was delivered with a frankness suited to the purity of their character. They unanimously resolved not to purchase the right of negotiation. If negotiations were opened, they professed a willingness to discuss any proposition made by the French government; if it exceeded their powers, they were ready, they said, to consult with all practicable expedition the government of the United States. They expressed their readiness, if the difficulties attending the proposition for a loan, and the embarrassments incident to a reclamation for illegal depredations on the commerce of the United States should retard an immediate completion of a treaty, to postpone these important subjects for future discussion, and place the present relations of the two nations on an amicable basis. They asserted the early and invariable attachment of the United States to republican France, and proposed to discuss any measures, which had given her offence, in the confidence of being able to make satisfactory explanations. On the advantages of neutrality, they said it was unnecessary to dilate. All the efforts of their government had been exerted to maintain it. Referring to other suggestions, the envoys remarked, that America had never contemplated a political connexion with Great Britain; whether the reputed danger of that government was real or not they could not decide, but it was evident to them that both the belligerents had much reason to wish for peace. They declared their conviction that France miscalculated on the state of parties in America; that her extreme injustice would unite all parties against her, and produce a common sentiment of hostility so soon as it should be ascertained that to past injuries, which she would not redress, were added new wrongs aggravated by contempt.

They complained of the embarassment of their condition. They were called to pledge their country to a great amount, for demands as extravagant as unexpected, without discussing the justice or the policy, on which they were founded; without assurance that they were not preliminaries to much greater yet concealed; without any promise that the rights of their country would thereafter be respected, and without a document to prove that persons to whom they were required to unbosom themselves, were empowered even by the minister, much less by the directory, to hold any conversation with them.

On the 21st October Mr. Gerry proposed to his colleagues to adopt the following resolution.

To the question, whether the propositions informally and confidentially communicated to us as private citizens, at the request, as is stated of Mons.

Talleyrand in his private capacity, will be adopted as the basis of a treaty, this answer is given, that it is highly probable some of the propositions communicated on 19th and 20th October will be considered as the basis of a treaty and others as inadmissible, but that it is impossible to discuss or come to a decision on them until they are presented to us in an official character.

The original of this note is endorsed " intended to be given Saturday, 21st October."* The endorsement is in general Pinckney's handwriting.†

On 3d November the envoys relate that they told one of these intrusive messengers that they should at any time be glad to see him as a private citizen, but " that they had determined to receive no propositions, unless the persons who bore them had acknowledged authority to treat." Nevertheless, either as private citizens, or in some other capacity, the anonymous gentlemen were received by the envoys; their conversation was noted in the private journal of Mr. Marshall, and the transcript of that journal communicated to the American government as late as the 17th December.

For a long period the American embassy had contented itself with listening to unaccredited agents, without seeking such interviews with the minister himself, as might, under ordinary circumstances lead to mutual good understanding.

---

* Mr. Gerry's MS. papers.

† Mr. Gerry's letter to president Jefferson, MS. 13th January 1801.

On the 22d October it was intimated to Mr. Gerry that the minister had expected to have seen the American envoys, and to have conferred with them individually on the affairs of their mission, and had authorized this communication to be made to him. Mr. Gerry sent for his colleagues, and general Pinckney and general Marshall expressed their opinion, that not being acquainted with M. Talleyrand they could not with propriety call on him, but that according to the custom of France he might expect this of Mr. Gerry, from a previous acquaintance in America. With this personal selection Mr. Gerry "reluctantly complied,"* and several interviews in the ordinary course of civility were had between them, in which, as the most interesting topic of the day, certainly one most interesting to his visitor, M. Talleyrand occasionally discussed the relations of France and the United States.

Meanwhile thirty days had elapsed and no communication in writing was received from the directory or its officers. It was proposed therefore by one of the envoys to address to the minister of foreign affairs an official note, calling his attention to their situation, and demanding that steps should be taken to open negotiations.

Proper as this measure would be under ordinary circumstances, it seemed to Mr. Gerry that in the present irritable state of the French government,

* Envoys' letter of 8th November 1797, American state papers vol. iii. p. 495, 2d edition.

no good could be expected by it ; that any urgency on the part of the Americans would serve rather to exasperate than to reconcile ; and he proposed therefore that communications in cypher should be made to their own government, describing in detail their present situation. The delay this would occasion did not seem to him a sufficient objection to it, inasmuch as it was not proposed by the envoys to quit Paris ; and the American government, by a timely knowledge of affairs, would be better able to select such alternative as was presented. The personal observation, which even his limited intercourse with the minister had afforded, enabled him to speak with more confidence on this point.*

This first disagreement among the envoys was not of serious consequence. Mr. Gerry, at their request, without yielding the opinion he advanced, that the letter would be useless, joined in one under date of 11th November, in which the envoys remind the minister of the promised communication, they had anxiously but in vain ex-

---

* Mr. Pickering, in his review p. 117, in stating this fact adds also that Mr. Gerry proposed to have "*six* copies made out and transmitted to his government." The perils of navigation, which then obstructed the ocean are in a great degree forgotten, and the readers of the review would be astonished at the folly of a pretence, which it is more than insinuated was a contrivance to waste time. Yet Mr. Pickering's own despatches to the envoys were transmitted in the *same number of sets*, and "one by a despatch boat sent on purpose." *American state papers*, vol. iv. p. 153.

pected to receive ; they repeat that the preservation of friendship with France was dear to the
American nation, the loss of it a subject of unfeigned regret, and that the recovery of it by
every means, which consist with the rights of an
independent nation engages their constant attention ; that the president of the United States had
given it in charge to the envoys to discuss candidly
the complaints of France, to offer frankly those of
the United States, and to review and alter existing
treaties, so as to consist with the mutual interest
and satisfaction of the contracting parties ; that
they were anxious to commence this task and
would be truly happy to restore that harmony,
which it was their wish as well as duty, if possible
to effect between the citizens of the two republics.   To this letter no answer was returned.   The
envoys were given to understand that it had been
laid before the executive directory, who would
command their minister what steps to pursue.

Previous to the writing of this letter, the envoys addressed to their government a minute account of all their discourse with informal agents,
" in thirty-six quarto pages of cypher and eight
pages of cyphered exhibits."

At the first interview between Mr. Gerry and
the French minister, at which the other two
envoys, " because they were not acquainted with
Mons. Talleyrand," had refused to be present,
that minister distinctly stated that the directory

had determined not to treat with the envoys, unless they previously made reparation for some parts of the president's speech at the opening of congress, that an arrette declaratory of this intention would be communicated in a few days; but if the envoys had any propositions to offer, he would with alacrity communicate them to the directory; that considering the circumstances and services of the same kind, which France had formerly rendered to the United States, the best way for them would be to offer to make a loan to France, either by taking Batavian inscriptions for fifteen or sixteen millions of florins or in some other way, which might be devised.

The good effect of this waiver of etiquette, if indeed any of the artificial forms of private society could exist between important official functionaries in such a situation, was thus distinctly seen. Two independent facts were learned with formality, precision and authority. First, that no treaty would be made with the envoys without an apology for the president's speech or an equivalent. Second, that a voluntary offer of a loan would be accepted as an equivalent.

Mr. Gerry on his return communicated these facts to his colleagues. Their consultation upon them resulted in desiring one of those mysterious prolocutors, who still attended them, to inform Mons. Talleyrand in substance that neither would be accepted.

In consequence of the visit made by Mr. Gerry to Mons. Talleyrand, the latter invited the former to one of his customary dinners ; the civility was returned by the American, and something like an intercourse that might give opportunity for conciliatory arrangements might have been effected, but the separation of one gentleman from his colleagues placed them all in so unpleasant a situation, that it was impossible he could consent to continue it. The minister's personal attentions, with a single exception, were afterwards declined, and affairs were left to the ordinary chance of official and diplomatic procedure.

The letter of 11th November remained without answer, and on the 24th December the envoys reported to their government their opinion, that if they were to wait six months longer, without they stipulated the payment of money and a great deal of it, in some shape or other, they would not be able to accomplish the objects of their mission, even if they were officially received, unless the projected invasion of England was to fail, or a total change take place in the persons, who directed the affairs of the government. In this conclusion all the envoys united, although on very different grounds.

So anxious were these ministers to supply the want of regular diplomatic proceedings by all the information in their power, that the idle prattle of a lady, who according to Mr. Pinckney, " was well

acquainted with Mons. Talleyrand," and by him
afterwards described as "known to be connected
with Mr. Pinckney," was transmitted by that gentleman in an official form to his government, as
additional evidence of the disposition of the directory to make the payment of money the basis of
negotiation.*

* "A lady understood to be Madame de Villette, the celebrated belle and bonne of Voltaire, was also concerned in this transaction." "As to the lady an intimation is given that that part
of the affair was not much to the credit of the Americans."—
Lyman's Diplomacy of the United States, p. 86. The able author
of this useful and generally accurate work, is here we think
under some mistake. The lady referred to was one acquainted
with general Pinckney, and her communication was made to
him and by him alone to the American government. Mr. Gerry
writes to Mons. Talleyrand, "I cannot give you the name of
any lady, for no one has made any political communications to
me since my arrival in Paris."

Madame Villette was the widow of a gentleman of fortune, a
colonel in the king's service. Her uncle was a general officer,
and her brother commanded the corps which defended the queen
at Versailles, where he lost his life. Madame was on Robes-
pierre's list of proscription, and was confined ten months in pris-
on, expecting every day to be summoned to the guillotine. Her
daughter, then only seven years of age, was her only companion.
She was not at this period remarkable for personal attractions.
The imprisonment had made great inroad on her health. She
is described by a gentleman in Paris, as "equally distinguished
for the goodness of her heart, her excellent morals, and the rich-
ness of her mind."

The intimations not much to the credit of the Americans,
should have been confined to one individual. Talleyrand ri-
dicules the folly, which saw any thing important in her remark, "lend us says she to him one day, money in our war,
we lent it to you in yours;" "and a conversation thus simple
is taken up by Mr. Pinckney, who finds it necessary to write

While affairs remained in this doubtful condition, the envoys faithful to their trust, and anxious
to leave no effort unattempted, which talents, industry and duty could accomplish, laid before the
French minister under date of 17th January, a
voluminous defence of the American policy, a justification of the conduct of the United States, and
a powerful appeal against that course of conduct,
which by the sanction of the directory, had sacrificed their mercantile capital, violated the privi-
leges of their flag, and exposed their mariners to
captivity.

The letter begins by declaring that the envoys
of the United States had been hitherto restrained,
by the expectation of entering on their mission in
the forms usual among nations, from addressing
the executive directory through the minister of foreign affairs, those explanations and reclamations,
with which they are charged by the government
they represent.   If that expectation was to be
relinquished yet the unfeigned wish of the United States to restore that harmony between the
two republics, which they have so unremitting-
ly sought to preserve, rendered it the duty of the
envoys to lay before the government of France,

every thing and to poison it, is mysteriously sent by him to his
government, as if it had any relation to the clandestine proposition made by the intriguers. Thus minute is distrust. Thus is
prejudice led astray in its reasonings. In this manner are the
politics of some men a pest to social intercourse."—*American
state papers*, 4th vol. p. 234.

however informal the communication may be deemed, some considerations in addition to those heretofore submitted relative to the subsisting differences between the two republics.

This admirable state paper, which may compare advantageously with the ablest diplomatic correspondence in the American archives, was draughted by general Marshall, and submitted to Mr. Gerry for revision and amendment.

During the time it was under his eye it underwent important alterations in its style and manner, to give it that softening and courteous form of address, which should neither contain, nor give reasonable pretence for a complaint that it did contain, any offensiveness of language, and although it was decidedly his opinion that there were reasons, which argument could not reach, for the unpromising condition of things, he agreed with his colleagues in subscribing the amended despatch.

While the most careful and successful regard appears to have been paid to the composition of this able performance to suit it to the temper of the haughty tribunal to which it was addressed, it lost nothing of the character, which belonged to a free and powerful people complaining of the injuries they had suffered, and describing the patience and the perseverance, with which they had peaceably sought redress. It displays every where the most anxious desire for an honourable recon-

ciliation, and affects not to conceal the grief of violated friendship in the unfortunate separation of the
only republics in the world.   The personal feelings of the writers, and the circumstances to which
they appeal for the proof of their sincerity, were
too forcibly expressed not to be true.

"Bringing with them," says the letter, "the
temper of their government and country, searching
only for the means of effecting the objects of their
mission, they have permitted no personal considerations to influence their conduct, but have waited
under circumstances beyond measure embarrassing
and unpleasant, with that respect, which the American government has so uniformly paid to that of
France, for permission to lay before you, citizen
minister, the important communications with which
they have been charged."

"If, citizen minister, there remains a hope that
these desirable objects can be effected by any
means, which the United States have authorized,
the envoys would still solicit, and still respectfully
attend the developement of those means.   If on
the contrary no such hope remains, they have only
to pray that their *return to their own country may be
facilitated*, and they will leave France with the
most deep felt regret, that neither the real and
sincere friendship, which the government of the
United States has so uniformly and unequivocally
displayed for this great republic, nor its continued
efforts to demonstrate the purity of its conduct and

intentions, can protect its citizens, or preserve them from the calamities, which they have sought by a just and upright conduct to avert."

These communications had no effect. There were points, which could not be overcome by any power of language ; obstacles, which the diplomacy of the French government, whose most familiar art was deception, raised in the road, by their willingness to transfer to the agents of the American republic imputations, which its own annals would prove to have been very frequently attributable to itself.

The directory believed, or affected to believe, that the American administration was wholly insincere in its pacific and friendly professions, that it was under English influence, and sought only a plausible pretence to join the " conspiracy of kings." They believed, or affected to believe, that the English cabinet, having by the power of France been obliged to acknowledge the independence of the states, aspired at least to influence their policy, and introduce monarchical establishments ; that it endeavoured to fortify, by similarity of constitutional forms, habits common to the English and American people. That many citizens of the United States could be found, who were seriously reconciled to the English system of government ; that men called by public confidence to the administration of affairs in the United States had written in favour of the British constitution, merely to prepare the way for such a system in their own country. That to men of these sentiments war was indispensable, and a war too with the French republic; that by means of a war they could raise armies and obtain supplies; that by means of war against their old friends, against brothers and republicans, it would be easy to accelerate their wishes, to excite civil commotion, to shock all former ideas of political morality, to stigmatize as seditious the honourable defenders of principles, and to crush, under the pageantry and force of monarchical institutions, the simple and unostentatious forms of representative government. *

Preposterous as these imputations now seem, they derived in the minds of the rulers of France, great confidence from the language and conduct of parties in the United States. Americans attributed such opinions to some of their fellow citizens, and in the war of recrimination, which was carried on in the gazettes of the day, all public spirit, all national pride and all sentiments of patriotism seemed to be lost for ever. The country was divided into factions, and would be ruined by the prevalence of either one over the other.

* If the opinion supposed to have been entertained by colonel Hamilton and before cited, page 62, had reached the ears of citizen plenipotentiary Genet as it had Mr. Jefferson's, it would undoubtedly have been communicated with additions and embellishment, and have served to confirm the imputations recorded in the text.

But the French directory chose to extend their erroneous suspicions to the characters of the distinguished citizens, who with equal purity of attachment to their own country were deputed to represent its interests with the government of republican France.

Two of these, it was said, if not believed, two of them were infected with the same anti-republican principles ; and any attempt at negotiation with them would prove abortive ; because it was a part of the political drama, in which they were actors, to close all avenues of honourable peace, and to give strength and popularity to their party at home by so managing affairs as to produce a rupture and throw the blame of it on the government of France.

Their associations and intimates, their oral and written opinions, known through the machinery of a vigilant police, justified as was said, all these suspicions. They did not come to make peace, but to prove that no peace could be made. Under the guise of a desire to negotiate with France, their real design was to show to America that there was no alternative but war.

These unreasonable and ill founded jealousies, it was apparent, could neither be written down by logical arguments on national rights, or eloquent complaints of public wrongs.

On 4th February, while these opinions were professed by the directory, Mons. Talleyrand invited Mr. Gerry to meet him, and having enjoined upon him profound secrecy, informed him that the executive directory were dissatisfied and embarrassed by the opinions and conversation of his colleagues ; that it had determined not to treat with them, but signified their willingness to enter upon negotiations with him ; and the minister added that his departure or refusal would produce an immediate declaration of war against the United States.

"Astonished," says Mr. Gerry, in a letter to Mons. Talleyrand, "at this communication, I informed you that I had no powers to treat separately, the measure was impossible, and that had my powers been adequate, a treaty made under such circumstances could never be ratified by my government. You differed from me ; we reasoned upon it, and each adhered to his opinion. I urged in vain the unreasonableness of admitting prejudices against my colleagues without informing them of the causes thereof, the good effect in removing them, which might result from such information, and the necessity of making known to them all that had now passed between us. You held me to the promise of secrecy, adding that if I would negotiate, we could soon finish a treaty, for the executive directory were not in the habit of spending much time about such matters. You desired another interview, in which, after a discussion of the subject, I confirmed and adhered to

my determination.   In this state affairs remained
some time, and I flattered myself with the hope,
that failing in the proposition for negotiating with
me separately, your next would be to accredit the
three envoys ; in such an event the secrecy mentioned would have been proper."

When Mr. Gerry returned from his first visit to
Mons. Talleyrand, he informed general Marshall
that communications and propositions had been
made to him by that minister, which he was not
at liberty to impart to general Pinckney or himself,
that he had also propounded some questions which
had produced changes in the proposition, but that
as soon as he could obtain liberty the whole matter
should be laid before him.

There needed nothing else.   Mr. Marshall in
his commentary on this extraordinary occurrence
in his private journal, expresses his conviction,
that the substance of this communication was a
determination to order his and general Pinckney's
departure from France.   The last named gentleman also in a few days assured Mr. Gerry that
he was apprized of the nature of this private interview, and immediately mentioned the fact.
Whether these gentlemen, by any such associations
or opinions as had been ascribed to them, had any
reason to apprehend such a measure, or whether
to embarass and divide the envoys, it was made
with the forms of privacy to one and covertly conveyed to the others, must be matter of conjecture.

On the 25th February Mr. Talleyrand's secretary called on Mr. Gerry and desired him to consult the other envoys, and inform him whether they would consent to a loan payable after the war, adding that this proposal had not before been made. The proposition with all its circumstances was submitted by Mr. Gerry to his colleagues and thoroughly discussed. The manner in which it was entertained will presently be stated.

Preceding these circuitous and extraordinary events, that is to say on the 18th January, as a prelude to the threatened war, which Mons. Talleyrand had assured Mr. Gerry, he alone had power to avert, the two legislative councils had decreed that every vessel found at sea and loaded in whole or in part with merchandise, the productions of England, should be declared prize, whoever the owner of these goods or merchandise might be.

The pressure of this decree on the commerce of their country induced the envoys to rescind their determination not to make an informal visit to the minister. On the 27th February they demanded an audience, and were received on the 2d March.

At this and the interviews which followed, the French minister reproached the envoys for the distance and the coldness they had observed in their intercourse with him, and asserted in answer to their vindication, that it was neither friendly or usual, but had increased the displeasure of the

directory.   He adverted again to the effect produced by the president's speech, and of the necessity of a loan of money, as an evidence of the sincerity of their professions, which must be tested
by something of more value than words.

All the envoys reprobated a loan as a measure,
which would entangle them with other nations, as
a departure from their neutrality, as unjust, impolitic, and a violation of instructions, which it would
be useless for them to transcend.

Talleyrand again remarked that his government
insisted on some proposition, which would prove
that it was not about entering into arrangements
with a people or their agents, who were unfriendly
to its interest, but finding that a loan as at first
proposed would not be acceded to, he changed his
ground, and suggested what his secretary had before communicated to Mr. Gerry, that it should be
contracted to be payable after the war, and in
supplies to St. Domingo.   So constructed, he said,
it would effectually prevent any just complaint by
other belligerents.   At any event this was the
only condition, on which the directory would open
negotiations, and this acceded to, the adjustment
of complaints would be easy.   If wrong had been
done to the United States it would be repaired,
but if this was not admitted, the distance and coldness between the two governments would be increased.

The envoys having had two interviews with

Mons. Talleyrand on 2d March, although he was not authorised by the executive directory to hold them officially, desired another on the sixth, which was accordingly appointed. At this last interview they rejected absolutely his new modified proposition, declining any loan in whatever terms, time or manner it should be made.

Between the 2d and 6th this matter was discussed, as after the 27th February it had before been by the envoys. The separate opinions of the members are not disclosed in their voluminous communications; nor in the statement made to Mons. Talleyrand does it appear, but that their resolution was unanimous. Such however was not the fact. A difference of opinion existed among the envoys. That of the majority has been commended to the admiration of the world, while the dissenting individual, whose error if it was one, was a mere error of judgment, and wholly harmless because it was unknown at the time both in France and America, has been calumniated, misrepresented and abused, as if he were ready to sacrifice his country's interest, honour, character and independence.

In the conferences of the envoys relative to the condition of things thus presented by the minister's secretary and confirmed by their direct application to the minister himself, it was acceded to by all of them that the haughty temper of the republic demanded as a preliminary, what with more propriety should have been the subject of negotiation.

Their instructions were in the following terms, " that no aid be stipulated in favour of France during the present war," and it was admitted that they excluded all power in the envoys to negotiate a loan during its continuance. Mr. Gerry thought that as to a loan payable after the war, the instructions were ambiguous. Messrs. Marshall and Pinckney maintained that they were as peremptory in the one case as the other.

" I considered," said Mr. Gerry, " that as our instructions contained not a word respecting a loan after the war, it was not manifest from them either that the government would approve or disapprove such a loan if made by the envoys, as a necessary measure of accommodation, and although the providing that no aid be stipulated during the war, might imply that aid might be stipulated after the war, yet it appeared probable to me such a contingency had not been anticipated by our government."

To the objection that whatever might be the terms, yet in effect a loan payable at any time, would be a loan, on which money could be raised for present use, Mr. Gerry said that he could consent to the proposed loan under no circumstances unless in the treaty to be made this possibility could be prevented; that if this treaty contained a stipulation to avoid the loan in case any such use

was made of it, such provision he thought would
do away the objection.

But it was after all a question of expediency.
France had made a series of vexatious captures of
the ships and merchandise of the United States,
to an amount of many million of dollars. By actual war, the undoubted right of the United States
for a reclamation of all that vast amount of property would be lost forever. A treaty with the dis-
advantage of a loan might give restitution to the
suffering merchants, whose property to this immense amount had either been already paid over
to the captors, or was now in progress of condem-
nation. That war with the French people in addition to all the misery, which necessarily attended a resort to arms, in the destruction of human
life, in the interruption of domestic pursuits, and
in the dangers which might be apprehended to the
new government and almost untried constitution
of the United States, would as a mere matter of
pecuniary calculation, be of vastly more damage
to the finances of their country. Its amount would
be incalculable, and its consequences on the credit
and revenues of the union, just now beginning
to recover themselves from the disasters of the
revolution, could hardly be well anticipated. The
power and resources of France prevented all danger of loss from the loan, which would be repaid to us according to the stipulated terms, and
might be negotiated on our credit merely without
any considerable advance.

Mr. Gerry adverted to the divided condition of the American people, as an argument that would prove almost any sacrifice less dangerous than a war not supported by the public will, and which might produce the most serious civil dissensions.

A war with France, he said, would throw the United States almost of necessity into the arms of England, already struggling for its existence under circumstances of unparalleled embarrassments. It was this connexion he feared much more than the force, great as it was, of the French arms.

On the point of honour Mr. Gerry did not admit that he felt less sensibly or delicately than either of his colleagues, but by no means conceded that the modified proposition of a loan under the existing circumstances of the case, could be injurious to the honour, or derogatory to the independence of the United States.

The honour of a country, he contended, could never be consulted by adopting a measure, which hazarded its existence. In the valour of his countrymen, in their firmness, resolution and enduring courage, he had unlimited confidence; he had been a witness of their wonderful efforts in the darkest periods of the revolutionary contest, but there were limits to all human ability. If France succeeded in her vast efforts for the subjugation of England, our destruction as the ally of England was certain; if she failed, we had contracted an alliance in no degree less productive of ruin.

There could be no point of national honour in such a dilemma. A jealous honour, he contended, would before now have involved us in a quarrel with both the belligerents. We had suffered wrongs from both of them, not less insulting in manner than serious in amount. With one we had effected a negotiation by yielding a principle not less vital, and probably not less embarrassing, than the loan now demanded by the other. Was it now necessary to our character to become of a sudden so nicely fastidious, and having without war borne all kinds of injuries, voluntarily incur the most awful calamity of nations upon a doubtful question of national honour ? If the Roman pride, which permits no second injury, had in our case already been violated, if the true interest and happiness of a young nation, feeling sensibly its wrongs, and rapidly acquiring the strength, which it now wanted to avenge them, was its best and highest honour, in which all the duty of all its citizens concentrated, was that not best preserved by a little longer patience in the path we had travelled ?

Mr. Gerry added that it was well to speak plain. He had not found in the opinions of his colleagues that flexibility, which persons earnest after peace would have practised. That their demeanour was cold, reserved and distant at least if not backward. That had they yielded to the conferences proposed by the minister, it might have been possible that some modification of the proposed terms could have been effected. He did not assign to them any other than the most honourable and patriotic motives, but they seemed to him to act on the conviction that France was insincere in her proposals, and never intended to do more than amuse us with the appearance of accommodation, without intending to make a treaty that would reconcile the two nations on terms compatible with our independence. He differed from them altogether.

They stood now on the brink of an awful responsibility. He willingly encountered it. He would have his own determination known to the American people. They must pay the expenses of the war, and their blood must flow in expiation of its causes. It was true he was outvoted, and his colleagues had a right to deliver the opinion of the commission. He would not embarrass them by informing the French government of this difference of opinion, but it must be remembered, and to this end he desired to record his solemn protestation, that no part or share of this refusal was attributable to him.*

Notwithstanding this, Mr. Gerry declared, he would not at present agree to a loan, nor at any time accede to it without the sanction of his govern-

---

* The private journal of Mr. Marshall, for the inspection of which the author is indebted to colonel Pickering, attributes substantially most of the foregoing arguments to Mr. Gerry, which are extended and confirmed in his papers.

ment. His only difference with his colleagues
was narrowed down to this. They absolutely refused to consider the proposition, and met it with
an unqualified negative. He was willing to open
negotiations on the basis of a loan, to be made
after the war, and to prepare a treaty *ad referendum*,
reserving to himself the right of a decision on the
whole matter, when a decision should be eventually necessary.

It was obvious that the loan was a small matter.
In a pecuniary light to the French nation it was a
trifle. It was solicited as proof of a friendly spirit
on the part of a people, with whom the directory
pretended to be irritated, and as a conciliation to
the French nation, whose attachment to the Americans had very greatly diminished.

In the subsequent stages of this negotiation,
Mr. Gerry endeavoured to persuade the French
minister that the loan ought not to be insisted on.
At a conference on the 6th of March, he urged
the impolicy of this demand, and maintained that
a treaty on liberal principles, such as those on
which the treaty of commerce between the two
nations was first established, would be infinitely
more advantageous to France than the comparatively trifling benefit she would derive from a
loan; such a treaty would produce a friendship
and attachment on the part of the United States
to France, which would be solid and permanent,
and produce benefits far superior to those of any
loan which might be made.

In this effort he was equally unsuccessful, and affairs seemed rapidly tending to a crisis.

On the 13th of March, a distinguished citizen of the republic, supposed with good reason by general Marshall,* to be deputed for the purpose by Mons. Talleyrand, called on the general, and under injunctions of secrecy, except as to his colleagues, informed him " that the directory was determined to give passports to general Pinckney and himself, and to retain Mr. Gerry; that this order would be kept up a few days to give time to make propositions conforming to the views of this government. That if they were not made Talleyrand would be compelled to execute the order. General Marshall told him if the proposition in expectation of which the order was kept up was a loan, it was perfectly unnecessary to keep it up a single day ; that the subject had been considered for five months, and the opinion with respect to the injunctions of positive duty concerning it were incapable of being shaken; that as to himself, if it was impossible to effect the object of the mission, he did not wish to stay another day in France, and would as cheerfully depart the next day as at any future time. The messenger reasoned, as often before, on the propriety of assuming the powers, which were required, as being indispensably necessary for the welfare of the country. He did not pretend to

* General Marshall's Journal, MS.

say that the demands of France were just, nor did the minister pretend to place the demand on that ground, or to expect compliance on that account, but because a compliance would be useful to our country ; that France thought herself sufficiently powerful to give the law to the world, and exacted from all around her money to enable her to finish successfully her war against England. All the nations around her, (and he enumerated them) had been compelled to contribute to this object. There was no instance in which France had desisted from a demand once made, and it might be relied on she would not desist from the demand made on us. After some further conversation, in which general Marshall persisted in the declaration that no money proposition could or would be made, he returned to the subject of retaining Mr. Gerry. He said it was expected America would consider this as manifesting an unwillingness on the part of France to break entirely with us, and that the government of the United States would annex to Mr. Gerry two other persons, who might do what was necessary for our country, or have a stronger disposition to reconcile the two republics. He hinted a desire that some propositions of the sort should come from us. General Marshall told him, " if two of us should return, our government would act as its own judgment should dictate. That if France was desirous that two of us should return to represent fully to our government the state of

politics in this country, and meant to leave to our
decision, who should stay or go, we should arrange
that matter as might comport with our own opinion of propriety and the interests of our country ;
that if on the contrary, France chose to decide for
us, and select for the United States the minister
who should represent them, the act must be entirely the act of France, and they would not have the
smallest concern with it."

"You know very well," said the general, " if any
of us returns to the United States, I am resolved to
be one ; but that I would contribute to no arrangement of the sort proposed, because I conceive that
a minister ought to represent the country and the
interests of that country which deputed him, and
not that to which he was deputed, and consequently he ought to be chosen by those who deputed
him, and not by those to whom he was deputed.
He replied, that my observation was very just in
itself, and would apply if France rejected us all,
and demanded a fourth man from America, but
that we were all three equally trusted and chosen
by the government of the United States, and
France only selected from among us one, whose
dispositions were believed to be friendly to this
government, and who might safely be permitted
to stay among them. That general Pinckney and
myself, and especially myself, were considered *as
being sold to the English.* He would not conceal
from me that our positive refusal to comply with

the demands of France, was attributed principally to me, who was considered entirely English. That he had assured the minister, he was mistaken. That I was restrained from agreeing to the loan, from want of power, and not by want of will, but the opinion was persisted in. I felt some little resentment, and answered, that the French government thought no such thing; that neither the government nor any man thought me English, but they knew I was not French; they knew I would not sacrifice my duty and the interests of my country to any nation on earth, and therefore I was not a proper man to stay, and was branded with the epithet of being English."*

This indecent and disreputable imputation, which while it glanced from, without injuring the honourable character of the upright and virtuous statesman to whom it was addressed, reflects on its author the disgrace it was vainly intended to affix on general Marshall, was soon after followed by an official letter from the minister to the envoys. It bears date the 18th of March, and was intended as an answer to their letter of 17th January.

In this letter Talleyrand assumes a style suited to the haughty temper of his government. He maintains that the priority of grievances and complaints belonged to the French republic; that all the grievances of which the American envoys

* MS. Journal of general Marshall.

complained grew out of measures, which the conduct of the United States had justified.   He complains that the republic was deceived in the negotiation, and sacrificed by the treaty of London
of 1794 ; that in this treaty the federal government had made to Great Britain concessions the
most unheard of, the most incompatible with the
interests of the United States, and the most derogatory to their alliance with France ; that by it
every thing had been calculated to turn the neutrality of the United States to the advantage of
England, and that France was thereby left free to
avail itself of the preservative means, with which
the law of nature, the law of nations and prior
treaties furnished her.

He complained that American newspapers under
the direct control of the cabinet had since the ratification of that treaty redoubled their calumnies
against the republic, against her principles, her
magistrates, and her envoys.   The executive directory had seen itself denounced in a speech of the
president, as endeavouring to produce anarchy and
division in the United States.   He accuses the
government of the United States of a desire to
adhere at every hazard, to the spirit of the treaty
at London, without giving to France an opportunity for equal advantage, as evidence of which he
adverts to the instructions of the envoys, which
he says were not drawn up with the desire of at-
taining pacific results.   The intention, which he

attributes to the government of the United States, he says, is so little disguised that nothing seems to have been neglected to manifest them to every eye. It is probably with this view that it was thought proper to send to the French republic persons whose opinions and connexions are too well known to hope from them dispositions sincerely conciliatory. He adds the following paragraph.

" It is only in order to smooth the way of discussions, that the undersigned has entered into the preceding explanations. It is with the same view that he declares to the commissioners and envoys extraordinary, that notwithstanding the kind of prejudice, which has been entertained with respect to them, the executive directory is disposed to treat with that one of the three, whose opinions, presumed to be more impartial, promise in the course of the explanations more of that reciprocal confidence, which is indispensable."

The replication of the American envoys was presented on the 3d of April. In clear and forcible language, with firmness, frankness and plainness suited to the character of the United States, this reply meets, answers, refutes every topic in succession, which was contained in the minister's letter. It denies his accusations, it corrects his mis-statements, it overturns his arguments, and presents another splendid instance of the powerful defence, which integrity and talents and learning

are capable of making for the injured rights of the
country.

To the part relative to themselves the letter
replies, " The opinions and relations of the undersigned are purely American, unmixed with any
particle of foreign tint. If they possess a quality
on which they pride themselves, it is an attachment to the happiness and welfare of their country ; if they could at will select the means of
manifesting that attachment, it would be by effecting a sincere and real accommodation between
France and the United States, in promoting the
interests of both, and consistent with the independence of the latter."

To the offer of the directory to treat with one
of their number, the envoys reply, " The result of
a deliberation on this point is that no one of the
undersigned is authorized to take upon himself a
negotiation, evidently intrusted, by the tenor of
their powers and instructions to the whole, nor
are there any two of them who can propose to
withdraw themselves from the task committed to
them by their government, while there remains a
possibility of performing it.

" It is hoped the prejudices said to have been
conceived against the ministers of the United
States will be dissipated by the truths they have
stated.

" If in this hope they shall be disappointed, and
it should be the will of the directory to order

passports for any number of them, you will please accompany such passports with letters of safe conduct, which will entirely protect from the cruisers of France the vessels, in which they may respectively sail, and give to their persons, suit and property that perfect security to which the laws and usages of nations entitle them."

This letter of the envoys to Mons. Talleyrand was followed by one from him to Mr. Gerry, intimating a belief that his colleagues had withdrawn from the territories of the republic, and expressing a desire to resume with him reciprocal communications upon the interests of the United States of America and the French republic. To this Mr. Gerry replied.

MR. GERRY TO MONS. TALLEYRAND.

PARIS, APRIL 4, 1748. (GERMINAL 15th, an 6.)

I had the honour, citizen minister, of receiving your letter of the 14th Germinal (the 3d inst.) and Mr. Deutrement, who delivered it, informed me, that it was intended to be shown to general Pinckney and general Marshall.

Whilst my colleagues and myself, to whom the government of the United States have intrusted the affairs of the embassy, had a joint agency therein, I have carefully imparted to them all the propositions which you have requested, and the relative conferences, and to yourself our decisions thereon ; regretting at the same time, the unfortunate and embarrassing circumstances which imposed on me this disagreeable task. But as by the tenor of your letter, it is now expected that they will quit the territory of the French republic, it will be impossible for me to be the medium of, or to take any measures which will be painful to my colleagues, or not to afford them all the assistance in my power ; and it would be moreover inconsistent with the line of conduct, which you well know, citizen minister, I have uniformly observed, for removing the unfavourable impressions which existed on the part of this government against them. Indeed in our last letter, there is a conditional application for passports, which as it appears to me, supersedes the necessity of a hint to them on this subject ; and general Marshall is waiting impatiently for an answer to that part of it, which respects a letter of safe conduct, for the vessel in which he and his suite may take passage for the United States, to determine whether he shall embark from France or from Great Britain, but the unfortunate situation of general Pinckney with respect to the critical state of his daughter's health, renders it utterly impossible for him to depart under existing circumstances.

You have proposed, citizen minister, the 5th or 7th of this decade for me to resume (*reprendre*) our reciprocal communications, upon the interests of the French republic and of the United States. The reciprocal communications, which we have had, were such only as I have alluded to in the beginning of this letter ; unless your proposition accompanied with an injunction of secrecy, for me to treat separately, is considered in that light. To resume this subject will be unavailing, because the measure, for the reasons which I then urged, is utterly impracticable.   I can only then confer informally and unaccredited, on any subject respecting our mission, and communicate to the government of the United States the result of such conferences, being in my individual capacity unauthorized to give them an official stamp.   Nevertheless every measure in my power, and in conformity with the duty I owe to my country, shall be zealously pursued to restore harmony, and cordial friendship between the two republics.   I had the honour of calling on you last evening, for the purpose of making this communication verbally ; but as you were absent, to prevent misconceptions, I have thought it best to reduce it to writing.

Accept I pray you, citizen minister, the assurances of my perfect esteem and respect.

E. GERRY.

To the minister of foreign affairs
of the French republic.

The joint agency of the envoys had now terminated. After divers perplexing embarrassments respecting passports, general Marshall at length received them about the 12th of April, and immediately embarked for the United States.* Mr. Pinckney detained in Europe by the sickness of a member of his family, as speedily as possible quitted Paris. Mr. Gerry on the positive declaration of the minister, by order of the directory, that his departure from Paris would be attended by an immediate declaration of war, which would be suspended by his remaining till the sense of his government could be obtained, consented under these circumstances not to demand his passports. On the departure of Messrs. Marshall and Pinckney, Mons. Talleyrand proposed, as already mentioned, to proceed immediately on a separate negotiation with Mr. Gerry, which proposition he rejected without hesitation, declaring, and against the minister's repeated efforts, maintaining the position that his whole power terminated with the departure of his colleagues.

* Some difficulty occurred in general Marshall's obtaining a letter of safe conduct for the vessel in which he proposed to embark, which induced him to express a design if it was refused, of returning through England. The same confidential agent of Mons. Talleyrand, with whom he had formerly conversed, said to him on learning this, that it would give great offence to the government of France, and injure him in the opinion of his own countrymen; and that it would be immediately published by this government, that he had gone to England to receive the wages he had earned by breaking off the treaty with France !

On the 20th April he addressed to Mons. Talleyrand the following letter, which distinctly discloses the peculiar and painful situation in which he was placed, and the terms which by a perfect understanding with the minister, were to be the conditions of his continuance in the French capital.

MR. GERRY TO MONS. TALLEYRAND.

PARIS, APRIL 20, 1798. (1 FLOREAL, an 6.)

CITIZEN MINISTER,—My colleagues having been under the necessity of departing from Paris, have left me in the most painful situation : as it respects themselves, the government and nation which I had the honour with them to represent, and my personal circumstances. The alternatives presented to my choice, were the continuance of my residence here, or an immediate rupture on my departure ; I have chosen the former, prompted by every consideration of the duty I owed my country.

The object of this government in my remaining here, as announced in your official note of the 14th Germinal, (3d April) was " to resume our reciprocal communications on the interests of the French republic and of the United States." My answer informed you that " I could only confer informally and unaccredited, on any subject respecting our mission, and communicate to the government of

the United States the result of such conferences;
being in my individual capacity, unauthorised to
give them an official stamp." This then I consider as the line of conduct well understood to be observed on my part; and in the present state of
affairs, citizen minister, I flatter myself, that propositions for terminating all differences, for the
restoration of harmony and friendship, and for the
reestablishment of commerce between the United
States and France, will be promptly made on the
part of the latter; that they will be such, as corresponding with the justice and magnanimity of
this great nation, and with sound policy, will ensure success; that I shall have an opportunity of
soon embarking for the United States, and presenting them to my government for their consideration; and that all further depredations on our
commerce, by French cruisers, will in the interim
be prohibited. If in forming this arrangement I
can render any services, you may be always sure
of my immediate and cheerful cooperation.

Measures like these will at once extinguish those
coals of discord, which kindled into a flame, must
be destructive of the respective interests of the
two republics; will not only restore, but increase,
if possible, their former confidence; and terminate
in a competition for excelling each other in mutual
acts of generosity and kindness.

In any event, citizen minister, I flatter myself
it will not be thought necessary for me to remain

long in France, as the state of my family and affairs requires my immediate return to the United
States; and as their consul-general will continue
his residence here, which, pending negotiation,
will answer every political purpose. I pray you,
citizen minister, to accept the assurances of my
most perfect esteem and regard.

E. GERRY.

To the minister of foreign affairs
of the French republic.

Things had hardly settled on these new terms,
when the publication of the despatches of the envoys to the American government returned to Europe, and put the people as well as government
of France in a flame.

Talleyrand demanded the names of the intriguers, who taking advantage of the insulated
situation in which the envoys had kept themselves,
had endeavoured to deceive them, and of whose
devices he felicitated Mr. Gerry in not having
been the dupe. The avowed object of this demand was to ascertain for the official information
of the directory, by whom had been made the proposition of money for corrupt distribution.

In compliance with this request, Mr. Gerry
communicated the real names of the parties, who
in the published communications of the envoys,
had been by the American secretary of state distinguished by letters of the alphabet.

On the 26th July, Mr. Gerry quitted Paris.
The interval between the departure of his colleagues and his own, was passed in an effort of
the minister to enter upon negotiations with him,
although he had professed his entire want of authority to engage in, and his determination under
existing circumstances, even if he had the authority, to decline its exercise.

In the letters which passed between them,
Mons. Talleyrand in the name of the directory,
announced the pacific disposition of the French
government. He announced the willingness of
that government to give Mr. Gerry a public reception, the obtaining of which he declared rested
solely on himself. The demand of a loan, and
explanation for president's speeches, were abandoned ; a regret too earnestly urged not to have
been sincere, was expressed by action as well as
language, that Mr. Gerry determined to depart,
and positive assurances were given of the reception of another minister in his place, with the respect due to the nation he would represent. To
favour the belief of a better disposition, than had
before existed, an arrete was forwarded to Mr.
Gerry at Havre, restraining the irregular and vexatious conduct of French privateers in the West
India seas, and assurances given that all other arrangements should conform to the just expectations of the United States.

The despatches of the American envoys had
produced a wonderful excitement. In England,

as well as in America, they were supposed to display the corruption and profligacy of the government of France, and unexampled assiduity was discovered to print and circulate with the utmost possible publicity copies of these despatches through every part of Europe. The indignation of the directory was excited, but a cooler judgment suspended its effects.

The over zealous anxiety of England to involve the two nations in war, indicated to the rulers of France the great advantage which was expected by her ancient enemy from an alliance with the United States. The causes from which so great good was anticipated, were examined and appreciated; the power, the influence, and the character of the American people were more carefully ascertained. The strength which such an union would bestow on the last enemy, which remained to her, and a growing respect for the fortitude and resources of that enemy, changed the councils of the politic directory and produced that successful negotiation, which by a change of their own policy, the United States were subsequently able to effect, and after a short interval of ambiguous hostility confirmed the two nations in the relations of peace.

The excitement occasioned in the United States, by the publication of the despatches of the envoys, was almost unexampled.

The demand of money for corrupt distribution,

was considered not merely as evidence of the baseness and venality of an unprincipled government, but resented as an insult on the integrity of the United States. The proposed loan, which certainly was no uncommon thing in national diplomacy, was connected without much judgment in the public mind with the bribe, which was to precede it ; and those who were not influenced by questions of pretended honour, were terrified by danger of national ruin.

A war fever, producing that delirium which is the usual accompaniment of such an epidemic, spread rapidly through the country, and was inflamed and aggravated by men, who in a subsequent period of our history discovered war to be among the most terrible of all national calamities.

An impression was made on popular opinion favourable to the administration of the national government, so that the opposition, which had before nearly or quite divided the physical strength of the country, rapidly lost its numerical force. In the excitement, and under the delusion of the moment, the residence of Mr. Gerry at Paris, was severely censured by the administration, and his immediate recall announced by the secretary of state, in a letter which hardly preserved the form of official civility.*

* This letter bearing date 25th June 1798, was communicated to congress with the president's message covering Mr. Gerry's despatches, and to most readers not particularly attentive to dates, it would seem that his remaining in France was in viola-

Preparation was made for a war, which was intended to demonstrate the greatness and glory of the United States. Its burthens could hardly be felt at such a moment of unnatural irritation. The condition, which the great party who had been in opposition to the then administration had endeavoured to avert, appeared now rapidly approaching, while they had for a time at least, lost that hold on the good opinion of the public, which could alone enable them to prevent it.

Mr. Gerry arrived in the United States on the 1st October 1798, and communicated to the secretary of state the letters which had passed between him and the French minister since the departure of his colleagues from Paris, with other proceedings already adverted to.

These despatches were laid before congress on the 15th of January 1799. Unwilling however to permit them to go alone, and apprehensive of the effect, which they might produce on the republican party, broken in a good degree and disabled, but by no means annihilated, the secretary followed them by a commentary, intended no doubt to overwhelm Mr. Gerry with irretrievable disgrace, to support the high and lofty pretensions of the government, to keep up that fervour without which armies, navies, taxes, and the appendages of milita-

tion of its order. But this letter was never received by Mr. Gerry. If it was ever sent to Europe, it passed him on his return. " My first knowledge of its existence," he says in a letter to the president, " was in the public newspaper."

ry institutions could not derive support, to gather round the administration the pride, patriotism and wealth of the nation, and to expose its opponents to disgrace, as aliens to the interest and welfare of their country.

There commenced at this moment a series of measures which has marked the succeeding period as the epoch of the reign of terror. The leaders of the dominant party were carrying their policy to extremes, which alarmed the eminent citizen who presided in the councils of the country, and although checked and controlled by his firmness and the reproof which he bestowed on the most distinguished of those concerned, and particularly on the secretary of state, whom he dismissed from his station, it produced such reaction in the public mind, as to destroy forever the ascendency of the federal party in the United States.

CHAPTER VII.

Commentary on the mission to France, and strictures on colonel
Pickering's publications in relation to it.

THE most obvious subject of remark, on a review of this extraordinary mission, is the submission of the envoys to communications with individuals producing no evidence of official rank ; the
affected secrecy of these intrusive agents ; and
the great consequence given to the affair, by the
minute recapitulation of every trifling circumstance, in official despatches to the American
government.

If the conduct of the envoys in these undignifi-
ed conferences was evidence of their anxiety for
peace, the detailed communication, which they
made of it, was not less calculated for war.   It
is a single instance in the history of public missions that so much should be recounted, where
so little was performed ; although it cannot be
believed that the republican envoys were indeed
the first on whom the arts of European diplomacy
were essayed.

But the censure, if deserved, is divisible among
all the members of the embassy.   In the report
of the secretary of state, the dissent of one of
them is no where intimated, although he was

aware that on the 20th October Mr. Gerry proposed to his colleagues that they should put an
end to all informal negotiation.

It was so determined ; and the only subject of
regret, for which all of them are to account, is
found in their departure from this judicious resolution.

The preference and selection of Mr. Gerry
from his colleagues, by the minister of the directory, is the next subject of remark, and has been
most adroitly used to the injury of his fame.

To be selected by an enemy implies treachery
to a friend. It has been said with sarcastic imputation, that if the French government could treat
with him and not with his colleagues, he must
have been less attached to America than they
were, or more subservient than they would be to
the interests of France. The insinuation is made
with something of temper in the journal of one of
the envoys, it is brought forward in the report of
the American secretary, and alleged in plainer
terms in his subsequent review.

Could the inference be well drawn the fact
would indeed be disgraceful ; but it is not perceived why, if any dependence is to be placed on
the allegations of the French minister, his whole
statement should not be received with equal credit,
and why therefore his refusal to receive Messrs.
Marshall and Pinckney as envoys of the United
States, on the pretence that they were English-

men in their principles and policy, does not as well
establish that position, as his readiness to receive
Mr. Gerry proves him to have been French? The
truth is that no fair deduction, except a desire to
sow discord in the embassy and the country, can
justly be made from the conduct of this artful
diplomatist.*

Neither his language nor his conduct should be
received as evidence against the agents of the
United States. It was not what he thought, but
what they did ; not his imputations but their conduct, which establishes their character. The two
honourable men, on whom his offensive neglect
and pretended suspicion would fasten the traitorous charge of being Englishmen at heart, refuted
the slander by the patriotism of their lives ; and
the other, whom his insidious flattery chose to indicate as devoted to France, held the same shield
against his disreputable imputation. The rejection of the two envoys, on the pretence of their

---

* Mons. Talleyrand's own reasons for his preference of Mr.
Gerry, and rejection of his colleagues, were thus subsequently
stated.

"The advantages that I prized in him, are common to all
Americans who have not manifested a predilection for England.
Can it be believed that a man who should profess a hatred or
contempt of the French republic, or should manifest himself the
advocate for royalty, can inspire the directory with a favourable
opinion of the government of the United States. I should have
disguised the truth if I had left this matter ambiguous. It is not
to wound the independence of that government to point out to a
sincere friend of peace the shoals he ought to avoid."—*Talleyrand
to Pichon, 28th August* 1798.

affiliation with English politics, was in accordance with the language of intemperate passion, with which a party in their own country charged a whole class of their fellow citizens ; the selection of the other, on the suggestion that he was more attached to the schemes of the directory, was another form of perpetuating those libels, with which another class of the American public was assailed at home. They are solemn warnings of the effect produced abroad by internal dissension. In other respects they are entitled to no regard. They are equally unfounded and despicable. The triumvirate had but one heart, and that was American to its core.

The minister of foreign affairs, in the name of the directory, announced, " that they were disposed to treat with that one of the three, whose opinions, presumed to be more impartial, promise in the course of the explanations more of that reciprocal confidence which is indispensable."

What were those opinions? The secretary of state infers that they regarded points in connexion with the embassy, and would imply some willingness to yield in negotiation what the others would withhold. This imputation is unfair and gratuitous. Mr. Gerry, in a commentary on this part of the secretary's report presented to the president, remarks :

" Whatever was presumed of my opinions, no person at that time knew any thing of them in

regard to the embassy, except the envoys, and
therefore no comparison could possibly be made
between our opinions, if different in this respect.
But Talleyrand was informed of some opinions of
my colleagues, as he said, not relating to the embassy, which had produced embarrassment and
dissatisfaction. I carefully avoided uttering or
writing any thing in regard to France, that might
offend either the government or people. When
I mixed with French citizens, I treated them with
attention and civility. If this conduct of mine
led the French government to think that my
opinions were more impartial than my colleagues
it is not a matter, which Mr. Pickering was authorized to censure. "As to the prince to whom he
is sent, the ambassador should remember that his
ministry is a ministry of peace, and that on this
footing alone he is received ; this reason inter-
dicts every evil practice to him. Speaking ill
of the French government or nation would have
been an evil practice. I was justified in avoiding
it. Civility required a return of courtesies and
attention ; I could not dispense with the claims of
decorum. Some letters of the other envoys were
intercepted ; what they contained I know not, but
we were all alarmed on the occasion, and thought
it best to conceal our papers, lest a general order
for seizing them should be the consequence. It
was generally understood that the opinions, which
rendered the other envoys obnoxious in France,

were irrelevant to the embassy, fraught, according to the French representations, with prejudices against the French government and nation. Nothing can therefore be more untrue than that the disposition of the directory to treat with me was the result of my not having as invincible a determination not to surrender the honour, the interest, or the independence of my country, as either of my colleagues."

It would seem from the foregoing remarks, that a belief of Mr. Gerry's impartiality, in comparison with the other envoys, resulted less from any knowledge of his opinions, than by the discovery of theirs ; less from his being supposed to be friendly, than because they were known or suspected to be hostile.

Upon the subject of opinion however, which under the management of the secretary of state, in his official and subsequent publications, did much to impair the reputation of Mr. Gerry, it may be well to enquire how far it enters into the appropriate character of a minister of peace. Why, it may be asked, was Mr. Gerry selected by the president, or opposed by his cabinet, but because they believed his opinion of the proper American policy differed in some respects from the party in power? Why did Mr. Hamilton propose Jefferson or Madison as one of a mission to France, to be joined by two citizens of the federal party, with whom, on great questions of American policy,

their opinions essentially differed? Why was Mr.
Jay selected for a previous negotiation with England but for this, among other reasons, that his
opinions presented no such obstacles to a treaty,
as would be found in the opinions of Jefferson,
Madison, or their friends? Why was not Mr.
Cabot selected, who had been recommended by
Mr. Ames? "Because," says president Adams,
"I knew his character and connexions were as
well known in France, particularly by Talleyrand,
as Mr. Gerry's were. It would have been inex-
cusable in me to hazard the success of the mission
merely to gratify the passions of a party." Hence
because of a difference of opinion between Mr.
Cabot and Mr. Gerry, the latter was preferred by
the president of the United States. When Mr.
Monroe was sent to France, it was distinctly intimated that he was selected because he had entered
into the measures of her policy, and had repeatedly expressed his wishes for her success. When
that gentleman was recalled, "the choice of a
person in all respects qualified for the mission was
not without its difficulty. While a disposition
towards the administration, in which implicit confidence might be placed, was a requisite not to be
dispensed with, it was also desirable that the person employed should have given no umbrage to
the French government. No individual who had
performed a conspicuous part on the political theatre
of America fitted both branches of this descrip-

tion. All who had advocated in public with zeal and with talents, the measures of the American government, had been marked as the enemies of France, and were on this account to be avoided."* Personal opinions, not unfavourable to France, were qualifications essential to a candidate, in the opinion of Washington; and the historian, who mentions the circumstance, does it in a manner, which admits its obvious propriety.

Notwithstanding the odium, which the well disciplined enemies of Mr. Gerry were able to cast upon him, because his supposed opinions recommended him to the favour of the government of France, they knew that this favour was not personal to him, any more than his opinions were; but that both opinions and favour belonged to the whole political class, of which he was a member, and whom the French statesmen ignorantly believed to be attached to their interest. Thus Mr. Pinckney wrote to the department of state, " Those who regard us as being of some consequence, seem to have taken up an idea that our government acts upon principles opposed to the real sentiments of a large majority of our people, and they are willing to temporize, until the event of the election of president is known; thinking if one public character Adams is chosen, he will be attached to the interests of Great Britain, and that if another character Jefferson is elected, he will be

* Marshall's Washington, 5 vol. p. 618.

(to use the expression of Dupont de Nemours in the council of Ancients,) devoted to the interests of France."

The opinions, for which Talleyrand chose to prefer Mr. Gerry, were those for which Mr. Monroe had been selected, those which Washington supposed his colleague Pinckney entertained; for the selecting of whom on that account, his other colleague Marshall had lauded the first president of the United States. Why the favour shown to him by the French ministry, because of those opinions, should be supposed to imply a dereliction of duty, is to be accounted for only by that intemperance of party spirit, which first excites popular vengeance, and then devotes its victims on its unappeasable altar.

That the French directory failed in its just respect to the government of the United States, by pretending to doubt the competency or the honour of the colleagues of Mr. Gerry, because of their opinions, is readily granted. The disgrace does not attach to them. That the haughty ministers of the republic might be expected to take such course, seems to have been anticipated, by care in other instances to prevent it. Its indecorum was no security against its adoption. Nor was it applied solely to the United States. When negotiations were proposed by lord Grenville on the part of England, in June 1797 to conclude peace, " the directory being informed, that the same minister, lord Malmsbury, was deputed, Mons. De la Croix signified the consent of the directory that negotiations should be opened with lord Malmsbury, another choice would however have appeared to the directory to have argued more favourably to the speedy conclusion of peace." *

It is no where alleged, in express terms, that any opinion of Mr. Gerry favoured a compliance with the demand of money for corrupt distribution, but the language of Mr. Pickering's publications authorizes the inference, that in this respect Mr. Gerry was more practicable than his colleagues.

Upon this subject, Mr. Gerry who saw only the secretary's report, as he died before the review was written, has the following memoranda. The injustice of Mr. Pickering's language is still more manifest in regard to the much talked of doceur, inasmuch as the envoys, when it was first proposed, replied, "if we could see in France, a temper sincerely friendly to the United States, we might not regard a little money, such as is stated to be usual, although we should hazard ourselves by giving it." I am content to bear my proportion of blame in this respect, although I did not make the declaration or propose the answer; but I can see no fairness in attempts to load me with censure, while this, which was the most reprehensible measure of the embassy, is passed in silence, because it came from my colleagues.

* Belsham's Geo. 3. vol. v. p. 379.

From the history of the embassy already narrated, occasion was taken to allege that Mr. Gerry was improperly engaged in separate interviews and secret negotiation with M. Talleyrand. Such charges make a figure in the report of the American secretary, are set down in the journal of his colleague, and are enlarged upon and censured in a commentary on his conduct, subsequently published by Mr. Pickering.

There is something disreputable in secrecy and separation; and the charge is odious enough to gain attention, for whatever is vituperative excites curiosity, and there is always malignity enough to delight in defamation.

With how much exaggeration this matter has been stated, will be seen by the following extract from the controversial publication of Mr. Pickering. He says :* " Thus slighted, thus insulted, and kept at an offensive distance, Pinckney and Marshall would not make to Talleyrand, what he desired, inofficial visits to discuss official business. Mr. Gerry however because he had seen Talleyrand in the United States, in the form of an emigrant was pleased, *contrary to the opinion of both his colleagues*, to make him an early visit."

This statement is in contradiction to the official despatches of all the envoys, in which they say that general Pinckney and general Marshall not

* Pickering's Review, p. 116.

being acquainted with M. Talleyrand, could not
with propriety call on him; but that according to
the custom of France, he might expect this of Mr.
Gerry, from a previous acquaintance in America.*
A singular reason truly for either going or refusing
to go, but an absolute negative of the injurious allegation before cited. Separated as the envoys
were from any regular intercourse with the agents
of the directory, and suspected as they knew
themselves to be of a disinclination to practicable
terms of peace, a scrupulous regard to etiquette,
and a voluntary seclusion from favourable chances
of breaking down unreasonable prejudice, were not
calculated to accomplish the object of their mission.†

* American state papers from 1797 to 1801, p. 199.

† Personal intercourse between diplomatic agents and the
government to which they are sent, has ordinarily been considered so important, that forms of etiquette and ceremony have
rarely prevented its being enjoyed. "Inofficial visits to discuss
official business" have greatly expedited desired results. For
reasons satisfactory to itself, the American government notified
Mr. Jackson the minister plenipotentiary of the king of Great
Britain to the United States, that all future discussion was to be
in the written form. His majesty's envoy chose to treat it as a
great indignity. "Considering that a very few days have
elapsed since I delivered to the president a credential letter from
the king, my master, and that nothing has been even alleged to
deprive me of the facility of access, and of the credit to which, by
immemorial usage, I am entitled, I believe there does not exist in the annals of diplomacy, a precedent for such a determination between two ministers who have met for the avowed purpose of terminating amicably the existing differences between
their respective countries, but after mature reflection I am in-
ced to acquiesce in it by the recollection of the time that must

In a note on the separation from his colleagues, as the charge stands in the secretary's report, Mr. Gerry remarks, " If my conferences are complained of because they were separate, the other envoys were the cause. On the 30th December, when Talleyrand expressed a wish to see me on 5th January, in order to make some communications, I noted the particulars, and soon after imparted them to my colleagues, informing them that the conference proposed by Mons. Talleyrand was a measure, which I could not accede to, unless sanctioned by them ; that if they conceived no injury could result from it, and that it might give some information to them, which might be useful, I would meet the minister, otherwise I must decline, let the consequences be what they might to myself, since good intentions are not all that is expected of negotiators, who are often calumniated

necessarily elapse, before I can receive his majesty's commands upon so unexpected occurrence, and of the detriment that would ensue to the public service if my functions were in the interval to be altogether suspended. I shall therefore content myself with entering my protest against a proceeding, which I can consider in no other light than as a violation in my person, of the most essential rights of a public minister when adopted as in the present case, without any alleged misconduct on his part. As a matter of opinion, I cannot own I assent to the preference which you give to written, over verbal intercourse for the purpose of mutual explanation and accommodation. *American state papers*, vol. 4. p. 11. These " inofficial visits to discuss official business," which Mr. Jackson deemed it essential to preserve by solemn protest, and which two of the envoys to France would not permit, because they were not acquainted with Mons. Talleyrand, is charged as a great fault on Mr. Gerry ! *Pickering's Review*, p. 116.

for measures truly meritorious. These were my words to the other envoys, and they sanctioned the meeting. Attempts to meet the minister between the 25th of January and 2d February, having failed, I informed general Pinckney that it was again proposed I should call on M. Talleyrand on that day, and that I wished to confer with him and general Marshall on that subject. We all met, and I desired the other envoys to express their opinions, because if they thought best, I would excuse myself directly, if not, I wished to know how to conduct myself in case of new propositions. We all agreed that I ought to go, and were decisive against a loan. On the 1st March, the last of the days of the conferences, the secretary of Mons. Talleyrand called on me, and said the minister wished to see me. I waited on him and he stated that he had appointed an interview for the envoys on the 2d, but he would confer with me on the subject then. I answered no. I prefer a conference in company with my colleagues, but that if he would give his ideas of the general principles of a treaty, such as France desired, I would propose to my colleagues that we should return him a counter project, but he declined it, saying it would give the directory unnecessary trouble, that if the proposition of a loan was adjusted, every thing else could be accommodated without difficulty. On this we parted. Every thing that passed at these interviews, except what related to the inadmissible proposition to me to treat separately, was communicated to my colleagues, and the October and December conferences are published."

Terrible as seemed at first to these ceremonious envoys, the degradation of making inofficial visits to discuss official business, they nevertheless afterwards solicited and accepted an opportunity of doing the very thing. " Events of magnitude affecting the United States induced them to depart from this determination."*

The difference then between Mr. Gerry's conduct and his colleagues was, that he did early what they did late.   He found events of magnitude affecting the interests of the United States on his first arrival ; they did not permit them to influence their conduct until the animosity of the French government burst into a storm.

There can be no principle involved in this form of intercourse, for certainly principle could not yield to events differing only in a few degrees of magnitude.

It is not easy to perceive why the envoys might not as well see, converse and confer with Talleyrand, as write to him.   The minister was not the government, nor as far as the Americans were concerned, the authorised agent of the government. The directory, the supreme power of the state, it was well known to them, had not authorised communications usual between ambassadors and

---

* Pickering's Review, p. 116.

the nation, to which they are deputed. Yet unaccredited and unacknowledged, they were willing
to write ; but to two of them, and to the American
secretary, inofficial visits seemed vastly objectionable, and letters, which could merit no other appellation, quite admissible.

The reluctance of Mr. Gerry was not to an interview with the minister, which he much preferred
to a conference with his agents, but to a separate
interview, which divided him from his colleagues.
His attempts to prevent a separation were incessant, and as curious as they were unavailing.

Mons. Hauteval, designated in the despatches as
Z, introduced the American and French minister
as stated by him in his printed account.

The civility, thus paid by one member of the
embassy in his private capacity to the individual
holding the portfolio of the foreign department,
was returned by the customary politeness of an
invitation to a dinner. Mr. Gerry accepted it,
chiefly that on returning it he might break down
that wall of partition, which a misjudged ceremony prevented the envoys from attempting to pass.
This dinner will furnish a subject for remark, but
here it is proper to attend to the one given by the
American in return.

Mons. Talleyrand accepted an invitation to dine
with Mr. Gerry, and both his colleagues, the ladies
of their family, and several Americans and French-
men were collected at the festival.

The culinary art was taxed to make the company agreeable. "I considered it," Mr. Gerry remarks in his diary, "a dinner of business, and hoped if my colleagues could not write, and would not visit, they might possibly eat and drink themselves into notice; but it was a terribly dull affair. I tried what I could at a compliment, and gave as a toast, The government and citizens of the French republic; in expectation it would be drank cheerfully, and the sentiment reciprocated, but it was not till after some delay, and as was suggested not very great satisfaction, the minister gave *La liberte de mer.*

Mons. Darchè who is at the head of the bureau for American affairs was present. It is since said he is placed there as a check on Talleyrand, but whether his presence or that of any Americans who were there, or what else marred the freedom of this interview, I know not."

The displeasure, if any existed, was not personal to Mr. Gerry. After dinner an intimation was made to him that Talleyrand was about to give a grand ball to general and madame Bonaparte, at which Mr. Gerry would be invited to attend.

"I desired Mr. Bellamy, who communicated this notice," Mr. Gerry continues, "not to allow a card to be sent to me, as I should be obliged to decline if it came to me alone. Afterwards I informed my colleagues candidly that my situation was painful beyond all conception; that when I left the United States I determined to make every possible personal sacrifice for the great objects of the mission, and to accord with my colleagues, or quit the embassy ; that when it was deemed proper for me, having had with Talleyrand some acquaintance in the United States, to pay him a visit, I had submitted to it as a sacrifice of my own feelings ; that the minister's attentions to me separately, which have been the result of that visit, have been extremely painful, however obliging under existing prejudices, they may be thought here on the part of Talleyrand ; that I have spared no pains to promote an extension to my colleagues of the same attentions trifling as they are, under an impression that personal interviews with the department of state might cure existing personal prejudices, that this dinner is the only one I have been able to accomplish or am likely to; that as to the proposed compliment from Talleyrand, I shall do as the envoys advise."

A card was sent to Mr. Gerry for this ball, and none to his colleagues, who notwithstanding the introduction made at the dinner, had neglected calling on the minister, and according to French etiquette were not entitled to expect an invitation. Mr. Gerry's diary proceeds, " I had of course determined to send my apology; 14 Nivose being the day appointed, the secretary of Talleyrand came in while I was at breakfast, and said he was from the minister, who had charged him to inform

me that he depended on seeing me in the evening,
that the directory would be there, that they would
know of the invitation, and might consider my absence as a want of respect; that Mons. Talleyrand
would probably introduce me to them, and that it
might advance the business of the mission ; at the
same time he presented a card of invitation to my
secretary, which he said was an extraordinary civility. I was distressed by the information, and
asked general Marshall's opinion on the proper
measure to be pursued. He said he thought I
ought to have been left to accept or not without
being thus urged, and that the decision must rest
on myself.

After weighing the subject, and reflecting that
it was an invitation from Mons. Talleyrand, (not
as minister) to me as a private gentleman, and
that a refusal might be seized as an excuse for
making our situation worse, which was now bad
enough, I determined to go to the ball, and to
avoid all political conversation.   *   *   *

In the course of the evening, I had some conversation with the Danish minister, He said he
was glad to see me here, as it looked like a prospect of accommodation. On my enquiring what
was the state of Danish affairs, he said, very
bad, that the French continue to take Danish
vessels, and they give a reason curious enough,
that American vessels were not met with in such

numbers as they used to be, and it was necessary to take Danes in their room."

Whether an effort to pave the way for reception and conciliation was judiciously made by such compliances, and whether the ambassador who conformed to the custom of the country, or those who covered themselves from observation behind the shield of etiquette and ceremony, best consulted the obligations, which devolved on the ministers of peace, must be settled by the judgment of their fellow citizens.

" In my opinion," Mr. Gerry remarks, " the American envoys were emphatically the ministers of peace. Such were our instructions, such was the avowed object of the administration, such was the interest of the country, and such was the temper of our people. There was no need of sending us here to make war. For any belligerent relation, which our country was willing to assume, there needed no apology. Wrongs almost innumerable justified an offensive attitude. We had causes enough for war. But policy advised to peace, and we came to make it, and it was in my mind right to accomplish that object by all practicable means. A concession of insignificant ceremonies could not injure the honour, which had survived the rejection of one minister and the neglect of three; or had submitted to be robbed on the ocean and bearded under the very eye of the government. The honour of our government best consisted in its preservation.   Destruction to the finances, or ruin to the confederation would not preserve its honour.   Some matters were indeed of vital consequence.   I would not submit to degradation, nor express satisfaction at imposition ; but a man in the hands of robbers best consults his honour in taking the surest means of self preservation."

Of the secrecy imputed to him Mr. Gerry has remarked, " My separate conferences with Talleyrand were six in number, viz. on 28th October and 17th December 1797, and 4th, 6th, and 7th of February, and 1st March 1798.   Those which were secret, were the inevitable consequence of their being separate.   On 4th February, when Talleyrand informed me he had something of vast importance to communicate, it was impossible for me to divine what it was.   It seemed probable that it related to the government or the envoys.   If it should disclose the impediments to our being received, the knowledge of them might tend to dissipate them ; if some stratagem lurked in the cover, it would be best broken by being known. No minister, I apprehend, would ever lose information because it was confidential, nor could any injury arise to the people, the government or agents of the United States from any intelligence, which could be communicated to me."

The suggestion that there were *negotiations*, separate and secret, between Mr. Gerry and Mons.

Talleyrand is the invention of the enemy. He heard Talleyrand's objections to his colleagues, and endeavoured to remove them. He listened unofficially and informally to the propositions made to him, and refused to give them an official character. The conversations between these personages were as wholly extra official, as any conference, which Mr. Marshall entered on his journal with the nameless gentlemen who spoke with him on American affairs.

Whatever steps Mr. Gerry took were to prepare the way for a joint negotiation with the whole embassy, and not to conduct one himself. Against his public declarations, and the conduct observed by him after the departure of his colleagues, in which he resists all efforts at negotiation, declaring and reiterating the declaration that a separate negotiation was impossible, it bears as little the marks of honesty as truth, to charge upon him the fact of a separate negotiation. His whole course was marked by a strong disposition to secure an honourable peace; a task the more difficult, because in the sincerity of the other ministers the French government professed to feel no confidence, and because their distance and coldness and ceremony, unfortunately gave countenance to the charge; a task, which the spirit of his instructions prescribed, his own principles enforced, the great party of his countrymen solicitously desired, and the best interests of his country demanded him if possible to secure.

It was a task personally perplexing, inconvenient and laborious, but it was the sacrifice of private feeling to public duty, and the hazard of reputation in the service of the state, as a gallant soldier exposes his life for his country.

Mr. Gerry remained in France after the departure of his colleagues, and the secretary of state in his official report says, "unfortunately Mr. Gerry was induced by the threats of an immediate war against the United States, to separate from his colleagues and stay in Paris, threats which viewed with their motives, merited only detestation and contempt."

The three envoys, in their joint letter to the French minister of 3d April 1798, address him as follows. " It is hoped the prejudices said to have been conceived against the ministers of the United States will be dissipated by the truths they have stated. If in this hope they shall be disappointed, and it should be the will of the directory to order passports for the whole or any number of them, you will please to accompany such passports with letters of safe conduct, &c."*

On this application passports were furnished to

* General Marshall left France 16th April 1798. Mr. Gerry demanded his passports on 10th June, but could not obtain means to leave Paris until 26th July. His departure from France was so obstructed by the government, that the United States brig Sophia, in which he took passage, was unable to sail from Havre until 8th August. Every possible interruption was given, which might retard his return home.

Messrs. Marshall and Pinckney, but none were sent to Mr. Gerry. The joint letter implies a joint assent to such an act in this regard, as France, without any agency on the part of the envoys, might choose to observe. Mr. Gerry could not leave France without permission. An attempt to have done so would probably have been a pretence for a haughty and unprincipled government to have violated the law of nations, and to have seized the persons and papers of the entire embassy. "It has appeared to me," said president Adams, at a subsequent period, "that Mr. Gerry was as much a prisoner in France as any individual in the walls of the Bastile."

So far as not peremptorily insisting on his passports was evidence of a voluntary continuance in the French capital, he is amenable to the charge.

The reason alleged by him was the positive threat of an immediate war.

If this threat was serious, and would have been executed in case of his departure, the propriety of his conduct depends on the question, whether the then condition of the two countries was better for the United States than open and declared hostility.

If the declaration made was believed by him to have been seriously intended, the propriety of his conduct depends on the reasonableness of his belief.

The secretary of state declares "suspense was

ruinous." His remaining did then suspend actual war. Was it ruinous thus to protract hostility ? Mr. Gerry and his political friends conceived almost any thing was less ruinous than
war. To prevent that calamity, to preserve the
young republic he represented from the waste
of treasure and life, which would be the consequence of a contest with the gigantic victors of
Europe, to protect her from an alliance, which
would transfuse her young blood into the wither-
ing arteries of a decaying and debilitated associate,
and to prevent the collision of those fierce passions
which threatened the American people at home,
were the objects, which right or wrong detained
him at Paris, and brought down upon him the vengeance of a political adversary, who found that
the victim, which his party required, was fortunately the individual, whom his own prejudices
would most readily select for the sacrifice.

But the secretary adds, " These threats should
have been despised. Four or five months before,
the threats of immediate orders to quit France and
the terrors of war in its most dreadful forms had
been held up to all the envoys."*

By whom ? Not by the minister, but by individuals without a document to prove their authority. The declaration of war to be made, which
induced Mr. Gerry to remain in Paris, was official,
from the minister of foreign affairs in the name of

* American state papers, vol. 4, p. 253, 2d edit.

the directory. The condition of France gave credibility to the declaration. Continental Europe was at her feet. England she was preparing to invade. It was her habit to ensure the success of her schemes by the certainty and celerity of execution. The credulity charged on Mr. Gerry, did not arise from any respect for the justice, or any admiration of the character of this formidable adversary. He had declared to his colleagues that "France was the proudest as well as most unjust government on the face of the earth, so elevated by victory as to hold in perfect contempt all the rights of others, and that with this disposition she would make war if we refused to comply with what her pride would insist on because it had been proposed."*

To one who might have anticipated the publication of the envoys' despatches to the government of the United States, a residence at Paris long enough to wait their return could not have been a very desirable position.

Haughty and unaccommodating, the rulers of France regarded neither the laws of nations nor the security of public ministers.

Before the arrival of the American plenipotentiaries, they had sent off thirteen foreign ministers, and in the insolence of their pride were not likely to regard the Americans as entitled to more respect than Geneva or Genoa. At that period the Portu-

* Marshall's Journal, MS.

guese minister was in the Temple, the Roman envoy confined to his house under guard, the Spanish ambassador was ordered beyond the boundary of France, and the envoy of republican America, who had discovered and disclosed the cupidity and profligacy of the directory and its minister, might reasonably expect one of those domiciliary visits against which his public character afforded no protection, and which led to the conciergerie or the guillotine. Of such a position of affairs the American secretary was satisfied. A despatch boat had left the United States with instructions to the messenger, who sailed in her, containing the following significant notice.

"It is important that the envoys be out of France, (unless as before mentioned, they have treated or are in treaty) because it is very probable their despatches No. 1 to 5, will in a few days be laid before congress."

An interval of ten days between the reception of this notice and the arrival of the printed communications in Paris, enabled the American minister to secure his papers from being violated and to prepare for meeting in his own person whatever the insolence or rage of the government might denounce.

It came in the moderated form of a demand for the names of the intrusive intriguers, who taking advantage of the isolated situation of the American envoys, had played on their credulity and amused them by pretences of influence or agency. It suited the policy of the French minister to deny for himself all knowledge of the concern, and to laugh at that easy credulity which had converted the babble of a court and the prattle of ladies into grave matters of public interest and deep schemes of crafty diplomacy. That there was some shrewdness in this movement of the French Machiavel cannot be doubted. Whatever of folly was justly imputed to the Americans, belongs not exclusively to the subject of this memoir, but to those colleagues of his " whose respectable talents"* none of their fellow citizens ever ventured to deny.

While the situation of Mr. Gerry in France was thus unpleasant and hazardous, his family, left under the protection of his country and her laws, were exposed to every measure of indignity. It suited the excited passions of the people, or rather the policy, which was busied in causing this excitement, to invoke maledictions upon him, and as he was beyond the reach of their personal operations, to visit his political sins upon an unoffending lady and her harmless infants, as in the barbarous periods of English history families were swept off for the conduct of their chief.

Letters anonymous or feigned, imputing his continuance in France to causes most distressing to a wife and a mother, in such forms as would give them the appearance of real correspondence,

* Pickering's Review.

were conveyed to her by almost every post. On several occasions the morning's sun shone upon a model of a guillotine erected in the field before her window, smeared with blood, and having the effigy of a headless man.   Savage yells were uttered in the night time to disturb the sleep of this family of females, and the glare of blazing faggots suddenly broke upon its darkness, to terrify them with the apprehensions of immediate conflagration.

In a land of law and civil liberty these were the penalties, which were awarded to the helpless family of a distinguished citizen; this the protection of a community to whose independence his early life was devoted.   This that refinement of manners, which expressed its abhorrence of the jacobins of Paris, and denounced contemptuously the democrats of New England !   Truly the age of chivalry was gone !

Nor is such unmanly and dishonourable conduct to be charged merely to low and vulgar villains, who were the immediate perpetrators.   More eminent citizens, by a conduct as unfeeling, though less exposed to legal animadversion, added to the wounds which the common principles of humanity would have endeavoured to soothe rather than inflame, and countenanced by silence, indifference or scorn, the wantonness of insult, in which their pride would not allow them more actively to engage.

Mr. Gerry's own view of the benefit to be obtained by residing in France after the departure of his colleagues, is explained in his correspondence. To the president of the United States he says, " I expected my passport with my colleagues, but am informed the directory will not consent to my leaving France, and to bring on an immediate war contrary to their wishes would be in my mind unwarrantable."

To Mr. Murray, minister of the United States at the Hague, who had expressed a desire for particular information he replies, " Your information as respects my consent to stay in Paris for the present is just. Your inference ' to be accredited' is wrong. The alternative presented to my choice having been my residence here or a rupture, I have chosen the former. I flatter myself you know me too well to suppose that an official reception, a mere civility, could have the weight of a feather in forming in my mind so important a decision ; if I had an ambition of that kind it has been and is now in my power to gratify it, but for this I would not give a sol. All personal considerations are against my remaining here."

To Mr. King, minister of the United States at London, who adopting the views of his political party, with the freedom of long friendship pressed him not to remain, he writes on the 3d May, " Whether the directory have settled a plan concerning America, and what it is, I am still to learn, but sure I am, our independent rights and just pretensions shall not be impaired by my conduct. I am sorry you are so severe on this government, or being so disposed, that your letter was not in cypher, because I have hopes our affairs will be amicably settled, if not rendered desperate by suspicions and prejudice. I cannot say what will be the opinion of the president, or of his constituents respecting my conduct in remaining here, but I will do nothing that I cannot justify to my own mind, and which I am not clearly convinced ought to merit their approbation. I have no personal views in remaining, and the moment I can reconcile this government to my departure, I shall embark for the United States; in the mean time with due attention to your friendly councils, I must be governed by my own judgment.

My situation, from a short period after my arrival, has been extremely painful, and has only presented a prospect of censure from one or other of the political parties, which divide our country and its councils. Thus circumstanced I could only determine to pursue as primary objects, the honour, interest and welfare of the United States; our independence I flatter myself is not in the least danger. These I have invariably pursued, and I believe this government is so well convinced of it, that was I to enter into negotiation, no proposition would be made to me with the hope of success, which would militate against them."

To Mr. Murray again he thus writes. "I am favoured with your's of the 20th May, and have been prevented from answering it sooner by the embarrassments, resulting from the arrival of the newspapers here containing our informal negotiations with persons presenting themselves as agents of this government. Before this event I was officially informed that France had no disposition for hostilities, that an arrangement of our affairs then under consideration would soon be made, and that I should find it perfectly agreeable to me. This information was accompanied with the prospect of completing the business in the United States by a person to be sent out for that purpose. What will be the consequence of these publications time only will determine."

To a gentleman who had forwarded him by express the despatches published in America, advising him to withdraw from France before their contents were made known, and urging upon him the danger of his situation he writes,

"I have received your letter with the copies of the despatches enclosed. The prospect of a ten years' imprisonment would not induce me to quit this country as a fugitive."

The benefits actually resulting from his residence in France were, to use his own language, first, an express renunciation on the part of France of loans; second, of reparation for president's speeches; third, of a renunciation of a demand upon the United States to assume debts due her citizens ; fourth, a disclaimer of any wish that we should dissolve the British treaty ; fifth, an admission of our claims for captures, founded on the want of a *role d'equipage ;* sixth, advances towards a new negotiation ; and seventh, the actual preservation of peace.*

While Mr. Gerry's object, at the expense of personal comfort and hazard of fame, was to give his country the option of peace or war, the government of the United States was pursuing its course with decision and energy, and having selected their alternative, do not seem to have found that suspense was ruinous. There was no suspense. The executive acted as if all the envoys had been ordered from the French territory, and it may well be doubted whether any personal hazard to Mr. Gerry would for a moment have obstructed the measures of the secretary of state.

On 22d May an act of Congress was passed authorizing the president of the United States to raise a provisional army,† and soon afterwards

* Minutes of conference with the president.—*MS.*

† In prospect of a war with France, Mr. Hamilton had recommended "an army of fifty thousand men, ten thousand of them to be horse."

"Such an army without an enemy to combat would have raised a rebellion in every state in the union. The very idea of the expense of it would have turned president, senate and house out of doors.———Yet such was the influence of Mr. Hamilton in congress, that without any recommendation from the president, they passed a bill to raise an army, not a large one indeed,

Washington was commissioned lieutenant-general. On 28th of the same month, authority was given to the navy of the United States to seize vessels under the flag of France, which had committed any depredation on the American commerce. On 13th June the commercial intercourse between the United States and France was suspended. On 7th July the treaties concluded with France were declared no longer binding on the United States. On the 9th, under the title of an act to protect the commerce of the United States, authority was given to issue letters of marque and reprisal. To this measure followed, as a necessary consequence, other acts for increasing the naval force, for direct and indirect taxation, and for appropriating the revenue among the new officers of government. The alien law was passed on 25th June, and the sedition law on 14th July. All this was done during a period when the "suspense," created by Mr. Gerry's residence in France was declared to be "ruinous." The meaning of which, if any meaning be attached to the phrase, is that the uncertainty of peace or war, created by his conduct, retarded or diminished preparation for hostility. It is difficult to understand how the most positive assurance and certainty of a belligerent attitude could have expedited or increased military preparations sooner or more extensively

but enough to overturn the then federal government.—*Adams' letters*, p. 68.

or what stronger position could be taken to place in the power of the administration the force and wealth of the nation.

Of a measure resulting from so serious an act as a division between the members of a joint embassy, in which one of them remained in opposition to the opinion of both his colleagues, it is feeble praise to say only that it was not wrong. It involved a great and hazardous responsibility, not lightly to be assumed, and not to be justified by trifling advantages. But under the circumstances in which the government and people of the United States were situated, it is not possible that a proceeding, which might change the neutral relations of the country for a belligerent attitude, could be indifferent to its most vital and permanent interests.

Had Mr. Gerry demanded his passports, or returned in defiance of the threats of the French government, the war, which they menaced, might not indeed have been waged by them, but the condition of affairs in the United States must inevitably have produced it. Negotiation would have ended. The first minister was rejected. A solemn and dignified embassy was repulsed, and insulted, and driven from the country. The causes of complaint for past injuries were not diminished; new evils were accumulating, and the only alternative would have been the humbleness of submission or the activity of resistance. War was inevitable.

To speak lightly of such a condition of the

country comports as little with the wisdom of a statesman as it does with the piety of a Christian. If in itself war be not the greatest misery that could fall on a community, it certainly has an alarming tendency to produce it. The courage, the patriotism, and the self-sacrifice of a generous people may, by the blessing of heaven, carry them safely through its storms; but its clouds then threatened wider devastation than its ordinary ravages. There was danger of civil commotion; there was apprehension of foreign alliance, as fatal as the embrace of the disguised statue to her ignorant admirers. There was hazard that the young tree of liberty planted on our shores, whose branches now luxuriantly expanding, were then but beginning to spread themselves, and whose root was scarcely fixed in the earth, would be blown down in the whirlwinds that must prematurely assail it. There was danger that an inconsiderate rashness would, like another Erostratus, sacrifice the last temple of rational liberty.

By remaining in France, Mr. Gerry kept open the door of negotiation. He received and communicated assurances that the French directory were not obstinately determined on hostilities; that they would negotiate, whenever the character and sentiments of the American agents should satisfy them they could do so with prospect of success. In the short period that elapsed between the departure of his colleagues and his own, Mr.

Gerry acquired a persuasion of this fact, and succeeded with some difficulty indeed, but nevertheless succeeded in making this known to his own
government, and the people of his country.

In brief space after his return a new embassy
was appointed ; the secretary, who had found in
his conduct an obstacle to his views or his policy,
and laid out his official strength to prostrate his
good name, had himself been made to drink of the
waters of bitterness, and to find the poisoned
chalice commended to his own lips.   Peace, firm,
honourable, lasting peace was concluded with the
French republic, and the popular sentiment so
thoroughly changed that the whole administration,
chiefly by the impetus given by their war councils,
was overthrown.

The peace, which the American government
preserved, has been claimed as the consequence,
not of negotiation but arms.   It has been said the
preparation for war prevented it.   But the operation of the public sentiment refutes this opinion.
Preparation for war unhorsed the riders of the war-
steed, while to the dominant and victorious nation,
against whom it was directed, it was too small an
addition to the vast force they had subjugated, to
create any sensation of alarm.

The executive chief burst the bonds, with which
his cabinet had endeavoured to bind him, too late
for his personal elevation indeed, but soon enough
for his country and his fame.   Against their advice

and approbation he acted on the prospects, which negotiation held out, and acted with success ; and might well say, in relation to this and another incident of his administration, not connected with this subject, that " they were two measures that I recollect with infinite satisfaction, and which will console me in my latest hour."* " He [Mr. Gerry] was nominated and approved and finally saved the peace of the nation ; he alone discovered and furnished the evidence that X, Y, and Z, were employed by Talleyrand ; and he alone brought home the direct formal official assurances, upon which the subsequent commission proceeded and peace was made."†

Long before this satisfactory declaration was offered to Mr. Gerry, by the distinguished chief from whom his appointment had proceeded, and while yet the public mind was abused by the philippics, which had been launched against his conduct and character, his own conscious rectitude of intention was gratified, and his wounded spirit consoled, and cheered and comforted by high testimonials of approbation bestowed upon him by the great head of the republican party, whose encomiums may be placed in contrast, although they overwhelm by their incomparably superior value

* President Adams' letters, No. 10, p. 47.
† Ibid. letter 13, p. 65.

the vituperations of an angry and mortified political rival.*

If it has been the lot of few indivinuals, against
whom neither treachery nor corruption could be
alleged, to be more severely censured than was
Mr. Gerry for his share of this memorable embassy, so probably no man can boast of more ardent
or honourable praise. The testimony of the two
great statesmen, who by different parties were
placed at the head of the nation, and thus together
may be said to have represented each separate
part of the people, is placed in credit against the
charges of that bold account, by which a few intemperate partizans would have made him bank-
rupt in character and fame.†

How well he discharged the duty assigned to
him is yet an open question, which neither the au-

* The great length of Mr. Jefferson's letters would of itself
prevent their insertion, but there are remarks in them, which
communicated as they were under the seal of confidence the
author does not feel at liberty to disclose. He represses his
desire to publish them with great reluctance.

† A petty punishment was devised by Mr. secretary Pickering
for the contumacy of Mr. Gerry.

On June 20, 1799, he thus addresses him, "I consider your
stay in France after the 12th of May, when my letter of March
23, 1798 was delivered to you as perfectly gratuitous, and consequently that your salary ceased on May 12, excepting the al-
lowance of one quarter's salary for your return according to
usage."

On an appeal to the president, after Mr. Marshall was secretary of state, this decision of the former secretary was reversed.

thority of Adams and Jefferson in his favour, nor of Pickering, such as it is, against him, will conclusively determine. There is an appeal to the people; not to a people excited by intemperate political feeling and party zeal, but to a people calm, intelligent and dispassionate; to posterity, who will sit in judgment on the great men of the past age, when the little causes of private hostility shall have been buried in the silence of the grave; posterity who will be able to mark the difficulties, which any measure would have presented, and the thousand roads of deviation with the one solitary and obscure path, which the wise political traveller should have selected and steadily maintained.

CHAPTER VIII.

Commentary on the mission continued.......Further strictures on Mr. Pickering's publication.

Of the circumstances occurring after the departure of the two envoys, the most important are those, which ensued when their despatches had returned from America. These probably changed the whole complexion of the case. Mr. Gerry communicated to Talleyrand at his request the names of those individuals, whose discourse about loans and doceurs was conveyed to the American government. This forms another allegation against the propriety of his conduct.

There is something so ludicrous in finding in the diplomatic despatches of an important embassy grave discourse with people, who have neither local habitation nor a name, save at the end of the alphabet, that it is almost forgotten; these diminutive appellations were inserted not by the envoys but by the secretary of state.*

On the return of these despatches to France and to Europe, the envoys were exhibited as the subjects of an intrigue too base to permit even its agents to be named. But the implication, for in diplomatic arrangements insinuations often supply

* American state papers, vol. 3. p. 475. 2d ed.

the place of facts, plainly was that the French directory or its minister had endeavoured for their own corrupt purposes to impose on the unaccredited envoys, and taking advantage of the isolated condition in which they kept themselves, proposed to open a passage to the French government by bribery and fraud.

Whatever was the truth of the case, no course was left but for the French minister to pretend ignorance of the whole transaction, and demand, with the show of indignation, who it was that thus had offended the government, and tampered with envoys at its court?

The demand being made of the only individual, who was in a condition to answer it, Mr. Gerry might have refused to reply; and his silence would have been trumpeted through Europe as evidence of the fabrication, which in the spirit of a war party its ministers had circulated to rouse the indignation they were desirous of producing.

Or Mr. Gerry might have said, you Mr. minister know who they were: you employed, authorized, countenanced and directed them. You saw them with the American envoys, you knew what they were saying, doing, desiring, soliciting. You knew we refused to accede to their propositions, and you would not receive us. They were your agents, and it is an insult for you to ask me their residence or their name.

To such an honest expression of the truth

Talleyrand would reply, Sir, if your allegations are true, produce me the credentials, which entitled them to be received by you as my agents, or in want of such evidence, be contented that you and your colleagues shall be deemed dupes to sharpers, who came to you without authority, and that you sir, in addition, should stand accused before Europe with aiding their machinations by a declaration that you cannot maintain. They were not my agents. Your assertions are not warranted by the fact.

In this issue of fact between Mr. Gerry and M. Talleyrand, to have called individuals within the reach of the gens d'armorie of Paris to testify to the truth of their agency, could hardly have been prudent, and the Frenchman by the advantage of position, which his sagacity originally foresaw, was enabled to stand securely on his defence.

There was a third course. It was to answer the question strictly and literally.

Who are the individuals intended by the letters X, Y, Z, &c. in your despatches.

They are Mr. Hottinguer, Mr. Bellamy, and Mr. Hauteval. If you knew them before, as I believe you did, my answer gives you no additional information; if you did not, punish them for an imposition mutually on you and us.

The whole error is to be traced to the informal conferences with individuals not bearing any credentials, and whose authority the French minister might affirm or deny at his pleasure ; and this error is to be shared in common by all the envoys. If their proportion is unequal, Mr. Gerry's is the least, as he first proposed its termination.*

To these material charges some others of inferior nature, to increase the weight of popular indignation, have at times been added. Thus it was gravely said that Mr. Gerry was at a private dinner with Mons. Talleyrand, where the business of the money was discussed.† A private dinner seemed to mark a degree of intimacy and unwarrantable compliance, which alarmed the minds of our plain republican citizens, to whom the corruptions and the manners of a court are equally matters of mystery. It was true that in the effort to establish that interchange of civility, which might lead to a mutual good understanding, Mr. Gerry dined at the table of the French minister, who in return

---

* Mr. Pickering intended in his report to have charged the whole of this informal mismanagement to Mr. Gerry.

As it was draughted it reads thus. Paragraph 34. " While we, amused and deluded by warm but empty professions of th e pacific views and wishes of France, and by *Mr. Gerry's* informal conferences might wait in fruitless torpor hoping for a peaceful result."

This part was amended by Mr. Adams, who caused the words, " Mr. Gerry's" to be erased, whereby the impropriety, if there was one, was attributed to the whole embassy, and not to any individual.

The disingenuousness of an attempt to charge the informal conferences on Mr. Gerry alone, who was the first of the three to propose their termination, is only a specimen of the whole of the secretary's report.—*See Pickering's Review*, p. 131.

† Pickering's Review, p. 141.

for this customary form of politeness, was invited
to the hotel of the American envoy. The dinner
at Talleyrand's was what is called a private dinner, in opposition to those dinners called public,
in which the ministers of the directory were accustomed to receive the public functionaries. It
was in fact as public as forty or fifty guests of
different classes, countries and sexes would permit. At such a private dinner was the money
concerns of the American embassy supposed to be
brought into discussion, and in such privacy was
it that the American envoy was plotting treason
against the rights of his country !

Mr. Gerry on two or three occasions failed of
finding M. Talleyrand at his bureau, and although
the secretary of the latter made an apology* for
his absence, the fact has been adduced to show
the slight regard he paid to the American envoy.†
In offset to this it has been alleged that he became the dupe of the French minister's threats,
mingled with blandishments flattering to his vanity. He had even the folly to imagine his colleagues envious of his good fortune.‡

* Mr. Pickering says, " one of Talleyrand's secretaries called
to make a slight apology." This slight mode of speaking shows
the temper of the party who uses it. How was it possible for
Mr. Pickering to ascertain whether the apology was *slight* or
formal, serious or delusive. It was an apology brought by the
principal secretary of the minister's bureau.

† By the barbarous calendar adopted in the country, it was
difficult always to remember when it was the Frenchman's sabbath. Mr. Gerry went once on a *decade* and the office was closed.

‡ Pickering's Review, p. 127.

Thus inconsistent is the hostility, which pursues an opponent without justice or principle.

The vanity to be flattered by slight apologies, by neglect and by studied disrespect, or the want of consequence which is subjected to repeated disappointments, and yet persuades a man to imagine others are jealous of his importance, is indeed a singular union of dissimilar materials. The imputations cannot both be true, although both may be unfounded. As circumstances occurred at one or another time they would serve like the artifices at the hustings to be played off before different auditories against a political rival.

In giving an account of the business of the embassy there are some curious suggestions by Mr. Pickering in his review, which serve further to explain with what temper and feeling he draughted his celebrated official report.

Thus he says, " A letter* having been prepared and submitted to Mr. Gerry, and he having employed a day in making *essential changes to adapt it to his own taste*, to which the other two envoys yielded for the sake of unanimity, on 11th November it was sent to M. Talleyrand. No answer however was given to it."

" Three months [meaning two] having elapsed, general Marshall draughted a long letter consisting of a justification of the conduct of our government in relation to France. This was done by 10th

* Review, p. 117.

January 1798. It was submitted to **Mr. Gerry,** (*whose humour it was necessary to consult to obtain his signature*) to suggest any alterations and amendments he might think proper." "Mr. Gerry's vexatious delays prevented the completion and translation of this letter until the 31st January, when it was signed and sent to the French minister."

The reading of these letters might satisfy any one that, as they stand, they have spirit and fire enough to vindicate the policy of their government, and are tart enough for messages of peace. Mr. Gerry's taste must have been gratified then by some modification of their causticity, and his humour, which it was necessary to consult, was not of that acrid and angry kind, which deemed irritating expressions to be means of accomplishing an object so judicious as less intemperate language.

But the suggestion that a minister's humour and taste must be consulted before his signature can be obtained to state papers of immense consequence to himself and his nation, is indeed wonderful! As if a man of independence and integrity would place his signature to papers that displeased him, or which he had not sufficiently examined. The reviewer, it would seem, calculated on Mr. Gerry's signature as a matter of course. Because according to his language in another place, "men of such respectable talents, untainted honour and pure patriotism as generals Pinckney and Marshall, and in whom their government and country reposed entire confidence," had prepared an official paper, the attestation of the remaining member of the embassy was to be given without delay.

This was not the mode of reasoning adopted by that member. Whatever slight was by political opponents thrown upon his talents, his patriotism, or his fame, he felt that his country had long and steadily reposed as great confidence in him as it had ever done in his colleagues, and that it was due to himself and his fellow citizens to examine and deliberate, and then to decide.

While however the reviewer complains of his vexatious delays, his health was suffering under the effect of continual exertions, and his secretary, absolutely unable to accomplish the task imposed upon him, resigned his office.*

The letter was indeed a "long letter" covering fifty-four closely printed pages of letter press,† and which, being drawn without previous concert, re-

* Extract from a letter of resignation of B. Foster, jr., Mr. Gerry's private secretary, dated March 30, 1798. "It has been a source of much uneasiness and regret to me that I have been under the necessity of declaring before my inability to get through so much voluminous writing, as has appeared in the course of the negotiation."

† American state papers, vol. 4. p. 27 to 80, inclusive, 2d edit. It may excite some surprise that in a joint mission long letters should be prepared by one or two of the members *apart from their colleague*, and before principles had been settled at a conference.

quired to be examined and compared with sundry authorities ; and finally, in conforming to the taste and humour of the colleague to whom it was submitted, to undergo discussion and alteration in some places, and to be preserved in its original form in others, after proposed amendments, " for the sake of unanimity," were withdrawn.

The review proceeds : " On the 18th January, at the instance of the directory, the two legislative councils passed a decree," &c.   " On 6th February, general Marshall put into Mr. Gerry's hands the draught of a letter to the French minister, remonstrating against that decree and closing with a request for passports.   But Mr. Gerry was too busily engaged with his secret negotiations with that minister to attend to the letter, though it would affect nearly every American vessel on the ocean.   On 14th February Mr. Gerry returned the draught of the letter with some amendments.   It was then put under copy and translated.   On the 18th, being fully prepared it was offered to Mr. Gerry to sign———which he declined."*

As no letter appears in the despatches of the envoys, without his signature, it is a just conclusion, either that the reasons, by which Mr. Gerry maintained his change of opinion, were satisfactory to his colleagues, or that they carried their desire to consult his taste and humour to an extraordinary length.

* Review, p. 119.

Something of the mode, by which the business of the embassy was managed, and how the delays complained of occurred, may be discovered in the following notes.

MR. PINCKNEY TO MESSRS. MARSHALL AND GERRY.

PARIS, APRIL 2, 1798.

GENTLEMEN,

I think it of importance that no longer delay should take place in transmitting our reply to the minister of foreign affairs. Duty to our country and justice to ourselves require that his letter should not remain unanswered; and I am very apprehensive, if we do not make it soon, we shall be prevented from making it at all. The latter part of the letter which Mr. Gerry took with him to consider, he said should be attended to immediately. If he cannot join his colleagues in what is there expressed, and cannot suggest such alterations as they can accede to, we ought then to determine what prudence and duty may dictate. But I am for avoiding an apparent admission, by our silence, of the unjust and injurious charges made against our country, our government, and ourselves. I see so much danger resulting from delay, that I am unwilling it should be imputable to me, I therefore think it incumbent on me to give you my sentiments freely on this subject, and hope by to-mor-

row morning we shall come to some decision.
Mr. Burling requests to have any despatches we
may wish to transmit by him to America the day
after to-morrow.

I have the honour to be, very respectfully,

Your most obedient servant,

CHARLES COTESWORTH PINCKNEY.

Messrs. Marshall and Gerry.

————

MR. GERRY TO MR. PINCKNEY.

PARIS, APRIL 2, 5 P. M.

Mr. Gerry presents his compliments to general
Pinckney, and informs him that he is ready at any
moment to finish the letter proposed as an answer
to the minister of foreign affairs. He has made
one attempt to obtain this object, but his propositions not having been entirely acceptable to general Marshall, he thought it best to present in one
point of view the draught as he proposes it, and it
is now ready. He has suggested no alterations but
such as appear to him indispensably necessary to
prevent further irritation on the part of this government : the charge on our part of wantonly plunging the United States into a war : and future embarrassments to our government and ourselves.
He shall certainly accord in this final measure with
his colleagues, if possible, as he deprecates a dif
ference of opinion with them, on the important

and embarrassing affairs of the embassy. Mr.
Gerry's health is not good at present, but he has
not from that or any consideration neglected a
moment, the business alluded to.

————

The letter referred to covers twenty-six pages
of letter press, and its review and examination by
one of the embassy, might reasonably require at
least, as much time as was demanded by the other
two for its original preparation.

So in respect to the others. A joint mission has
the advantage of combined learning and ability,
but it necessarily supposes the delay which is incident to difference of sentiment, and discussion of
opinion.

The vituperative spirit of the reviewer cannot
but be seen in the manner in which the delay is
stated.   Mr. Marshall and Mr. Pinckney prepare a
letter on the 10th January.   Mr. Gerry's vexatious
delays prevent the completion and translation until
the 31st.   The inference intended but not expressed would put the whole of this interval to his account.   But how many of the twenty-one days
were consumed in a revision, how many in acced-
ing to or rejecting the alterations, and how many
in making a translation and in copying the dupli-
cates is not exactly ascertained.

Not satisfied with speaking slightly of Mr. Gerry
in connexion with the French mission, which was

the only topic that introduced his name into the review, Mr. Pickering has seemed desirous of taking all opportunity to underrate the character of his mind, the value of his services, the estimate in which he was held by his associates, and the causes by which his public stations were procured. His mind is every where represented as diminutive, his services inconsiderable, his reputation exceedingly limited, and his place in the public councils accidental and fortuitous.

How much of this picture, made up of dark lines and gloomy colouring, is drawn from imagination by political animosity, or how truly it reflects the individual, whose likeness it pretends to exhibit, the facts stated in these volumes and the proof of those facts, under the hand of contemporary patriots, must be permitted to decide.

No claim was ever made by or for Mr. Gerry " to that gigantic and stupendous intelligence, which grasps a system by intuition, and bounds forward from one series of conclusions to another without regular steps through intermediate propositions," but it is not easy to see any thing in his public performances, at which a dismissed secretary was authorized to sneer. To sound good sense, and the improvements of a liberal education, to an uncompromising integrity, which even the most angry of his opponents has acknowledged, to long and arduous attendance in the school of the patriots, and to multiplied opportunities of being concerned in the responsible direction of great public affairs is he indebted for that estimation, in which he stood with his fellow citizens, and the relative rank, which the judgment of posterity will assign to him, among the illustrious companions of his life. In forming an opinion upon the character of his mind, no better rule can be adopted than one, which this adversary himself has proposed for another object of his censure.

"On the score of talents and learning the experience of five and thirty years in the United States has furnished ample proof that a practical knowledge of the interests of the country, a common sense deliberately exercised in forming a sound judgment, united with perfect integrity and pure and disinterested patriotism, are of infinitely greater value than genius without stability, profound learning, ripe scholarship, and philosophy."*

Of the value of Mr. Gerry's services, something has been shown in the facts already narrated. If the successive duties assigned to him in the general court of Massachusetts and the congress of the revolution do not prove the ability, with which they were performed, if " it was his good fortune to be present at the adoption of the declaration of independence,"† and was not equally the good fortune of his country that he was present when the project was first debated in congress; if he had

---

* Pickering's Review, p. 62.
† Ibid. p. 111.

merely "the honour of signing his name to that celebrated state paper,"* and had not the higher and
nobler honour of being among the earliest and firmest and steadiest of its adventurous friends, if he
was only "a member of the national convention
and member of the house of representatives in the
first congress, and in one or two succeeding con-
gresses,"† and has left in the journals of those
illustrious assemblies no evidence of having been
there, but the record of his name, he may justly
be exposed to those diminutive and sarcastic re-
flections, by which malevolence seeks to disguise
itself under the affectation of contempt; and cannot complain that he comes in for a full portion
of censure in a work, whose spirit of vituperation
includes John Adams, Thomas Jefferson and John
Quincy Adams, and loses no opportunity of sending an arrow of reproach at Madison and Monroe.

The estimate, in which Mr. Gerry was held by
his associates of the revolution, and his companions
in later political life, may be found in the intimacy
of their friendship. The intercourse maintained
by public men no where exhibits more implicit
confidence or warmer expressions of esteem than
the confidential letters, which the great and the
brave were daily addressing to him. The natural
consequence of this connexion was the public

* Pickering's Review, p. 111.
† Ibid.

stations, which he was called upon to fill. Popular sentiment was in unison with the opinions of the gifted and the faithful. The accident, to which some people attribute the talents that conducted the revolution, is by a more devout temper of mind ascribed to the special providence of God.*

* The writer of the review could not himself believe that Mr. Gerry was not one of the master builders in the temple of his country's freedom.

In 1774, Mr. Pickering compiled some insignificant formulary of manual exercise, which he would not venture to introduce without obtaining Mr. Gerry's approbation, although he was not in the military department. " I have been so extremely hurried with other business, that my plan of exercise remains incomplete. However, by writing in the evening and rising in the morning by candle light, I have made shift to finish the manual exercise, except only the planting, grounding and presenting, (that is, resting) the firelock. The whole plan you have enclosed, to execute which, I shall proceed with all expedition."— Pickering's MS. letter, November 23, 1774.

In November 1777, the colonel, apprehensive that some delay in his official returns would bring upon him the displeasure of congress, addresses Mr. Gerry as a friend by whose influence its irritation might be safely conducted from him. " I have given you this detail because I knew not whether congress may not have judged me negligent; but gentlemen of the family who have known my real situation, I trust deem me very excusable."—MS. letter to Mr. Gerry, Nov. 2, 1777.

In 1784, this gentleman, upon whom so many offices were conferred, and " all of them unasked for in any form whatever," (Review, p. 67) having some little place under government to solicit, thus writes Mr. Gerry on March 9. " In my last I begged you to deliver the letter therein enclosed, to general Mifflin. It respected the office in question. He has ever shown me marks of friendship, and I trusted to the continuance of them. The nomination you hint at, coming from the quarter it did, would not for that consideration, press on him with any additional weight. *You and the president are on such terms of intimacy,* I suppose he will have shown you my letter. If not, I wish you may see it and sound him on the subject, if you judge it expedient." In 1785, the same gentleman and his partner began a letter of business in the following strain. "With extreme pleasure we learn your arrival once more at York to take your seat where your services always have and always will be, valuable to your country."

While writing the defamatory insinuations in the review, general Marshall's private journal was lying open before him, which that eminent citizen commences, by speaking of Mr. Gerry's not having then arrived in Paris, and by expressing the highest expectation of the advantage to be derived from the ability, experience and character of the colleague, with whom he was to be associated.

CHAPTER IX.

Returns to Massachusetts.......Proposed for Governour of the Commonwealth......Private life......Pecuniary and domestic misfortune. ......Character......Member of the electoral college of Massachusetts. ......Presides at a meeting in relation to the Chesapeake.

MR. GERRY returned to the United States at a period of increased exasperation and violence.[*]

[*] The state of things at this period was so offensive and oppressive, that the patience of the party which submitted to them is a subject of wonder. The temples of devotion and justice became altars of desecration. In Massachusetts the chief justice of the supreme judicial court, addressed the grand jury in terms which are thus characterized by one of the leading journals of the day. "The learned judge, in a forcible manner, proved the existence of a French faction in the bosom of our country, and exposed the French system-mongers from the quintumvirate of Paris, to the vice-president and minority in congress, as apostles of atheism and anarchy, bloodshed and plunder."—*Centinel, Nov.* 24, 1798. A meeting of free citizens preparatory to the election of national representatives is thus described. "A convention of Parisian cut throats assembled in solemn divan for the purpose of selecting some devotee of republicanized France as a candidate for the democratic suffrages in this district, for federal representative at the approaching election."— *Ibid. October* 17, 1798.

The system of denunciation was placed in full contrast with the system of exaggerated praise. The birth days of the first public characters were celebrated quite as extensively and expensively, as the birth day of the nation, and toasts of extravagant adulation reciprocated. At one of these festivals in Massachusetts, where was present the dignified officers of the state, the following singular sentiment was proclaimed. The

He came back under a suspicion that he was inclined to pacification ; that he thought this object attainable under proper direction ; that letters addressed to him by the department of state and the expected tenor of its future movements would place him in hostility to the administration, and that he was to assume the rank of a leader in the northern section of the United States of that political party, which it suited the views of the dominant power to crush and annihilate. On the other side the most dissatisfied members of the opposition were aware of his confidence in the executive chief, and the difficulty there would be in his pursuing all those measures of aggression, which a partizan directs, not because they are all right, but because they are expedient movements in the tactics of faction. A cautious demeanour was observed with regard to him by both parties, each fearful of committing itself by attentions,

The Honourable Francis Dana, chief justice, and the learned associate judges of our supreme judicial court. While the political opinions delivered from the bench, are dictated by intelligence, integrity and patriotism, may they be as highly respected as have ever been its judicial decisions.

Political opinions from the bench of justice, and party politics too!

The plan of personal exaltation was carried so far, that on one of these birth days "a parade of artillery did themselves and the day, the honour to attend at the renaming of the fortress of the United States, formerly called Fort Williams, which now bears that of Fort Pickering."

which it might not be easy to retract.* The first public announcement of his course, was by his declining a proposition made on the part of his personal friends to place him again in the house of representatives of the United States. It was contained in the following card.

Mr. Gerry being informed from various quarters of the wishes of a number of his fellow citizens of this district, that he would stand as a candidate for a representative in congress at the approaching election, has a grateful sense of the honour they are disposed to confer on him, and regrets the indispensable necessity he is under of declining it. He nevertheless assures them of the continuance of his exertions in private life to support the federal government, as the only effectual measure of union, on which under providence rest the liberty, independence and welfare of ourselves and posterity.

His recent colleagues took other ground. Mr. Pinckney in answer to an address made to him at Trenton declared, " For my own part I believe the French directory are not sincere in the pacific declarations made by the minister of foreign affairs to Mr. Gerry. If we would secure the inde-

---

* A few days after Mr. Gerry's arrival, a gentleman of influence in the federal party waited upon him and said, that as soon as he had announced his opinion of the necessity of war with France, he would be complimented with a public dinner, of which this individual was authorized to inform him. The compliment was of course declined.

pendence of America free from the intrigues and ambition of France, I am convinced we must fight for its preservation." And again to another complimentary speech, "They [the French] are a people artful and insidious in policy, bold and powerful in arms; but having endeavoured to study their character with attention, I am convinced their intrigues are more to be dreaded than their force."

Something of a more discreet course, but sufficiently distinct to settle its identity, was maintained by his other late colleague.

In Mr. Gerry's view of affairs war might be averted. He would not proclaim an opinion that the French rulers were insincere because he did not entertain it; he was as little disposed to urge those measures of resistance by arms, which the majority were preparing, because he did not believe such policy best adapted to the objects it professed, but he was more unwilling to create dissension and controversy at home, or retard the movements of the government in its constitutional power.

If war was to be declared, it was his opinion that the duty of a good citizen was to make it successful. If the government in its wisdom saw fit to appeal to this last arbitrator of nations, it was his doctrine that no measure could be justified, that might weaken its chances of success. It was not as he believed then proper to quarrel about

the manner of navigation, which had brought the
ship among the rocks or exposed her to the storm,
but to engage with one heart and one common
exertion to carry her with safety through the battle and the breeze.

These sentiments, which patriotism cannot disapprove, were too sensible and too moderate to
meet the excited feelings of the community. They
left him for the moment without the honours,
which party and faction bestow on their leaders,
but they were remembered to his credit when passions, which then confounded the reason of the
community, had become tranquillized and still.

The progress of affairs and the happy termination of the difficulties with France justify the
correctness of those views, which Mr. Gerry had
entertained of the interests of his country. In the
midst of all the pride, pomp and circumstance of
war, of brilliant preparation on land and triumph
on the ocean, the executive chief saw fit to put
his own hand to the helm, and suddenly to change
the direction of his ship.

Against the advice of all his ministers, Mr. Adams on 18th February 1799, instituted 'a new
mission to France.

On the 12th May 1800, Mr. Pickering was dismissed from the office of secretary of state. On
the 14th the provisional army was disbanded. Mr.
Dexter superseded Mr. M'Henry as secretary of
war.

The apparently sudden decision of Mr. Adams'

mind was the result of care, examination, reflection and judgment. He had been at Quincy* a chief part of the summer and autumn of '98. His personal interviews there and at Cambridge had been most frequent, free and confidential with Mr. Gerry, who early succeeded in dispelling those prejudices at his own conduct, with which it was first surrounded, and afterwards in impressing on Mr. Adams the views of American policy in relation to France, which his personal observation had matured.   Mr. Adams departed for Philadelphia persuaded of the correctness of those principles, which Mr. Gerry had enforced, but alarmed and unhappy at the strength and combination, which in and around his cabinet pressed on his attention others of a different character. The language of his speech on the opening of congress, incites to military preparation, not so much for actual warfare, as a weapon of diplomacy. It is easy to perceive in it the change his mind had undergone. His expurgation of the secretary's animadversions on Mr. Gerry is of similar tendency. The repeal of the French arrette of 20th October '98, communicated to congress on 15th February '99, was in further aid of his new views. Talleyrand's letter to Pichon of 28th September 1798, which was indeed but a repetition of Talleyrand's constant language to Mr. Gerry, completed his conviction, and the new mission

* The president's residence in Massachusetts, seven miles from Boston.

was instituted, which in his own language saved the peace of the nation. The success of this mission, honourable as it was to the political character of the president, was yet in strong confirmation of the sentiments and policy of his opponents. It made their prophecy fact, and largely contributed to that change in public affairs, which in a few months placed the power of the government in their hands. The republican party rallied under the excitement of these new events.

In Massachusetts they offered their support to Mr. Gerry for the office of governour, in opposition to Caleb Strong, who was proposed by the federalists. Two years before, the republican party had but a single member in the senate of the state. On counting the votes it was now found that "the whole number was 39059, of which 19530 made a choice; that Mr. Strong had 19630 and was chosen."*

Mr. Jefferson was inaugurated president of the United States on 4th March 1801, and a new effort was made by the republican party to assimilate the political character of the state to that of the nation. Mr. Gerry very reluctantly consented again to permit his name to appear as a candidate for the chair, and a canvass of great animation and much virulence, terminated in the reelection of the former governour.† From these several ex-

---

* Report of Com. of Mass. legis.

† Mr. G. received 20169 out of 45816 votes.

ertions Mr. Gerry could derive no other satisfaction than in finding he still possessed the confidence of that great political party with whom he had always been associated, and whose physical weakness was the cause, and not any deficiency of energy or zeal, that he was not placed at the head of the state.

Retiring now from the turmoils of political affairs, Mr. Gerry was once again at liberty to attend to his favourite pursuits, to cultivate his farm, to superintend the education of his children and to enjoy the pleasures of domestic life. Unfortunately however, the peace, that would have followed this cessation of public labours, was interrupted by a circumstance that served to embarrass the whole future of his life. A friend, for whom he had become surety to a large amount, failed and left him with a weight of pecuniary obligations, from which he was never able afterwards to extricate himself.

The cares and anxiety, to which this derangement of his finances subjected him, checked his political correspondence and his connexion with the more animating scenes of society, but had no effect on his domestic intercourse, or the happiness, which was enjoyed in his family circle. Whatever were his disappointments abroad, and great as must have been his anxiety for the future prospects of a numerous and dependent establishment, the same serenity of disposition, the same amiable and endearing manners, the same animating and cheerful temper, which made him so much the object of affectionate interest, continued to disguise the agitation of his heart. The circle of his hospitality was diminished, the expensive assistance, which he had brought to his own efforts in education was curtailed, and its cares divided with his accomplished companion ; a necessary but still elegant frugality presided over his household ; his amusements and occupation, which had before extended over a wider circle, now settled within the family limits, which seemed to give them new strength by compression.

But another and severer misfortune awaited him. She in whose society his peculiarly affectionate feelings found their sweetest consolation, and who seemed, by the extraordinary attachment which bound him to her, not only a substitute for all other pleasures, but in herself almost the sole satisfaction of life, was visited by a dangerous and long continued malady, which engrossed all his solicitude and care.

The intervals of the distressing disease, to which she was a victim, served but feebly to recruit his own strength, which watching and anxiety undermined, and hardly allowed him any other relaxation or employment than his farm or his family demanded.

Notwithstanding these severe trials the occasional visitor at his friendly mansion was delighted with the assumed cheerfulness of his manners, the ease and freedom of his conversation, abounding with anecdote and the recital of by-gone events, piquant and full of wit, which under the control of good feelings never inflicted a voluntary wound.

It was at this period of comparative seclusion, that the author, then an undergraduate at Harvard University, first became acquainted with the individual of whom he is writing, and acquired those sentiments of respect and esteem, which matured in the course of a more intimate connexion may perhaps be thought to guide a too favourable pencil in giving this account of his public services and his private character. But the impressions, which he then received, were not made on him alone. No one was a greater favourite with the young than Mr. Gerry. He accommodated his manners to their feelings, habits and taste. With a dignity of deportment and an elevation of character that commanded their respect, there was a freedom of manners and an indulgent disposition, which won their affections and secured their confidence.

He has been called reserved and austere, but only by those to whom he was not personally known. The little arts, by which popularity is often secured, were indeed wholly unknown to him. He rested his claims to public favour on the merit that deserved it, without descending to court the applause of the people, by flattering their vices or ministering to their vanity. He was rarely if ever at their primary meetings, considering as below his rank in political estimation the management of the materials of a party ; and they who found themselves courted by other candidates for their favour, not unwillingly attributed his reserve to pride or disdain.

But nothing could be more inappropriately said of him than that he was austere. His fault was of an opposite kind. A fond and affectionate husband, a kind and indulgent parent, a friendly neighbour, most liberal in hospitality, and generous in his contributions to alleviate distress, he was entitled to high rank in the calendar of the humane and beneficent. His exertions to do good within the circle of his personal influence were limited only by his means. It was the habit of his life to consider nothing a sacrifice, which added to the comfort of his friends, and wholly to forget all self-interested motives in his endeavours to ameliorate the condition of the humbler members of society.

Two circumstances have contributed to the erroneous estimate, which in this respect has been made of his character. The furrows of care were early traced on his countenance. This appearance, with a singular habit of contracting and expanding very rapidly the muscles of the eye, gave to his features the appearance of sternness, which had really no connexion with his mind.

Another cause for this opinion was the severity

of his administration of the state government. Numerous removals from office produced much individual suffering, which was naturally enough charged to the governour. It is not proper to anticipate occurrences, which remain to be related, further than to say, that much of that course was in no degree attributable to him, and that his reluctant share in it caused him many of the most painful moments of his life. With all the clamour at the time, the objects of his party were not thoroughly accomplished, because the chief magistrate shrunk from inflicting personal distress; and many individuals were left in the enjoyment of official station, whom the stern decrees of political proscription had selected for sacrifice.

It was with more truth he was accused of obstinacy. Forming his opinions with deliberation, he yielded them with reluctance. Feeling the conviction produced by thorough investigation it was not easy to change his results. The tenacity with which he clung to such sentiments as his judgment approved, may at times have been too determined, and probably obstinate.

This tendency was increased by another, which was the weakest trait of his mind. He was habitually suspicious. Accustomed in the early period of his life to watch with a jealous eye, the actions and opinions of those who administered the government, to anticipate evil even for ostensible good, and to calculate on coming danger before even its shadow could be seen, he acquired an indisposition to give his confidence easily, readily or freely. This habit increased as he advanced in life, for "confidence is a plant of slow growth in an aged bosom." There was little of the art of acquiring popularity in entertaining such a state of mind; less in letting it be seen. They who were associated with him were often oppressed with a conviction that he was doubtful of their sincerity, and this feeling on their part generated a state of things which otherwise would not have existed. It is something anomalous in the history of character, that an individual punctiliously upright in his own conduct, should unwillingly admit the sincerity of others.

Mr. Gerry was an exemplary citizen in all the duties of private life. Adhering to the doctrines of the Episcopal church, he was serious without bigotry, and liberal enough to admit that although that sect was most satisfactory to himself, it was not entitled to arrogate superiority over others, into which the christian world was divided.

In his temper, he was naturally ardent and impetuous, but in the course of a most intimate acquaintance, and under excitements calculated to give full play to the passions, the writer never saw them break their boundary, or get the mastery of his mind.

Mr. Gerry was of middling stature and spare frame. A large broad head, high and prominent forehead, and a quick piercing and expressive eye, completed the outline of a striking physiognomy. Extremely temperate in all the indulgences of pleasure, he preserved a constitution, not originally robust, in a good degree of strength, so that to his latest day he never used a cane, and was able to read the smallest print without the aid of glasses.

The refined pleasures of intellectual life, the conversation of educated females, and the charms of polished society, were his most admired relaxation from the laborious and patient industry, which he was accustomed to devote to political duties; and in these circles of intelligence and taste, his own contribution to the general amusement, was readily bestowed and most highly appreciated. Belonging to that school of manners, which commenced under the royal government, and perfected its pupils in the camp and cabinet of the revolution, regulating the deportment with courtesy towards others, and a personal dignity that never lost its self-respect, lofty without arrogance, affable without familiarity, he was at all time and under all circumstances, entitled to the reputation of a perfect gentleman.

The retirement he enjoyed during the period under review, was varied by two incidents of a political character. In 1804, he was a member of the electoral college of Massachusetts, by the unexpected success of the republican party, and joined in the unanimous vote given by the electors of the state to Thomas Jefferson for president, and George Clinton for vice-president, of the United States. The venerable James Warren of Plymouth, long the correspondent and always the friend of Mr. Gerry, was president of this college, and in this act completed the public services of his valuable life.

The attack made in 1808 by the British ship Leopard on the American frigate Chesapeake, presented another occasion for his influence with his fellow citizens.

In order to give a full expression to the public feeling and to strengthen the administration in such measures of resistance as the exigency might demand, it was determined to hold a body meeting in Boston, as was the usage in the earlier periods of the colonial controversy.* The state-house was selected for this purpose, but the concourse of people soon filled the hall and the multitude collected on an open area at the north.

Upon the uppermost of the steps which led from the floor of the building, and exactly on the spot where now stands Chantry's magnificent statue of Washington, a table was placed for the moderator.

A gentleman announced that Elbridge Gerry was in town, and moved that " this patriot distinguished in the first movements of resistance to a haughty adversary" be invited to preside over

* Hutchinson, 3d vol. p. 430.

the present deliberations. The motion was carried by acclamation, and a committee appointed to conduct him to the chair.

Mr. Gerry then hardly recovered from a disease from which even fatal consequences had been apprehended, was at the house of a friend a short distance from the assembly, without having had any notice of the meeting, or the most distant idea of being called to preside. He readily accepted the invitation, and walked with the committee by the usual avenue to the gothic hall of the state-house. Nothing indicative of a convention was visible. Scarcely a solitary passenger crossed his path. As ignorant of the location assigned him, as the assembly was of his approach, he was conducted across the hall, when the folding doors were thrown open, and he found himself not only in the presence of several thousands of his fellow citizens, but in the place appointed for their moderator, and actually presiding in their councils.

Surprise could not be more complete either to him or them. Bowing in acknowledgment for the plaudits, which seemed to shake the very skies, and allowed him a moment to recover his self-possession, he addressed the assembly in the following animated sentence.

I had not anticipated that at my time of life, there could have been a scene like the present, but I yield to the call that is made on me, as I hold it to be the duty of every citizen, though he may have but one day to live, to devote that day to the good of his country.

This sentiment, indicative of the governing principle of his life, is the epitaph recorded on his monument, and was then reechoed by an approving multitude, who felt that the virtue of the revolution was resuscitated at a crisis, which called for a similar exercise of its energy and zeal.

CHAPTER X.

FROM this long period of repose, Mr. Gerry was unexpectedly awakened by a call on him again to become a candidate for the office of governour of the commonwealth of Massachusetts.

A nomination had usually been made during the sitting of the legislature, and the first suggestion of an intention of again presenting his name to the public, was communicated to him by a committee of gentlemen, who reported that he had been, with great unanimity, selected by the republican party. At the earnest solicitation of his political friends, but in his own language, " at the sacrifice of domestic and family interests, and with great personal inconvenience," he assented to the request.

A canvass now commenced, which exceeded in its violence whatever had before occurred of a

similar character. If in its progress the subject
of this memoir was assailed with every vituperative epithet, and presented to the public in the
most odious points of view, it does not diminish
the pain of the recollection, that his rival, the
then incumbent of the chair, was treated with
equal asperity.

Governour Gore had been elected the chief executive magistrate of the state, by the strength of
the federal party, and held his claim to their confidence and respect by a cordial cooperation in all
the essential measures of their policy. So far he
was the legitimate object of attack by those, who
differed from him in the principles of government,
and in their views of the political system ; but
there was an honesty of heart, a courtesy of manners, and a generosity of feeling in this distinguished civilian, which ought to have protected
him from the arrows of malevolence and slander.

The misty medium of party prejudice magnifies
the errors of public men, while it as often gives
them a factitious importance, which disappears
with the returning light of intelligence and reason.
Mr. Gore lived through the period of storm and
turbulence, and it has been said of him with equal
truth and elegance, that " his was a pure spirit,
high and looking upward. His taste was refined,
his sensibility acute, his feelings manly, generous,
independent. He had the most elevated ideas of

public and private duty, and his conduct was always in perfect conformity with his principles. In times of excitement he was calm and just; in times of corruption pure."

The election terminated in favour of Mr. Gerry, who entered on the duties of his office on the second day of June 1810.

It has been the misfortune of the United States that dissensions among their citizens, on the correct course of their own national policy, had such relation to their connexion with foreign powers, as to involve the separate parties in the imputation of attachments or antipathies wholly independent of any motive of patriotism. It was eminently so at this period. The conduct of the belligerents sacrificed to their own advantage the rights and interests of the United States whenever they presented obstacles to the great objects of their controversy, while the folly of a war with both at the same time, and the inconveniences and evils resulting from the necessary movements of diplomacy to prevent it, constantly gave fuel to the flames of that party zeal, which is the inseparable concomitant of liberty. From the period of Mr. Jefferson's election to the presidency, in March 1801, the government of the United States, in all its departments had been decidedly in the hands of the democratic party, and their strength had so rapidly and steadily increased, that the check, which opposition exerts on public measures, had

ceased to enforce its salutary restraint. The nearly
unanimous reelection of Mr. Jefferson in 1805,
and the triumphant majority, which in 1809 placed
Mr. Madison in the executive chair, had broken
down the federal party, which though still organized in the national legislature, and represented
by individuals of talent and character, was rather
calculated by its situation to irritate the dominant
party than control it.   In Massachusetts however,
the case was directly the reverse.   For nearly the
whole period, in which the people had divided
themselves into political parties, the government
had been in federal hands.   The restraints upon
commerce, which the national councils had deemed wise to impose, operated severely on a people
essentially commercial in their feelings, habits
and interest, and combined with other measures,
in which it was generally believed their advantage
was but little consulted, to array against the national government a very decided majority of the
citizens.   But the friends of the national administration had not been inactive.   Twice by the
election of governour Sullivan, they had succeeded
in acquiring power, which was wrested from them
almost as soon as possessed.   The time now
presented a favourable opportunity for another
effort, and the whole democratic party in the state
united in support of Mr. Gerry.   They were
opposed by the entire force of the federalists, who
clung to the government of this state as the chief

citadel of their strength ; and overthrown in the general and other local governments of the confederacy found it necessary to preserve here the last remnants of their power, until times more favourable to their views, should give them a wider field of operation. Their whole strength was accordingly exerted to prevent Mr. Gerry's election, and each party entered into the conflict with hearts of controversy. The parties thus engaged were too nearly matched, both in address and numbers, to have rendered it certain on which side the balance would incline, but a third party was found to take the field, and by their overpowering weight to settle the conflict.

This party consisted of the few but venerable survivors of the revolution, whose personal acquaintance had impressed on their minds the constant and important services of Mr. Gerry in the early days of danger and anxiety, together with a class of educated and ardent youth, who not having before mixed in political conflicts, brought with them those feelings and principles in favour of a patriot of the revolution, which the history of its times were well calculated to inspire. Mr. Gerry seemed to have been awakened from his long inactivity, and to come before the electoral population like the last of the Romans, the only one in the splendid assembly of revolutionary worthies whom the generation now enjoying the fruits of their labour, would, in the progress of events, be permitted to honour.

His rival Mr. Gore, had been too young to engage in the great struggle for independence.   His
friends remembered indeed, that when just leaving college, he had marched with a volunteer
corps to the defence of Rhode Island; but this
solitary instance of duty was almost ludicrous in
comparison with the long and splendid and eminent services of the associate of the patriots in
the congress of independence.   Attachment to
the principles and gratitude to the agents of the
revolution triumphed over the violence of political feeling, and the democratic party, assisted by
the fortunate selection of a candidate, were victorious at the polls.

It would have been well for them to have remembered in the exultation of success, the means
by which it was achieved, and to have moderated
their triumph by a regard to the insecure foundation on which it stood.

But the leaders of the party believed that the
state was revolutionized, and that their triumph
over their antagonists was the final overthrow of
the federal power in the last portion of its territory.   They were the more satisfied of this, because they had exactly divided the senate, and
had obtained in the house of representatives a
majority, which gave them the control of the
elections in joint ballot of the two houses.

The speech of the governour to the legislature,
the first measure of his administration was tem-

perate and conciliatory.   It inculcated the necessity of union.   In a review of the course pursued
by foreign powers, he justified the measures of
the national government, and exhorted the community to an union of effort in its support.   His
references to the revolution for illustration of the
several measures connected with state policy was
calculated to preserve the title, by which he acquired his situation, and to soften the asperity of
opposition.   In enumerating the advantages which
the country possessed, he said " When we reflect
that the United States are in possession of numerous blessings, political, civil and religious,
many of which are not enjoyed by any other nation, that we are remote from those scenes of
war and carnage, by which Europe is vested in
sable, that we enjoy the uncontrolled right on principles of true liberty, to form, alter and carry into
effect, our federal ands tate constitutions, that
founded on them and on law, there exists a spirit
of toleration, securing to every one the undisturb-
ed rights of conscience and the free exercise of
religion, that the people at fixed periods have the
choice of their rulers, and can remove those who
do wrong, that the means of education in all its
branches are liberal, general and successful, that
the national strength, resources and powers, by
proper arrangements may render these states invincible, that by our husbandry, commerce, manufactures, and mechanic arts, the wealth of this

country almost surpasses credibility, let us not be prompted by imprudent zealots of any description to hazard the irretrievable loss of all or of any of these inestimable blessings, but let us secure them forever, with the aid of divine providence, by rallying around the standard of our national government, and by encouraging and establishing a martial spirit on the solid foundation of internal peace, order and concord.

The answers of the two houses were respectful and affectionate, even beyond the common courtesy of the official style. The house of representatives say " to the course of your excellency's administration we look with pleasing anticipation. We consider the past conduct of public characters as the safest pledge of their future course. And with impressions of this nature we feel assured that under your guidance a spirit of harmony will pervade our councils, that the national government and sister states will receive the respect which is their due, and that the great interests of the commonwealth under the fostering care of the government will receive every assistance they may need, and every encouragement in our power to bestow."

The senate commenced their answer in the following language :

On the first meeting of the several branches of the government, the senate respectfully recognize in the person of the chief magistrate of Massa-

chusetts, the man who so eminently contributed
by his revolutionary services to establish the independence, and secure the peace and prosperity of
our country. The zeal and fidelity with which
these services were rendered, afford to us a pledge
that in discharging the duties of the high and honourable trust committed to you by a majority of
the people, your excellency will be uninfluenced
by the sinister suggestions of party spirit, but will
be guided by a sincere and single regard to the
great interests of the whole commonwealth.

This confidence is strengthened by the reflection, that during the conflict which for many years
has agitated almost every part of our community,
your excellency has been aloof from the scene of
contention, and we trust therefore has advanced
to the chair of government, unbiassed by those
passions and prejudices, which are in some degree
common to all who have been actively engaged in
the warfare of public opinion.

The suggestions here made were most perfectly true. With the directors of political parties the
long retirement of Mr. Gerry had given him no
opportunity to be intimate. The changes, which
time had made in the members of the different
departments of the government had left him almost without personal acquaintance with them,
and the desire, which his party had to place his
name as a candidate at their head, had itself, if
there had been no other reason, rendered his ad-

vance to the chief magistracy wholly independent
of all conditions, stipulations and expectancies.
In his own political sentiments, matured as they
were by time and experience, he was immovably
confirmed ; but in regard to individuals or parties,
other than as they came recommended by character and conduct, he was impartial, unfettered
and independent.

But after all, what is the worth of a victory if
the enemy are allowed to possess the spoils.
Of what consequence is it who are masters of the
field so long as the vanquished retain their pos-
sessions ? The battle between the great political
parties had been fought at the ballot boxes again
and again, and constant defeat had embittered and
exasperated the disappointed competitors. They
beheld for a long series of years the honours and
emoluments of office, the pride of place and dignity of station, held by their political adversaries
until the reproach of being a democrat was considered as impassable a barrier to public station, as
the want of moral character or intellectual ability.
The moment of their triumph was therefore a fit
time for retaliation, and the victory they at last
had won was to be consummated by its honours and
rewards. This determination, which was in some
respect the language of excited feeling and the
expression of natural passion, derived no little
support from the principles of justice.

The limited legislation of the states gives rise

to few questions of high character. The general policy of all parties is in most respects the same in time of peace. Changes in administration are marked rather by changing individuals who manage affairs, than by any great variation in the affairs that are managed. The party who now came into power, found all the posts of honour and profit in possession of their enemies, and this possession so confirmed by time and arrangement, as to be apparently the result of premeditated purpose.

The judicial department, the most stable and the most efficient in its operation, was from the chief justiceship to the crier of the court, wholly in federal hands. As a consequence of this, the bar, with hardly sufficient exception to be noticed, added all the force of professional character to the federal cause. The literature of the state, so far as it had official form, was under the same control. Colleges and learned societies seemed to have settled a sort of common law, that the honours of science would be as inappropriately bestowed upon democracy as the chef d'ouvres of taste upon the aborigines of the country. In its connexion with the national government, the state had always been represented by the same political class, their members in the United States senate having been invariably selected from the federal party. It had been the policy of the federalists to inspire the opinion, and it was their belief probably, for self-love is exceedingly credulous of praise, that in their ranks were contained all the talents and all the learning, and all the moral character of the country, and as the Romans looked upon the rest of mankind as barbarians, so they were pleased to consider their fellow citizens on the democratic side, as little better than the Goths and Vandals, into whose power had unfortunately fallen the heritage of the state.

The long period of submission to this contemptuous demeanour, which the democrats had been forced to endure, had not diminished those indignant feelings, which are excited in the minds of honourable men by injustice and insult, and it prepared them to take advantage of their success, without much regard to those considerations of prudence, which were calculated to preserve it.

The legislature set the example. Every appointment in their gift was bestowed on the individuals of their party, and strong intimations were given that the governour would be expected to follow the same path.

The equality of votes in the senate would have prevented the passing, and it consequently restrained the proposing of such laws as would change adversely to the federal interests any of the existing establishments, and the legislature after a short session adjourned to meet again in January.

The character of the governour, which was brought more distinctly into view, rose very much in the estimation of the public. There was an adherence to principle, which secured the attachment of his political friends, and an urbanity and liberality of manners, which disarmed his opponents.

The charge of pride and reserve, which had been made against him, was seen to be altogether fallacious. Accessible and familiar, the citizens found him ready to listen to their suggestions, and his house, always the abode of hospitality, was filled either by strangers whom his liberality attracted, or by constituents who felt gratified in having opportunity to make known their individual opinions to the governour of the commonwealth.

At the commencement in August, Harvard University conferred upon him the degree of doctor of laws, the honor of which, if in ordinary cases diminished by the prodigality of its bestowment on a certain political class, lost none of its original value, whatever that might be, when the leaders of a sect saw fit to make an unusual exception to the partiality of their favours.

In the November succeeding, the governour, as the head of the board of overseers, assisted at the splendid induction of the reverend John Thornton Kirkland, to be president of the college, and delivered an address in the latin language, in conformity to established usage on such occasions. The reply of the president was couched in flattering terms of respect; and the occasion, the place, and the speaker, would prevent them from being considered merely complimentary and insincere.*

The winter session of the legislature was marked by the same conciliatory spirit on the part of the governour, while the want of a majority in the senate still controlled the fiery temper of his party. In the nominations to office, the governour respected the claims of his political friends whom he found to have been heretofore almost entirely excluded, but of the incumbents holding their place at the will of the executive, no one was disturbed in the enjoyment of his situation. Strong effort was made by influential individuals to change the governour's policy in this respect, and there were not wanting those who expressed their dissatisfaction at the tolerance he was disposed to observe. But their disapprobation was without effect. He had proposed as the object of his policy to bring about a conciliation of temper between the people of the state and the national administration, and it seemed to him most likely to be effected by softening that asperity of feeling, which had separated the contending factions, and at times had threatened violence and almost civil war. The republican party, he was accustomed to say, by holding the government of the state, are restored to their rank as free citizens. They are no longer degraded or

* Appendix A.

proscribed. It is best for them not to incur reproach for the same conduct which has disgraced
their opponents. As they profess a liberality of
opinion, let them practise a liberality of conduct.

Causes for the change of this course were not
long delayed. Notwithstanding the courtesy and
kindness, which in outward forms of official intercourse were extended towards him, the mortification of a defeated party at the elevation of their
opponents, and the determination they had formed,
be his conduct what it would, to displace him from
the executive chair, was constantly observed, and
had its natural operation on those by whom he
was supported.

If the governour had supposed that conciliation
and liberal policy on the part of the executive
would so far repress the angry feelings of the opposition, that the republican party could keep the
government in their hands, and thus aid the general administration by a conformity to the policy
of the United States, he had not sufficiently calculated the depth and strength of that resistance,
which his opponents could exert. The tendency
of the measures of the United States, to bring
on a war with Great Britain, and the consequence
of such war to draw closer an alliance with the
ruler of France, allowing to each party in the
country, all the honesty of intention they could
claim, was in itself sufficient to have prevented
the success of a scheme desirable indeed, but

under the then existing circumstances perfectly hopeless. But when it was considered how small was the difference in the ballots cast by the two rival parties, that the annual accession by natural increase was enough to change the majority, and especially that the intimate connexion between the policy of the national and the popularity of the state administration would give hope of success to a party not in mass accustomed to defeat, the expectation of a decrease of the energies of an election campaign was hardly to be justified.

Every effort was accordingly made by the opposing parties to secure success at the election in April. The same candidates were presented by each party, and Mr. Gerry was after a hard struggle again elected governour of the commonwealth. The democratic party had made very strenuous efforts to gain the ascendency in the senate, and securing all they had acquired in the former year, and prevailing also in the county of Bristol, they had now the complete possession of all the executive and legislative departments in the state.*

* *Extract of a letter from a distinguished citizen of the United States, dated at St. Petersburg,* 30*th June* 1811.

"The Massachusetts election appears to agitate the Americans in Europe almost exclusively; of all the other elections going on at the same time in many parts of the union, I see paragraphs in the newspapers, but hear not a syllable from any other quarter. But American federalists in this city have received letters from their friends in London and in Gottenburg, in high exultation announcing the election of Mr. Gore by a majority of more than three thousand votes. Other Americans of different politics contest the validity of this return, and affirm that Mr. Gerry and

During the canvass preceding the election, the
federal party in the capital, at one of those meet-

Mr. Gray have been reelected, though by a reduced majority
compared with that of the last year.   Why this extreme anxiety
for the *Massachusetts* election?   Is it Mr. *Gore* for whose elevation all this enthusiasm is harboured?   I think it by no means
difficult to account for.   There is much foreign hope and fear
involved in these Massachusetts elections ; all the rest, even New
York are despaired of.   But the Massachusetts federal politi-
cians have got to talk so openly and with such seeming indifference, not to say readiness for a dissolution of the union; they
are so valiant in their threats of resistance to the laws ; they
seem so resolute for a little experiment upon the *energy* of the
union and its government, that in the prospects of a war with
America, which most of the British statesmen now at the helm
consider as in the line of wise policy, they and all their partizans calculate boldly and without disguise or concealment upon
the cooperation of the Massachusetts federalists.   The Massachusetts election therefore, is a touchstone of national principle,
and upon its issue may depend the question of peace and war
between the United States and England.   However hostile a
British ministry may feel against us, they will never venture
upon it until they can depend upon an active cooperation with
them, within the United States.   It is from the New England
federalists alone that they can expect it.   From the same view
of the subject, though prompted by very opposite feelings, I too
take a deep interest in the Massachusetts elections.   I have
known now more than seven years the projects of the Boston
faction against the union.   They have ever since that time at
least, been seeking a pretext and an occasion for avowing the
principle.   The people however, have never been ready to go
with them; and when in the embargo time they did for a moment get a majority with them, they only verified the old proverb
about setting a beggar on horse-back.   Mr. Quincy has been at
the pains now of furnishing them with a new pretext, which will
wear no better than its predecessors.   Mr. Quincy should not
have quoted me as an authority for a dissolution of the union.
He may be assured it is a doctrine that never will have my sanc-

ings peculiar to New England, in which the electors are accustomed to assemble for political
discussion, adopted resolutions of an inflammatory
character, and supported them by the premeditated
speeches of their most able men, among whom
the president of the senate was principally distinguished for his zeal.

The preamble to these celebrated resolutions
affected to draw a parallel between the oppression of the government of the union and that of
Great Britain before the declaration of independence ; and it intimated very plainly that the
course, which the fathers of the revolution pursued, though then termed rebellion, was a just
precedent for existing circumstances.   The resolutions themselves proceeded to declare that the
first flagrant violation of our neutral rights was
inflicted by the Berlin decree, in November 1806.
That the late offers or pretended proposals of
France to relax her decrees, were illusory and in-

tion. It is my attachment to the union, which makes me spe-
cially anxious for the result of the Massachusetts elections.
They are a contest of life and death for the union. If that
party are not ultimately put down in Massachusetts, as completely as they already are in New York and Pennsylvania, and
all the southern and western states, the union is gone. Instead
of a nation coextensive with the North American continent,
destined by God and Nature to be the most populous and most
powerful people, ever combined under one social compact, we
shall have an endless multitude of little insignificant clans and
tribes, at eternal war with one another, for a rock or a fish-pond,
the sport and fable of European masters and oppressors.

sulting. That neither reason, justice, policy, or law could justify either the president or congress in changing our relative connexion with the belligerents ; and they lastly resolved, " that such an unjust, oppressive, and tyrannical act they consider the statute passed by congress on 2d March inst. tending to the ruin or impoverishment of some of the most industrious and meritorious citizens of the United States, and that the only means short of an appeal to force, (which heaven avert) is the election of such men to the various offices in the state government as will oppose by peaceable but firm measures the execution of laws, which if persisted in must and will be resisted."

A contemporary journal, in the cause of the party, describing the scene at Faneuil Hall, where these resolutions were proposed, and giving a summary of the speeches, by which they were enforced, remarks, " The inferences from these discussions are that the men who now rule are corrupt and impotent ; that they are humbly submissive and obedient to France ; that they are inveterately hostile to Great Britain ; that they entertain a fixed contempt and detestation of commerce ; that they would sooner plunge this country into war with England and alliance with France, and consequently subject it to French dominion, than let the federal republicans again come into power, and expose the weak and wicked measures of the Jefferson policy.*

* Boston Centinel, 3d April 1811.

The declaration of this assembly, which might fairly be considered as speaking for the whole party, that a law of congress, if persisted in would be resisted, and the threat that if opposition by peaceable measures was unavailing, force—"which heaven avert"—would be resorted to, must seem to the calm reflection of more quiet times to approach too nearly to an act of rebellion. It seemed so to the governour, and he presented this assembly, the resolutions, which they passed, and very distinctly the individuals who were busy in their enactment, to the general court, in the address which he made to both houses at the opening of the session in the following June. After commenting on the preamble and resolutions, and exposing what he considered the erroneous positions and incorrect reasoning of the assembly, he remarked, " If our national rulers are justly charged as is stated by this assemblage, with having passed a tyrannical act, and laws that must and will be resisted, they have rebelled against the sovereignty of the people, are subject to punishment, and have forfeited forever a claim to public confidence ; but if the charge is unfounded, if they have conducted agreeably to our national charter, (which is manifestly the general sense of the nation) have not those who have denounced the government of the United States as oppressive, tyrannical and unjust, and who have declared an intention to resist the execution of their laws, unwarrantably adopted measures tending to excite a spirit of insurrection and rebellion, and to destroy our internal peace and tranquillity ?"

*   *   *   *   *

" To diminish and exterminate if possible a party spirit, the executive of this commonwealth, during the last year confirmed in his place or re-appointed when requisite every state officer under its control, who had been correct in his conduct and faithful to his trust, disregarding his politics and requiring only his support of the federal and state constitutions, governments and laws, with a due regard to the rights of officers and individuals subject to his official discretion. But it cannot be expected of any executive so far to disregard the sacred obligations of duty and honour, as to pre-serve in official situations such individuals as would abuse the influence of their public charac-ters by sanctioning resistance to law, or by such other conduct as would beguile peaceable and happy citizens into a state of civil warfare."

This bold and fearless denunciation of the lead-ers of the federal party ; the imputation which it threw upon their motives ; the criminality, which it charged upon their conduct ; and the interdict, which it placed upon their claims to public office, broke all connexion between the governour and that great class of citizens, who were in the politi-cal minority of the state.

A statesman who had more considered the

policy of public measures than their propriety, or regarded either his personal convenience or popularity, would have hesitated before throwing the gauntlet in defiance, among such numerous and powerful foes. An individual more conversant than the governour had been with the measures of the contending parties, and who had seen how harmless was the effervescence of that spirit, which subsided as suddenly as it rose, or how boldly and with how little meaning men were accustomed to use big words and formidable expressions; one more intimate than he had been with the machinery of elections, where it was necessary to excite a zeal, which would bring voters to the polls, might have been sensible that much less was meant than met the ear, or that at any rate error might be safely tolerated where truth was free to combat it, and that the whole of such magnificent tirade meant no more than to keep the party together, by persuading the followers of the party that there was something worth at least the exertion of an hour at the ballot box.

Intimations of this kind were made to the governour by some friends, to whom his speech was read before it was delivered to the legislature, and their opinion enforced by the fact that the two months, which had intervened, disclosed none of that awful hostility in action which this gasconade would imply. But the governour formed a different opinion of the character of the act.

He considered, however ineffectual at home, that it would be magnified and misunderstood abroad, and that in the negotiations with the belligerents, little effect could be produced if in the very bosom of the American people, rebellion had commenced, and revolution been solemnly proposed.

The reproof of the governour was not however confined to the political assembly in the capital. The clergy came in for a share, exceedingly well merited by any of them who perverted the religion of peace into a vehicle for the gratification of unhallowed passion, and disturbed the solemnities of the sabbath, by irreverent allusions to the political altercations of the week.

Most of the Congregational clergy in Massachusetts belonged to the federal party, and made it as much matter of conscience to avow their political as their theological tenets.　Nothing served more to embitter the condition of society, and as no ostensible remedy presented, nothing was more irritating and offensive than a constant exposure to this unhallowed conduct, which frequently mingled imprecation with prayer, and converted the temple of religion into a theatre of politics.　The right of a clergyman as a citizen to hold his own free opinions, and his duty to continue a patriot as well as christian, never was controverted by the republican party, but the propriety of his indulging himself in the opportunity, which his situation gave him, to wound the feelings by denouncing the motives, and censuring the conduct of any of his parishioners on matters of public concern, was denied by them to be either right in principle or decorous in practice. As part of a system to degrade the individuals of the democratic party, it was extensively pursued. To clerical influence thus improperly, and for the profession dangerously exerted, the federalists had been for a long period greatly indebted, and individuals in the sacred desk, marked by the honours of Harvard, were as distinguished for their zeal in the secular concerns of the state, as for their labours in the kingdom of their spiritual master. Seceders in escaping from such unchristian assaults to attend the teaching of more serious guides, were by the law as it stood, frequently subjected to a double tax, and the inconvenience was so seriously felt, as to become a subject of very general concern. The governour thus noticed the matter in his speech :

" It is a happy circumstance, and does great honour to our clergy, that there exists among them a general spirit of religious liberality and tolerance. They advance in the straight road of piety, which is always strewed with flowers. Should any wander into the devious path of party politics, the injury will not extend beyond themselves, and they will soon retreat from the lacerations of briars and thorns which will meet them at every step. A late solemn decision of our supreme judicial court has limited the right of protestant teachers of piety, religion and morality, to demand the taxes paid by their respective hearers for the support of public worship to those of incorporated societies, and has produced a great excitement; this may render indispensable an attention to the subject, and further provisions to encourage by every possible mean the liberty of conscience in relation to religious opinion and worship."

The temper of the governour's speech met exactly that of the two branches of the legislature. Answers were returned from the senate and house in accordance with its language and measures taken to secure by legislative means, the policy and power of the party, which at present controlled the commonwealth.

At the summer and succeeding winter session of the legislature, various statutes were enacted, and by the governour appointments were in the mean time conferred, which as they kept up through the year the highest excitement of party, cannot be passed here without notice. If flushed with victory, the dominant power exceeded the measures of prudence, or stung by indignities of long duration, they seized on the first moment of authority to recover from humiliation and enthralment, and proceeded too fiercely and too rapidly in their innovations, or imitated too exactly in their own favour the errors, which they complained of on the other side, the consequences may be a lesson of forbearance, and moderate the zeal of all future parties, as well in their rage for reformation as by inculcating feelings of respect for the minority opposed to them.

Of measures of a permanent character, the "act respecting public worship and religious freedom," deserves first to be mentioned, as the greatest alteration of the then existing laws, as complying with the recommendation of the governour to extend and secure liberty of conscience, as the overthrow of ecclesiastical domination, and as continuing to increase in the estimation of the community until, as at present, it is the most popular enactment in the statute book.

It provided that all moneys paid by any citizen of this commonwealth to the support of public worship or of public teachers of religion, shall if such citizen require it, be uniformly applied to the support of the public teacher of his own religious sect or denomination, provided there be any on whose instruction he usually attends. A further section provided for the citizens leaving one society and joining another, and thereby being exempted from taxation for the support of the one he had left.

That a law of such immense consequence should have then for the first time found the support of the government, is evidence of the attachment with which men cling to ancient abuses if they conduce to the advancement of political interests.

The extension of the right of suffrage as wide-
ly as the constitution permitted, was secured by a
law for that purpose.

With the avowed purpose of equalising the pecuniary facilities of the community, the entire
banking capital, strange as it may seem, having
hitherto been exclusively under federal control,
a charter was granted for the incorporation of a
state bank with a capital of three millions of dollars, the stock of which, upon a principle of reci-
procity, was secured to the friends of the party in
power.

To restore as far as possible the confidence of
the community in the administration of justice,
and to give some weight to the personal influence
of the republican party, which for many years past
had been systematically excluded from the bench,
the court of common pleas was abolished and a
circuit court established, consisting of five circuits,
with a chief justice and two puisne judges in
each. With the same view the law of 1809,
which had abolished the ancient court of sessions
was repealed, and a new law enacted, reviving the
court and directing a chief justice, and not less
than two nor more than four associate justices, to
be appointed. With the supreme judicial court
the party did not interfere. In respect for the
authority of the constitution, this forbearance was
observed ; it having been conceded, after due deliberation, by men having the confidence of the

dominant party, that neither the court nor the judges were within the power of the legislature. The result was very reluctantly acceded to, for the imposing influence of that court had been felt in the political agitation of the times, and some of its judges, like some ministers of the gospel, had been unwise enough to give to the extension of their political feelings the aid directly derived from their official authority.

Harvard college, which had very long been a powerful opponent to the republican party; which by making literary men federalists had made federalism popular, and with offensive aristocracy of manners had educated the youth under its care in the admiration of similar principles, did not escape the reforming hand of men, who considered that institution as the property of the state, and were unwilling that the state's pensioners should undermine the mansion in which they were domiciled.

So long had the federal party been in the habit of controlling the judicial, literary and religious institutions in the commonwealth, and so completely and habitually had all of them by long usage conformed to the views and sentiments of the federal party, that the principles and manner by which these institutions were conducted, seemed less the direction of that party than the natural and legitimate mode of their existence, and any alteration was therefore proclaimed to be not an alteration of a party system, but an overthrow of the institutions themselves. The federal party had been so long masters in the state, that it seemed to them quite natural they should be. Their intolerance and exclusiveness was so habitual as almost to be unknown to themselves, and they were as much astonished and alarmed at these innovations, as the West India planters would be at an insurrection of their slaves, or a claim by that class of the population, so to alter the laws of the land as to entitle them to participate in the rights of freemen.

These acts were therefore opposed in and out of the legislature, and an outcry set up that the days of the Visi-Goths had returned, and that a modern Alaric was about to scatter desolation and ruin.

Had the dominant party limited their operations to these measures of public policy and just retaliation, it is possible they might have been defended with success, but there were spirits among them too ardent to be checked by mere calculations of prudence, and too desirous of the trophies of victory to be satisfied with less than the field.

It was therefore further enacted that the clerks of all the judicial courts who had hitherto been appointed by the supreme court, should cease to hold their place, and that successors should be appointed by the governour with consent of council. The offices of sheriffs were declared vacant, and an appointment for four years unless sooner dismissed by the executive, was enjoined on the governour.

Nothing could be more unfortunate for a party situated as was the republican, than the condition in which these appointments placed it. The patronage of office, even if it be allowed to operate silently and quietly, is at best but of doubtful advantage ; for as the number of applicants always greatly exceed the situations to be filled, there are produced ten angry opponents for one lukewarm or ungrateful friend. Under existing circumstances, policy required the removals and appointments to be made without delay, that the effects of the convulsion might be sooner over, and not, by protracting anxiety and interest, continually keep alive the passions of the community. But this decisive and prompt movement was impossible. In the first place, the laws in some respects were not easily to be executed. In the second place, they would produce scenes of private misery, at which the governour relucted, and finally refused to inflict. Again his personal acquaintance with the influential men out of the capital, and especially in the eastern part of the commonwealth, was exceedingly limited, and the contradictory accounts given by the friends of numerous competitors, perplexing and unsatisfactory. Time therefore was allowed to those, who expected to be removed from lucrative situations, to exert with redoubled zeal their spirit of natural hostility, while the counteracting influence of place and power, which the party intended to wield, was not yet within their reach. The nonexecution of the law in some cases gave offence, the manner of its being executed was in others cause of complaint, so that probably a measure, or rather series of measures, contrived to establish by official influence the power of the party, and denounced and believed by its opponents to be conceived in a spirit of indiscriminate proscription, failed to conciliate the approbation of its friends.

Notwithstanding the general overthrow of the incumbents of office, a liberality was observed in appointments in the judicial department which had not before nor since been observed. On every circuit one federalist and two democrats were put on the bench. The solicitor general of the state, the clerks of the judicial courts in Suffolk and Middlesex, and the sheriff of Suffolk, were permitted to hold their places; offices whose aggregate value and consequence, was nearly equal to all that were displaced.*

If it was wise to have put nearly the whole appointments to office into the hands of the executive, the measure should have been executed with an unsparing and steady hand. If either from the consideration of the executive or the situation of the incumbents, it was impossible to carry such laws into immediate operation, it was unwise and

* Appendix B.

impolitic to have passed them. To seek power incurs odium. It is a fault therefore to acquire what it is impracticable to use.

It was hardly possible that a general removal could be made with satisfaction to the friends of the party who proposed it. There were attachments, connexions and interests, which made it not in all cases an agreeable task. Individual feeling and general interest were not always to be reconciled. In the arrangement the governour did not escape censure, but there were intelligent and candid men willing to bestow praise. A letter from a gentleman then of high consideration in the ranks of the party, and now eminently before the nation, contains the following paragraphs.

" I thank you very sincerely for your kind congratulations on my recent appointment, [by the government of the United States.] As to the appointment of sheriff, I cannot but express my thanks for the kind attention you have paid to the feelings and wishes of Mr. B's friends. His removal has been made as little painful to them as it could be, and I have no doubt the measure was the result of a careful deliberation, and a wish to promote the public good.   *   *   *

" I thought it right to state thus much to your excellency, that you might perceive that though my voice was decidedly for Mr. B. yet I was ready to acknowledge and to feel the strong motives, which induced a new appointment, and to believe them the dictates of sound deliberation.

" I beg leave to express my sincere acknowledgments for the personal favours, which your
excellency has been pleased to bestow on me, and
to assure you that I shall carry into my new situation the deepest sense of my obligations to your
friendship and patronage.

" Wishing you the enjoyment of domestic and
public happiness, a reward justly earned by a long
life, faithfully devoted to the public service, I beg
to subscribe myself, with great consideration," &c.

The dominant party made a much more fatal
mistake in a law for dividing the commonwealth
into districts for the choice of counsellors and
senators.

The constitution provided that " the senate of
the state should consist of forty members, chosen
by the inhabitants of the districts into which the
commonwealth may from time to time be divided
by the general court for that purpose," and in as-
signing numbers to be elected by the respective
districts, " regard should be had to the proportion
of the public taxes paid in said districts."

The right of the legislature to divide the state
into districts, provided the proportion between the
number of senators and the amount of tax was
properly observed, seems not to be doubtful. The
propriety of an alteration of the existing districts
was therefore a question of policy. In the new
arrangement, such contiguous towns were classed

together as ensured to the democratic party a small majority in most of the districts, and gave a large majority to the federalists in the others so that with an equal number of voters on each side throughout the state, the former party would, according to the votes of the two last previous elections be sure of a majority of senators. By increasing the number of their districts, it became obvious that they lessened their majority of voters in each of them, and although such an arrangement increased the number of their senators, it did no more than give them a majority, which even by parting with some they would still have retained. It was obvious too, that if there was only a small majority of voters in a district, the result of an election was exposed to hazard from the change of opinion even of a few individuals, and the consequence therefore was unnecessarily precarious.

But besides this, the new districts were arranged by breaking up counties, which had formed, as far as was possible, the ancient limits of senatorial districts, or by joining several counties together. They thus destroyed old associations and threw the electors into new combinations and connexions, in which local and territorial interests were confounded.

In all these respects the law was injudicious, but there was a stronger objection to it in the obvious motive to retain power in the hands of a party even against the will of the people. There was

an apparent management, too plain not to be perceived, and which being seen, was universally
reprobated.

It is true this was not the first instance of the
kind in state legislation. The districts for the
election of members of congress had always been
arranged by the federal party, as far as could be
done, with the same object and on the same system. But while the geographical line of counties was necessarily passed for those elections,
the intention, if in truth as certain, was less easily
brought home and fastened on its authors. In the
present instance it was too apparent to be denied,
and the design and management were instantly
reprobated by the opposition, as fiercely as if they
had themselves always been innocent of a similar
transgression.

To the governour the project of this law was
exceedingly disagreeable. He urged to his friends
strong arguments against its policy as well as its
effects. After it had passed both houses, he hesitated to give it his signature, and meditated to
return it to the legislature with his objections
to its becoming a law, but being satisfied that it
conformed to the constitution, he doubted whether
against precedents to the contrary, the private
opinion of a governour on a mere question of propriety or policy, would justify the interposition of
his negative, and he accordingly permitted it to
pass. Notwithstanding his hostility to the project

and his repugnance to its passage, the opposition had the address to have him in the public mind considered the author of the plan, and to affix to it a variation of his name to encourage the belief that it was his own individual invention.

The public feeling was by all these measures, by the ardour which on one side supported, and the violence which on the other assailed them, excited to a high and almost insupportable tone. It displayed itself in newspaper publications of a character the most pungent and severe. The speech of the governour to the legislature in June was followed by a series of essays under the signature of the Boston Rebel, in which all the usual forms of respect to a chief magistrate were violated; and his proclamation for thanksgiving published in October discussed in a similar series under the signature of a real christian, and old fashioned whig, which surpassed in intemperance of expression whatever before had been considered the limits of political severity. These and others of a like character were written with great force of talent and ingenuity, and being very extensively circulated, were calculated to produce powerful effects. Retorts were not wanting from the side of the administration, and a threatening letter having been anonymously sent to the governour, he thought fit to issue a proclamation for the detection of the author, in which he says, " such an attempt is an effort to pros-

trate at the feet of debased and slanderous printers, and of their more criminal employers, the
indispensable administration of justice; * * * *
to complete the triumph of calumny, falsehood,
injustice and malignant passions, crimes which by
means of incendiary writers and printers in this
state, have obtained an ascendency unparalleled
in any other; which have been principally directed
against the legislative and executive public functionaries of the national and state governments,
with a manifest intention to overthrow both, and
which also have been employed to destroy private
character, the inestimable property of both sexes."

The extraordinary latitude assumed by writers
in the public journals, in their commentaries on
the conduct and motives of the public agents, and
the recrimination to which it led, together with
some other circumstances connected with the
licentiousness of the press, naturally drew the
attention of the community to the power of the
law over this delicate subject, and the protection,
which the citizen might enjoy against calumny, as
well as the claim he had to receive intelligence
and information on matters interesting and important.

At the opening of the supreme court in Boston
in November, the learned judge, who presided,
deemed it useful to place the matter distinctly before the grand jury. With the principles, which
he stated to be law, no objection can be found.

The doctrine of libel was perfectly well defined; yet nevertheless, by the public generally, the charge was believed to imply the lawfulness of that kind of attack, which had been made on the functionaries of the government, and to secure from punishment, by the exceptions and limitations, which it disclosed, all or nearly all the authors and printers of the several pieces, which had attracted the particular observation of the community. The charge of the judge was published in the newspapers. If in the execution of his high trust a judicial officer correctly propounds the provisions of law, he is not responsible, most certainly, for the erroneous construction, which may be given to his opinions, or the wrong application which may be made of them. But if the existing law on any subject be unjust or unwise, it becomes the duty of the supreme executive magistrate to communicate his view of it to the legislature, to the end that it may be reformed by their authority. It is not however to be doubted that the high officers of government, keeping strictly in the path of their legitimate authority, may yet countenance opinions or measures, the direct agency of which they would deem it imprudent to assume; and that while the judges of the land were separated like the ancient Levites to a special service and a consecrated duty, it was not always possible for them to forget that politics as well as learning had been their qualification of admission to the temple of justice. The time had been, as already narrated, when the expression of a partizan temper was indulged with impunity. It was not now entirely safe, but the indirect influence of the judicial character was still powerful, and the individuals who wore the ermine knew they continued to be citizens, and felt themselves obliged to be federalists.

The governour was aware of the impression, which the charge of the judge was calculated to produce. It caused a correspondence between them, which is sufficiently original and amusing to be introduced here. There was a strong reluctance in the republican party to do any thing, which the constitution would not authorize in regard to the judicial institutions of the state ; but it is not questionable that they would gladly have taken advantage of any fair opportunity, to have placed a representative of their own sentiments and feelings on the bench of a tribunal, which deciding in the last resort on life, liberty, property and character, had for all the period of party passion been exclusively in the possession of the opposite political class.

MR. SECRETARY HOMANS TO JUDGE PARKER.

COUNCIL CHAMBER, JANUARY 7, 1812.

SIR,

His excellency governour Gerry directs me to present his compliments to you, with a request to be informed, whether the publication in the Boston newspapers or either of them, is a correct statement or copy of your charge to the grand jury of Suffolk on the subject of libels, and if so the governour requests you will be pleased to inform him.

I have the honour to be, &c. &c.

BENJAMIN HOMANS, *Secretary.*

———

JUDGE PARKER TO MR. SECRETARY HOMANS.

WEDNESDAY MORNING.

SIR,

I received your communication too late last evening to return an answer, being absent when it was left at my house.

I now request you to inform his excellency that not having the manuscript, from which my charge was read to the grand jury, in my possession, and not having read it in the newspapers, it is impossible for me to say whether it has been correctly printed or not. If however his excellency shall inform me that he deems it necessary in his administration of the executive department of government, to know with precision what has been done by me on the subject alluded to, in my administration of the judiciary department, I will as soon as the great mass of business with which I am pressed will permit, recover the manuscript, and transmit his excellency a fair copy of it.

Your obedient servant,

ISAAC PARKER.

B. Homans, Esqr.

GOVERNOUR GERRY TO JUDGE PARKER.

COUNCIL CHAMBER, FEBRUARY 8, 1812.

SIR,

Having been pressed by public measures on the 7th of January last, I desired Mr. Secretary Homans to request of you information in regard to the correctness of the publication of your charge to the grand jury of Suffolk, on the subject of libels ; and the next day he sent to me your answer, stating that you was also pressed by a great mass of business, and that, as soon as this will permit, you will inform me with precision, what has been done by you on the subject alluded to, in your administration of the judiciary department, if I deem it officially necessary. This I do ; but have waited to the present time, desirous of avoiding every measure that may have embarrassed or incommoded you amidst your important public concerns. Being informed that your session will probably close this day, I wish in the advanced state of the present session of the legislature for the earliest information mentioned in your letter, except the bills of indictments of which I have certified copies.

I have the honour to be, sir,
With great respect,
Your obedient servant,
E. GERRY.

The Hon. Isaac Parker,
A Judge of the Supreme Judicial Court.

JUDGE PARKER TO GOVERNOUR GERRY.

BOSTON, FEBRUARY 10, 1812.

MAY IT PLEASE YOUR EXCELLENCY :

I had the honour to receive your excellency's letter of the 8th instant, while on the bench in the discharge of my judicial functions, and perplexed with the multitude and variety of concerns which usually crowd upon a court towards the close of its session.

Having since the rising of the court, reperused your excellency's letter, together with those which by your excellency's order have been sent to me by the secretary of the commonwealth in the course of my arduous official engagements, I

now deem it to be a duty which I owe to the
public, to your excellency and to myself, to express with frankness the sentiments they have
occasioned, and to state the principles by which
I as a member of an independent branch of the
government, believe that I ought to be governed.

I need not point out to your excellency that
article in the declaration of rights prefixed to our
constitution, which was intended to establish a
complete and entire separation of the executive,
legislative and judicial powers of government,
nor need I advise your excellency of the importance of such a principle to the well being, if not
to the existence of a free government. I do not
apprehend your excellency has intended, in the exercise of the executive functions, to interfere with
those of the judiciary, nevertheless as it would be
your excellency's duty to resist even an unintentional encroachment by either of the other branches
of government upon the powers committed to you
by the constitution; so it is my duty to resist any
such encroachment, although the act which constitutes it, may not in the apprehension of your
excellency have the character which seems to me
to belong to it.

When I received from the secretary of the commonwealth his letter, written by your excellency's
directions, on the 7th of January last, requesting
to be informed whether a certain publication in
the newspapers was a correct copy of my charge

to the grand jury on the subject of libels, I
should have supposed it to have had for its object
the satisfaction of your excellency's mind upon
that point in your private capacity, had not the
supposition been forbidden by the formal manner
of the request, and the important public character
of the officer made use of to transmit it.

Being obliged therefore to consider it a public
proceeding, and not having before known an instance in which a judge had been called upon
when in the midst of his official labours, by the
chief executive magistrate, to avow or disavow
any proceeding attributed to him, and being left
to conjecture the motive which suggested the call,
your excellency will readily conceive that I had
reason to apprehend that some important public
measure was intended by your excellency to be
predicated upon the fact when ascertained, of the
genuineness of the publication.

The legislature being then about to commence
its session, the least important view in which I
could personally consider the subject, was that
your excellency intended to make my charge to
the grand jury the basis of some part of your
communication to that body, but on reflecting,
that if there was any thing in the doctrine advanced by me, which ought to excite the attention
of the legislature, every member of either branch
had the same means of seeing what had been
attributed to me, which your excellency had

possessed, and also, upon reflecting that whatever was stated by me to the grand jury to be the law upon the subject of libels, which differed from the generally known and received doctrine of the common law, was to be found in an opinion of the whole court, as declared by the chief justice in the case of the Commonwealth against William Clapp, since published in the authorized reports of judicial decisions, I was led to believe that a supposed amendment of the law was not the object for which your excellency required of me an acknowledgment of the charge, but that some object of a personal nature towards me was in your excellency's contemplation. It was for this reason, that in answer to your request I stated, that if your excellency would inform me that you deemed it necessary in your administration of the executive department of government, to know with precision what had been done by me on the subject alluded to in my administration of the judiciary department, I would transmit you a correct copy of the charge.

Having received no such information from your excellency, and having perceived in your excellency's speech to the legislature, a general reference to the subject of libels, and having also perceived in the newspaper account of the proceedings of the house, that a committee had been raised upon this subject, I was advised again to consider that all your excellency's views were in

the way of being answered, and that there was
no occasion for any information from me.

On January 31, however, I was surprised by
another communication from the secretary of state,
authorized by your excellency as he states, expressing your excellency's desire to see the letter
which was first received by me upon this subject,
and although I was unable to discern any motive
for the request, I forwarded a copy of it to the
secretary, which I presume has been laid before
your excellency.

I am now distinctly informed by a direct communication from your excellency, that the information wanted from me is for the purpose of pre-
dicating upon it some further communication to
the legislature, but whether with a view to effect
the general object of an alteration of the law, or
to inculpate me for any supposed error in my
charge to the grand jury, is still left for me to
conjecture.

If the former be the object, it is only necessary
for your excellency to be apprised of what the
law now is, which if not sufficiently explained in
the case decided by the whole court before alluded to, I shall be ready, as will my brethren,
(pursuant to a provision of the constitution,) to
assist your excellency in forming a definite opinion
upon.   My charge was intended to explain to the
grand jury, the law upon the subject of libels, as
existing according to the principles of the com-

mon law, and the decisions of the judiciary under the constitution. I presume it contains nothing beyond this intention; and if it does, it would be an unsafe basis to predicate a charge upon, because then it would be no evidence of the law as it now exists.

The principle adopted by the court, in the case referred to, naturally and necessarily flows from the nature of our government, and from our constitution. The same clause in the constitution which adopts the common law, rejects any part of it which may contravene the principles of the constitution, and although the legislature has an undoubted right to repeal the common law by express statute, yet until they shall have exercised that right, the courts of law are bound by their oaths to refuse operation to any principle of the common law, whenever such principle shall be found repugnant to the rights and liberties secured by the constitution. But it is a most remarkable fact in the history of a free people, that complaints should be heard against a doctrine so essential to liberty in an elective government; and that a departure from the common law (established principally under a monarchical government,) which departure is in favour of truth and freedom of enquiry, should be questioned in a country where the people are sovereign and all public officers are agents of the people.

If however the object of your excellency is to obtain from me facts whereon to predicate a charge against me, for any incorrect opinion delivered by me to the public through the grand jury of this county, your excellency must be sensible that I might avail myself of the common right of all persons accused to withhold any information which may tend to support charges made against themselves, and would therefore, on this supposition, readily excuse me for not complying with your request.

If the house of representatives, the grand inquest of the commonwealth, shall see fit to institute an enquiry into any of my judicial acts, I shall most cheerfully and unreservedly answer any question and acknowledge any act necessary to their investigation.

But I deem it to be my solemn duty to the public, and to such as may hereafter occupy my place, to protect, as far as in me lies, the independence of the department to which I belong, and never by any act of mine, to acquiesce in a claim of the executive to arraign the conduct or the motives of the judiciary, in a manner not authorised by the constitution.

In so conducting, I shall maintain the constitution which we are all sworn to support, shall promote the interest of the people for whose happiness it was made, and shall render the character of a judge in some measure, what the constitution declares it ought to be, " as independent as the lot of humanity will admit."

Upon these principles I should have been originally justified in declining to submit my charge to your excellency's scrutiny. But on recurring to the conditional engagement I made to your excellency, and being now informed that your excellency deems it officially necessary, I should were it in my power immediately transmit your excellency a copy. Upon enquiry I have learned that the manuscript was delivered over by one of the grand jury to the editor of the newspaper called the Patriot, with whom I suppose it still remains, having never seen it since it was delivered to the jury; and not having any copy of it, I enclose an order, by which I suppose it may be obtained, if your excellency thinks it important to have it. If I should have been mistaken in ascribing views and intentions which do not exist, (which the peculiar state of the times may have caused me to do,) your excellency I hope will pardon this interruption to your important labours.

I have the honour to be with respect,

Your excellency's obedient servant,

ISAAC PARKER.

The Editor or Printer of the Patriot

Will please to deliver to the order of his excellency governour Gerry, the manuscript from which a charge delivered by me to the grand jury, was printed.   ISAAC PARKER.

Boston, 11*th Feb.* 1812.

Messrs. Munroe & French,

The governour wishes to have the original here-in alluded to, as soon as convenient.   Your's,

BENJAMIN HOMANS.

17th Feb. 1812.

————

Mr. Farley, who handed to us the charge, ob-served that it would be called for the next day. We laid it aside and carefully preserved it for sev-eral days.   It not being called for, we neglected any further care of it, and an observation of Mr. Farley some days after, that " it was printed cor-rectly," inducing a belief that it would never be wanted, it has been mislaid, and we are sorry to say, is possibly destroyed.

Respectfully,

MUNROE & FRENCH.

————

GOVERNOUR GERRY TO JUDGE PARKER.

CAMBRIDGE, MARCH 2, 1812.

SIR,—On the 7th of January last, I presented through the secretary of the commonwealth, to yourself as an honourable judge of the supreme judicial court, a respectful request for information, " whether the publication was correct, of your charge to the grand jury of Suffolk, on the subject of libels," and received the next day your answer to him, that "not having the manuscript or read the charge in the newspapers, you could not say whether it has been correctly printed or not, but that if I deemed it necessary in my administration of the executive department, to know with precision what has been done by you, on the subject alluded to, in your judicial capacity, you would as soon as business would permit, recover the manuscript, and transmit to me a fair copy of it."

On the 8th of February, I informed you by letter, that I deemed the information requested, " officially necessary," but had waited till the close of your session, " having been desirous of avoiding every measure, that may have embarrassed or incommoded you amidst your important public concerns." A day or two after, the secretary delivered me, when much occupied, a manuscript of two sheets which were not enveloped, and took from them a scrip, which perusing, I found to be your order on the editor of the Patriot for the manuscript of the charge, and concluding that the two sheets contained the charge itself, I hastily put them into a file, and did not until the 17th of February, discover that they contained your answer of the 10th to my letter of the 8th of February. Immediately after this discovery, the secretary by my desire, sent your order to the printer of the Patriot, who stated, that the manuscript containing the charge, was mislaid or destroyed.

The subsequent circumstances, immaterial in

my mind, are mentioned to relieve your's from the
uneasiness you expressed, at your having received
on the bench, my letter of the 10th of February.
This was an unavoidable accident and contrary to
my order, which directed the delivery of the letter
at your house, on the presumption that you would
receive it after the rising of the supreme judicial
court. The frequency of such errors on the part
of messengers usually renders unnecessary explanations of this kind. But this complaint, sir,
is enforced by your solemn notice, that two letters
were by my " order" sent to you by the secretary,
in the course of your arduous official engagements.
One of these letters, that of the 7th of January,
already referred to, you had mentioned as having
received at your house ; where the other was delivered, I know not, but had supposed at the same
place ; indeed it did not appear to me material, as
both letters consisted of but few lines, and the
object of the last was to obtain a copy of the first,
to ascertain whether it contained any thing offensive to yourself. On perusing it, I was happy to
find it free from such a charge. Having taken so
much of your time, sir, in explaining accidents and
matters which unexpectedly had disturbed your
mind, I now deem it to be a duty, which I owe to
the public, to you and to myself, to enclose a
printed copy, which I presume is correct, of my
message on the 27th of February last to the legislature, and to state, that it was for the purpose of

making this communication to the legislature, at an early period of its session that the information in regard to your charge was requested. I do not apprehend the supreme judicial court has intended in the exercise of its judicial functions, to interfere with those of the legislature or executive. But I perfectly agree with you, sir, " that it is my duty to resist an unintentional encroachment, although the act which constitutes it, may not in the apprehension of that court, have the character which seems to me to belong to it."

It was surprising to me to learn by your letter, " that you was led to believe some object of a personal nature, toward yourself was in my contemplation," conscious as I was of never having expressed a sentiment or opinion in regard to yourself which could have authorised that belief, or that had not made a very favourable impression. It was impossible then for me to conceive what other reasons could exist in your mind for such a belief, or for supposing me capable of attempting to draw from you information, to criminate yourself. No part of my conduct, I trust, could warrant such a suspicion.

What has been stated, sir, I presume is sufficient to show, that altercation on my request in regard to your charge was unnecessary; that you was at liberty to comply or not with that request; and that it resulted from a sense of official duty.

I regret, sir, that " the peculiar state of the

times may have caused you to ascribe to me views and intentions," which did not, and could not exist, and the more so, as in the case of your refusal to admit John Shirley Williams, Esq. commissioned by me (and duly qualified) as a clerk of the judicial courts of the county of Norfolk, your conduct was not considered as an opposition to law, or to the executive authority; but was viewed and treated by me as an inadvertence on the part of the supreme judicial court, too minute to make any serious impression.

My desire and intention are to support the dignity and authority of the judicial, as well as of the other departments of government.

I have the honour to be, sir, respectfully

Your obedient servant,

E. GERRY.

Hon. Isaac Parker,
    An associate Justice of the Supreme Judicial Court.

———

Before the close of the legislature the governour made a communication on the subject of libels and the charge of the justice of the supreme court in connexion therewith. In this message he remarks:

" The honourable judge Parker in his charge, states that a more important variance (than had been by him mentioned) from the strict common law principles relating to libels, has lately been adopted here as resulting *from the nature of our government* and the express provisions of our constitution; this is that in trials of indictment for libels upon persons holding offices, which depend upon an election by the people or permitting themselves to be candidates for such offices, the accused is permitted to give the truth in evidence. The judges have not confined themselves in their variance from the common law, as it is conceived they ought to have done, to the express provisions of our constitution, but have taken an indefinite rule for their conduct, namely, " the nature of our government." They have also implied if not expressed that in the support of libels upon judges and executive officers not elected by the people, the truth is not to be given in evidence; but their reasons for these positions are not stated. " If a bad man is at any time held up for the office of governour, senator or representative," it may be desirable, as judge Parker states, " to let the people know, through the medium of the press, that they cannot elect such a man without disgracing or ruining themselves." And is it not equally true that if there are in office bad judges, they ought to be placed precisely on the same ground, that their mal-practices being publicly exposed, may meet prompt investigation and produce their removal and punishment? Can it be denied that as great a proportion of judges as of other public functionaries, in all countries and ages, have been bad men, although by their professional address they may have been more successful in escaping punishment; and if the conduct of a judge is to be exempt from the press, may not the judicial department by the power, which they are now exercising, and by the doctrines, which are and may be promulgated by them, establish an unconstitutional and dangerous influence in the state."

" If the judicial department of the state should at any time consist of bad men, who are desirous to oppose and overthrow the national and state governments, or either of them ; to favour or frown on individuals according to their political opinions ; to punish one individual severely and another lightly for the same offence ; to protect the guilty and punish the innocent, or to commit under the garb of justice any other atrocities, ought not such mal-practices to be exposed by the press in order to procure the removal of every such offender from office, as well as the misconduct of individuals who are in, or may be candidates for offices, to prevent their election by the people."

These pregnant intimations were communicated to the legislature at too late a period of the session to be very thoroughly and extensively understood, and the change of administration prevented any further proceedings.

There were men in the confidence of the governour, who would have been willing and able to have prevented any very serious attack on the judicial functionaries, though they might have been contented to alarm the possessors of that delicate power with the apprehension that it was not in future to be used, if ever in past time it had been, with partiality or favour.

The matter, however, already disclosed had too distinctive a character not to intimidate those, whose *esprit du corps* attached them to the judiciary establishment, and added another phalanx to the party, who would be desirous of changing the administration of the state.

The war between Great Britain and the United States, which was not declared by congress until 17th June 1812, was already seen to be in progress. Indications of the approaching storm had been clearly discernible from the proceedings of the national councils.   To all the local concerns, which have been enumerated, and to numerous others of high excitement at the moment, which swell the history of party contest in Massachusetts, was added the connexion between the government of the nation and the interest of the commonwealth.   Federalists were a peace party.   War with England was, by their code of national honour, unjust and unnatural.   Those lofty sentiments of pride, those chivalrous feelings which at a former period sounded boldly and gallantly at the prospect of hostility, if they had not subsided, were silenced, and gave place to grave questions of prudence and close calculations of economy.   The

governour belonged to the war council. To the
measures of the national administration he gave
his most cordial approbation, and disregarding his
own personal popularity or interest, made the
whole object of his efforts to consist in giving to
the general government all the aid that could in
any way be derived from the wealth, the power
and concurrence of the state. In his address to
the legislature, on their assembling in January, he
had discussed the various subjects of controversy
existing between the United States and foreign
governments, insisting on the correctness of our
own conduct, the impossibility of any other, consistently with self-respect or public interest, and
on the duty of our citizens of every party to gather
round the standard, which the government had
raised. With a boldness suited rather to his own
character than to the policy of the times, he imputed in plain terms a deficiency of patriotism and a
defect of public spirit to whomsoever, in the approaching contest, should hesitate to strengthen
the arm of his country. Coming directly to the
point at which all the arrangements of the government tended, though they had not then been
announced, he says : " If Great Britain had been
wise and just, a war with her would be contrary to
the mutual interests of both nations. Under existing circumstances it will be a wonderful event to
be explained only by her political blindness or
obstinate injustice. Will it not accelerate her

own destruction? This, which is in her power to prevent, is not the object of the United States. They would deeply regret it. But their existence as an independent nation depends on their maintaining their rights or repelling a further invasion of them and obtaining justice for past injuries. In support of the dignified and energetic conduct of our national government, will not the citizens of this state be *ardent*, to pledge *their property, their lives*, and *their sacred honour?* The present state of our country, the spirit of the nation, the union of her citizens, her ability (in her zenith) to enforce her rights, the hazard on the part of *Great Britain* of refusing justice ; all conspire to confirm the policy of decision and vigour, by the United States, and the individual states.—If at this momentous crisis the nation should cease to *respect herself*, and shrink from the indispensable duty of *self-preservation*, shall we not be urged soon by the advocates of vassalage to supplicate his Britannic majesty to admit us again into his royal favour as penitent subjects, to grant us his kind protection, and to cheer us with his paternal smiles, and above all, to recommend us to the patronage of his faithful royalists in these his dutiful provinces ?"

In the contest, which the governour's personal and official influence was incessantly exerted to accelerate, the power of the enemy, which it suited the policy of the opposition to enlarge, did not alarm him. He felt a confidence in the resources of the country and spirit of the citizens, which on every occasion he earnestly endeavoured extensively to inspire and diffuse. The evidence among other measures is in the communication of the following message to the general court, on 21st January 1812.

> *Gentlemen of the Senate, and*
> *Gentlemen of the House of Representatives.*

It being officially announced that the Indians complain " they cannot receive the usual supplies of goods, by reason of the nonimportation act, and that they are not to be purchased within the United States," I submit to your consideration whether it is not incumbent on this state to use the means in its power for enabling the national government to rise superior to such an humiliating circumstance.

In the year 1775, when our war with Great Britain commenced, and when immediately preceding it a nonimportation act had been strictly carried into effect, the state of Massachusetts apportioned on their towns respectively to be manufactured by them, the articles of clothing wanted for their proportion of the army, which besieged Boston, and fixed the prices and qualities of those articles, and they were duly supplied within a short period. Thus before we had arrived at the threshold of independence, and when we were in an exhausted state by the antecedent voluntary and patriotic sacrifice of our commerce, between thirteen and fourteen thousand cloth coats were manufactured, made and delivered into our magazine within a few months from the date of the resolve, which first communicated the requisition.

Thirty-six years have since elapsed, during twenty-nine of which we have enjoyed peace and prosperity, and have increased in numbers, manufactures, wealth, and resources beyond the most sanguine expectations.

All branches of this government have declared their opinion, and I conceive on the most solid principles, that as a nation we are independent of every other for the necessaries, conveniences, and for many of the luxuries of life. Let us not then at this critical period admit any obstruction, which we have power to remove, to discourage or retard the national exertions for asserting and maintaining our rights ; and above all let us convince Great Britain that we can and will be independent of her for every article of commerce, whilst she continues to be the ostensible friend but implacable foe of our prosperity, government, union and independence.

By calling on the inhabitants of this state and offering them reasonable prices, there exists no doubt in my mind of our ability to supply every article of clothing, which may be wanted for our proportion of troops, that may be wanted to carry on a defensive or most vigorous offensive war, and at the same time every article that may be wanted by the Indians.

But if this should appear in any degree a doubtful point, cannot the wealthy and manufacturing states of Massachusetts, New-York and Pennsylvania, and those north of the latter, effect the object?

The question requires not a moment to give a prompt affirmative answer.

The legislature then having a thorough knowledge of the resources of this commonwealth, of her ability and her disposition to draw them forth on such an important occasion, leave nothing necessary to be added on this subject.

E. GERRY.

Council Chamber, Jan. 21, 1812.

———

It was not by words merely that the governour proved the strength of his attachment to the policy of the national cabinet. On 10th of April congress passed an act " authorizing the president of the United States to require the executives of the several states and territories to take effectual measures to organize, arm and equip according to law, and hold in readiness to march at a moment's warning, their proportion of one hundred thousand militia, officers included." The requisition was made by the president on Massachusetts, for ten thousand men, as the quota of that state, and the general orders of the governour and commander in chief were issued on the 25th of the same month, containing the entire details of the service; so promptly did he deem it necessary to meet the exigency of the case. Nice questions of political casuistry, as to the relative rights of the state or the nation over the citizen soldier of the country, had not been invented to disturb the harmony of the people, and surely if they had arisen they would have been treated like the fancies of an unsound mind. Under his administration the force of the state would have been willingly and even earnestly displayed, in whatever position it could render the most effectual service. "We have been," said he, in a private letter of this date, "long enough at peace; we are losing our spirit, our character, and our independence. We are degenerating into a mere nation of traders, and are forgetting the honour of our ancestors and the interest of posterity. We must be roused by some great event that may stir up the ancient patriotism of the people. Policy has kept us quiet until it ceases to be policy. Weakness and exhaustion prevented us from noble daring, and it was wise in us to temporize until we gained strength and vigour. We have now grown to manhood, and it will be shameful in the man to bear what the child might submit to without dishonour."

But there is some difficulty in raising the temper of a people long lapsed in indolence and ease to the energy or the spirit of belligerents. Preparations for war alarm them. Taxes and loans, and the personal services, and the cessation of commerce, which precede it, will always hang a dead weight on their gallantry. The task is rendered more difficult when the causes of war may be impugned, and the evils which it threatens may plausibly be charged, not on enemies abroad, but on mismanagement at home. To a war with England, and to that course of administration which now rendered it inevitable, the whole policy and feeling, and all the zeal and passion of the federal party had been steadily opposed, and now that the crisis had arrived, and before the splendours of conquest and the shouts of victory had inspired animation and roused the spirit of the community, they found it easy to enlarge the circle of their forces, and to become popular as a peace party by whatever considerations peace might be preserved.

The annual election of state officers presented a favourable opportunity to regain the power they had lost. Identifying themselves with the opposition, as the governour had identified himself with the administration of the national government, they declared that by electing federal rulers in Massachusetts, a change would be made in the national executive, that a settlement would be then made with England that would give new energies to commerce, that an unrestrained com-

merce would give activity to the pursuits of agriculture to all the mechanic arts, to the fisheries and
to all departments of industry, and that the election of federalists would deal a death blow to the
standing army, direct taxes, immense loans, dis-
gusting excises, stamp acts and other evils, which
hang like a black cloud on their devoted heads.

" If the democratic candidates are elected,
nothing on earth can prevent the continuance
for years to come of all the deprivations, distresses,
decay of business and other evils, which now
spread calamity in every quarter of the country,
and which have been hourly increasing ever since
the country has been governed by democratic
rulers."

As preparation for the coming war, an embargo
was decided upon by the committee of foreign relations in the house of representatives of the United States, and notice of the yet immature purpose
communicated by some of the Massachusetts
members of congress by express, which arrived in
Boston on the eve of the annual election. The
news was immediately sent through the state.

In an embargo there was something dishearten-
ing and discouraging. It had the misery of war
without its benefits ; the sacrifice incident to battle with no chance for the exhilaration of victory.
To the local matters herein before enumerated
and to the connexion between the executive of the
state and the nation, was now added the paralysis of

another embargo upon all enterprise and exertion. These circumstances of the election called out a larger vote than had ever before been given in the commonwealth, and resulted in the success of the federal candidate by a majority of 1370, out of 104156 votes.

The immense difference between the policy of him who had been removed, and of him who had been placed in the chair, had not been overstated by the friends of the successful chief magistrate. The former had scarcely been settled again as a private citizen on his farm, before the war, which had so long been apprehended, was declared in form by the constitutional act of the lawful authority. Had he continued in office, he would have reechoed the declaration in the enlivening tones of patriotism and pride, inciting the people of his state by bold and vigorous exertions to crown the conflict with honour, and animating their courage by reciting the example of their ancestors, displaying the responsibility they held to the country, and urging them to make their own names as famous in future annals as were those who fell at Bunker Hill or conquered on the plains of Monmouth.

His successor was pleased to announce it in a manner characteristic of the new party in power. He ordained a day of public fasting, humiliation and prayer, because of the great calamity of being engaged in war against " a nation from which we

are descended, and which for many generations
has been the bulwark of the religion we profess;"
He exhorted the people " to ascribe righteousness
to our Maker when he threatens us with the most
severe of all temporal calamities, and to beseech
him to avert the tokens of his anger and to remember us with his former loving kindness and tender
mercy;" and " that the inhabitants of this state
may be the objects of his peculiar favour, that he
would take them under his holy protection, and
hide them in his pavilion until these dangers be
past; that the chastisements with which he may
think proper to afflict us may serve to humble us
and do us good, and that we may not be like those
who are hardened by his corrections, and who in
the time of their trouble multiply their transgres-
sions against him."

The policy of the ex-governour of Massachusetts would have elevated the spirits and animated
the confidence and cherished the hopes and nerv-
ed the courage of his countrymen. If he had
called them round their domestic altars, it would
have been for thanksgiving and not to fast; he
would have called them there not in humiliation
that calamity had fallen upon them, but in gratitude that they possessed the pride of freemen and
the resolution to maintain their liberties; he would
not have begged to hide them from danger, but
advancing at the first signal of an enemy, asked
of the God of armies " *to teach their hands to war
and their fingers to fight.*"

Little effort is necessary to create terror and alarm. Dangers that are unseen may be made to terrify the imagination with illimitable horror. The cry of *sauve qui peut* once raised, confusion and dismay will overwhelm those who raise it.

The desponding and affrighted tone of this first proclamation of the Massachusetts executive, the deplorable and abasing sentiment with which in an act of religious service, purified from all political design, the whole people of the commonwealth were directed to unite as if they were expecting the dissolution of the globe, and the day of final retribution, had its effect in restraining the generous and gallant and lofty spirit of a high minded and patriotic people, so that aided by other measures of the peace party their majority, which in the contest with governour Gerry scarcely exceeded thirteen hundred voters, amounted at the election of electors in November to 24023.

CHAPTER XI.

THE loss of the chief magistracy of Massachusetts was amply compensated to the ex-governour
by the vice-presidency of the United States. The
republican party through the country had beheld
with the highest satisfaction the steadiness of his
attachment to their principles, the fearlessness
with which he had advanced them where they
were least popular, and the aid, which his character as a distinguished actor in the war that acquired independence, would give to the contest which
in their opinion would secure it.

At a meeting held by the members of congress
of that party, on the 8th June 1812, at Washington, he was proposed by nearly an unanimous
vote* for the suffrages of the electoral colleges,
and on the first Wednesday of December of that
year, was elected vice-president of the United
States.†   It was not possible to have imagined a

* More exactly 74 to 3.

† This election was entirely on party grounds throughout the
United States, excepting only that Mr. Gerry received one vote

more splendid reward for the aid he had given to the political principles of his party.

To his friends in Massachusetts the nomination was particularly pleasing, and the result of the election was received with great exultation and delight.

They felt the compliment thus paid to their exertions under circumstances calculated greatly to depress them; and the honour reflected on themselves added new zeal to their efforts in support of the national administration. " The republican members of the senate and house of representatives of Massachusetts and other citizens," assembled in Boston, presented to the vice-president elect an address of congratulation, in the most respectful and affectionate terms, in which they thank him for the open avowal of his attachment to the national and state constitutions, while he exercised the office of chief magistracy of the commonwealth, and felicitate themselves on the evidence of the cordiality of their southern fellow citizens, " in selecting a character so fully comprising the essential qualities of a republican, and so adequate to maintaining the great principles of the revolution in their original purity."

The answer of the vice-president acknowledges the kindness of his friends in Massachusetts, and

in New-Hampshire and two votes in Massachusetts, which were withheld from Mr. Madison. One of these was given by his old friend in the revolution, general Heath.

his sensibility to this high proof of the confidence of the country.

Indeed this election seemed to him as an appeal from the decree of the state to the tribunal of the nation, a reversal by their authority of an unjust decision, and the consequent restoration of his character to its former elevation.

Since the peace of 1783, he had reluctantly engaged in public life. Every situation he had occupied was a sacrifice of his own inclinations to the calls of his country ; but in the present honourable distinction he felt the highest sensations of gratified ambition ; and cheerfully assumed the duties of a station, which in addition to its inherent dignity, had the cheering appearance of a reward for past labours of patriotism, and a compensation for the consequences of political fidelity.

A statesman, if there be one, who always sails with the breeze of popularity, knows not the keenest delights of his eminent profession. The most exquisite enjoyment of a servant of the people is at the moment when they make their acknowledgement for sacrifices submitted to in their service, and recall him to new and greater honours, more generous confidence and more conspicuous station. It is then that the pursuits of civil life have the animation and excitement of military glory. In the cabinet and the field, men are equally exposed to misfortune, but a gallant spirit lightly feels a wound, which is repaid by the consolation and applause of his country.

On the 4th of March 1813, the oaths of office were administered to the vice-president at his residence in Cambridge, Massachusetts, by the judge of the district court of the United States, and on 24th May succeeding, at a special session of congress, he took his seat as president of the senate.*

On this occasion he addressed that body in a speech, unusual indeed, if regard be had to precedent, but consistent enough with the natural frankness of his character and the earnestness with which he was ever ready to bring all the resources of his mind and all the influence of his station to the aid of his political principles.

Instead of the few complimentary phrases which usually serve the ceremony of introduction, the vice-president entered into somewhat of a formal review of the state of the country, bestowing a panegyric on the exalted personage who filled the supreme executive, not disguising a reproof of any who would distract the unity of the public councils; and exciting a spirit that should " meet with ardour an indispensable war."

* On his journey to Washington an incident occurred, which serves to show the natural amenity of Mr. Gerry's disposition. He and colonel Pickering were in the same stage coach. Arriving late at Hartford, Connecticut, the house afforded but one unoccupied bed, which was of course assigned to the vice-president, while his fellow passengers were destined to pass the night on a table or chair. He could not permit a person of the colonel's age to be thus incommoded, but offered him the half the accommodation appropriated to himself, which was gladly accepted; and the old gentlemen passed the night in the same bed as quietly as if they had always been personal friends.

" The United States," he says, " are now the enemy of Great Britain. And is it not easy to foresee that if the war should continue, the Canadas will be rendered independent of her, and as friends or allies of the United States, will no longer be instrumental in exciting an unrelenting and savage warfare against our extensive and defenceless borders ? To such inhuman acts in former times were the Canadians urged by France in her Albion wars ; and by our colonial aid Great Britain obtained jurisdiction over them. She in turn has abused this power and has justified the United States in their efforts to divest her of it. And is not their energy adequate to the object ?

" Will not this be evident by a view of their effective national and state governments ; of their great and increasing resources ; of the unconquered minds and formidable numbers of their citizens ; of their martial spirit ; of their innate attachment to their rights and liberties, and of their inflexible determination to preserve them ?

" But if any one still doubts, will he not recollect that at the commencement of our revolutionary war the united colonies had not a third of their present population, nor arms, nor military stores for a single campaign ; nor specie in their treasury, nor funds for emitting a paper currency, nor a national government, nor (excepting in two instances) state governments, nor the knowledge of naval or military tactics. Will he not also remember that Great Britain was then in the zenith of her power, that neighbouring nations trembled at her nod, that the colonies were under her control; that her crown officers opposed every mean of resisting her, excited among the colonial governments over which they presided unfounded jealousies of each other, and embarrassed every measure of their union; that she was loaded with less than a fifth of her present national debt, that she was at peace with all the world, and that she is now at war with a great part of Europe as well as with the United States. If Great Britain herself reflects on these things may we not hope she will relinquish a vain attempt to awe the citizens of the United States by exaggerated statements of her military and naval power, by delusive views of our unprepared state for war, of the great expense of it, and of the difficulties we are to encounter in defence of all that is valuable to men? If instead of fruitless artifices she will make rational and equitable arrangements, which the government of the United States have always been ready to meet, the two nations will be speedily restored to their wonted friendship and commerce."

The station of the vice-president is that which may enable an ambitious man most adroitly to conciliate the public favour. Called to express no opinion unless by a concurrence of circumstances, which places him in the majority, the odium of unpopular measures may always be avoided, and the credit of those, which are successful, easily secured. But no such cautious and calculating prudence marked the conduct of Mr. Gerry. There was no desire on his part to play the double game, which might win the favour of his adversaries by sometimes leaving the cause of his friends. He deemed the duty imposed upon him by the favour of his fellow citizens to consist in using all the influence of his office, not in advancing his own personal comfort, but in boldly, strenuously and invariably aiding the policy of the administration, and in making all his efforts subsidiary to the advancement of the great cause, in which they were engaged.

The situation of the United States, when the vice-president took the chair of the senate, was indeed critical. War had been declared with Great Britain, and time enough had elapsed to bring home to the knowledge of the people the condition and consequences of their novel situation. During that period an election of national and state officers had been made, and the popularity of the administration policy been put to severe test. The result was a strong support of the party in power. In the electoral colleges the president had received 128 out 217 votes. There was a majority in the house of representatives and in the senate on the same side.

In the national government therefore the dominant party might look down opposition.

In most of the southern and western states the same sentiment prevailed. In New England however the opposition had an overwhelming force, the direction of which was assumed by Massachusetts. This division of parties by geographical lines, augured ill for the stability of a government, whose principal of vitality was yet the subject of experiment.

The course of the opposite opinions of the two parties is well illustrated in the message of the president of the United States, and the remonstrance of the Massachusetts legislature.

The president says, " The contest in which the United States are engaged, appeals for its support to every motive that can animate an uncorrupted and enlightened people, to the pride of liberty, to an emulation of the glorious founders of their independence by a successful vindication of its violated attributes, to the gratitude and sympathy which demand security from the most degrading wrongs of a class of citizens, who have proved themselves so worthy of the protection of their country by their heroic zeal in its defence, and finally to the sacred obligations of transmitting entire to future generations that precious patrimony of national rights and independence, which is held in trust by the present from the goodness of divine providence."

The remonstrants, after declaring and urging their reasons in proof that the " contest" was im-

proper, impolitic and unjust, add, " To the constituted authorities of our country we have now
stated our opinions and made known our complaints; opinions, the result of deliberate reflection, and complaints wrung from us by the tor-
tures of that cruel policy, which has brought the
good people of this commonwealth to the verge
of ruin. A policy, which has annihilated that
commerce so essential to their prosperity, increased their burthens while it has diminished their
means of support, provided for the establishment
of an immense standing army, dangerous to their
liberties and irreconcilable with the genius of their
constitution; destroyed their just and constitutional weight in the general government, and by
involving them in a disastrous war, placed in the
power of the enemy the control of the fisheries,
a treasure of more value to the country than all
the territories for which we are contending, and
which furnish the only means of subsistence to
thousands of our citizens; the great nursery of
our seamen, and the right to which can never be
abandoned by New England."

The contending parties in the country had gone
too far in mutual crimination to veil even under
the forms of courtesy their conviction, real or pretended, of the motives and objects by which they
were severally actuated. Each claimed for its
self the purest patriotism and the highest intel-

ligence; and each accused the other of premeditated treason, and private aggrandizement.

The causes of the war, say the legislature of Massachusetts, and more particularly the pretences for its continuance, " fill the minds of the good people of this commonwealth with infinite anxiety and alarm," and the government of the United States is charged in regard to the information by them given " with a suppression too serious to be overlooked or forgiven,"—" ambition and not justice, a lust of conquest and not a defence of endangered rights are among the real causes of perseverance in our present hostilities," and with the qualification made by an hypothetical form of expression, they charge that the war in which they have been rashly plunged, was undertaken to appease the resentment, or secure the favour of France.

By the administration these denunciations were declared to be the wiles of a faction, eager to regain the power it had lost, feigning a fear that it did not feel, and ready to spring into the arms of England, if her friendship would restore them to their past authority. They asserted further, that the repeated declarations that the eastern states had lost their just weight in the confederacy; that the provisions of the constitution had failed to secure the objects for which it was adopted; and that a power, adverse to their interest had arisen in the formation of new states, were not merely calculated, but intended to prepare for a division, and the establishment of a more favourable condition of things, a separate peace and alliance with the public enemy.

These offensive imputations mutually cast with reckless prodigality, by opposing parties, were eagerly caught by the enemy, equally ready and interested to have all of them prove true; though nothing but the exasperation of political feeling could have induced any one to suppose they were merited by those to whom they were applied, or believed by those who applied them.

But the course of an opposition, which *flagrante bello*, could thus weaken the only means that might bring the war to a favourable termination, is certainly a matter of surprise. The vice-president was of the party who believed his country to be right, and who wished it to be successful wrong or right, and with this view he lent the whole influence of his character and station to support the executive department in the senate and before the people.

If the advantage of a strenuous cooperation by the second officer of the nation, is in proportion to the embarrassment resulting from an adverse movement, the administration had great reason to be satisfied with the selection they had made.

During every day of the first special session of the thirteenth congress, which continued until the 2d of August, the vice-president presided in the senate; and he kept the chair until its actual adjournment.

In this there was a departure from the usage of that body.

In case of the decease or other inability of the president and vice-president of the United States, the constitution has provided that congress may by law designate what officer shall act as president, until the disability be removed, or a president be elected. And in pursuance of that power, congress has devolved that contingent but possible rank on the acting president of the senate, and if there be none, on the speaker of the house of representatives.

To place this reversionary right in some member of the senate, it had been and yet is usual for the vice-president of the United States to retire before the close of a session, that a president pro tempore may be selected by that branch of the legislature, who, in the course of events, might in preference to the speaker of the house of representatives be called to the executive office.

But notwithstanding the administration was strong in the senate, the choice of a president pro tempore might, as the vice-president apprehended, devolve on an individual not invariably found among their friends, and he therefore preferred keeping his seat until the end of the session.

The vice-president of the United States is not

a member of the executive cabinet. The constitution indeed in its theory knows no such organization; but convenience, necessity, and at last
custom established one, which is consulted on
great questions by the executive chief; who while
he listens to its advice is yet governed by his
own judgment, and responsible for the measures
of his administration. This cabinet consists of
the secretaries of departments, and the attorney
general of the United States.

The first vice-president considered his exclusion
as a want of proper respect; the second regarded
it as a necessary incident of his legislative character, which could neither require nor permit him to
mingle in executive deliberations.

Mr. Gerry was not called to the regular meetings of the cabinet, but his advice and council
were solicited, and most confidentially and freely
given to the distinguished statesman on whom
then devolved a weight of responsibility, and an
anxiety of mind greater than at any other period
crowded the chief magistrate of the nation.

The opposition in the eastern states to all
the measures of the national administration, the
strength with which this opposition bore upon
every effort for a vigorous prosecution of the war ;
the obstacles it presented to the raising of supplies,
either of money or men ; and more than all, doubts
and apprehensions as to the extent of an understanding, which its leaders were suspected of main-

taining with the public enemy, were calculated to disturb the government, and render most unhappy the public functionaries, whom the majority of their fellow citizens expected fearlessly to meet the responsibility of the times.

The long embargo, which preceded the war of 1812, had been changed into a system of nonintercourse, partly on the persuasion confidentially inculcated by a distinguished citizen of Massachusetts, that the former measure would be resisted by force.

The intercourse of a British political missionary with the leaders of the federal party in New England had been watched with the same jealous but futile expectation that it would present a developement of unlawful designs, and the subsequent more alarming because more practicable evils put in the way of a claim for the military aid of New England was naturally enough assigned to the same anti-patriotic propensities.

Ardent as were the feelings, and strong as have been seen to be the political and party attachments of the vice-president, he had learned better and judged more truly the sentiments of his countrymen. Accused as he has been of strong antipathies, and prejudice and animosity to the party, which had opposed his own administration of the state government by every measure of personal and public hostility, he yet was able to examine more candidly, and was willing to express more favourably his construction of their conduct.

In the many and anxious deliberations of the cabinet as to the measures of New England policy, and the extent of the opposition of the federal leaders to the government of the United States, it was known that the vice-president had entirely acquitted them of all traitorous design. He believed, and he did not hesitate to express his conviction, that all their efforts, unwise and ill timed, and dangerous and unfortunate as he considered them to be, were the efforts of a party to regain political power, and not indications of hostility to the government, or a desire either to calculate the value of the union or to place any part of it within the domination of Great Britain. The effect of this persuasion, and the willingness with which the vice-president announced it, had its proper weight in softening some of the measures, which to a party believed to be in hostility to the government and constitution of the country, the administrators of that government under the constitution might have been bound to display.

Condescension might however, as he thought, be carried too far, and he felt obliged on one occasion at least to restrain it.

The exceeding embarrassment which the national administration experienced by the construction which the governour of Massachusetts, encouraged by the official opinion of the judiciary of his state, put on the relative power of the state and the nation over the militia of a state, induced the executive of the United States to try every possible measure to change it.

As a plan that might reconcile conflicting opinions, it was proposed that the governour of Massachusetts should be commissioned a major-general in the army of the United States; and it was supposed therefore, that while in the former capacity he could call out the militia of his state, he would be bound in the other to obey the national executive. The good effect of such a plan had been experienced, particularly in New-York. The decided opposition it met with from the vice-president induced the government to give up the scheme in Massachusetts.

Among the most fatiguing labours that devolved on the vice-president of the United States, was the necessity of attending to a vast mass of correspondence, which overwhelmed him from all parts of the country.

The right of a private citizen to address the public functionaries may not be disputed; but when that right is exercised in its extreme, the inability of the public agents to encounter it admits not of doubt. In those offices where clerks are employed, a great part of this labour may devolve on them, but the vice-president has neither clerk nor secretary, and the reading even without answering the numberless epistles of his fellow citizens, was enough to break down a constitution of iron.

Probably at that period there was more imposition in this respect than at other times. The war gave rise to numerous classes of office, and to local interests of great extent and variety. It seemed to be taken for granted, by each individual applicant for notice, that if he could get the vice-president's recommendation he was sure of success, and to be forgotten that every other citizen had the same right with himself.

Until the extent of this evil became so great that it was physically impossible to meet it, the courtesy of the vice-president extended to the answering of his numerous correspondents ; and when this labour became impossible, it was often his misfortune to find that the omission was cause of offence.

The vice-president continued to give his strenuous support to the administration, and his aid to a vigorous conducting of the war during the second session of the thirteenth congress. In the new situation in which he was placed his former acquaintance with the financial affairs of the country, and the experience he had in the congress of the revolution and that of the early period of the existing government was of advantage to himself and his associates. As *ex officio* a commissioner of the sinking fund, and presiding at that board, the duties of the vice-president, though secluded in a great measure from the public eye, are not of the less importance or value. Amid all the pressure of the war, with all the embarrassments, which attended the procuring of the means for its energetic prosecution, and the raising by successive loans the ample funds, which it required, the policy of the administration never lost sight of the grand object of repayment, or failed to see through the dark clouds, which hung around them, that bright star of promise, which foretold the future greatness of their country. The debt, which it was necessary to incur, they did not hesitate fearlessly to contract; but at the same time the funds, which were afterwards to discharge it, they were equally solicitous to preserve. Hence in all their laws for a loan, provision is made for a sinking fund, and the administration of this fund under commissioners was carefully secured by the vice-president's concurrence.

He had taken his seat in the senate, at the third session, and presided during the whole of a long debate on the 22d of November 1814, with his usual spirit, and in the enjoyment of accustomed health. On returning to his lodgings he complained of slight indisposition, but amused himself through the evening in arranging the letters of the day, and in a cheerful conversation with the inmates of the house.

There has been thought to be sometimes a premonition of approaching dissolution, even when the corporeal frame discloses no appearance of the crisis. Mr. Gerry's discourse was of his family in

Massachusetts ; and taking from his bosom a miniature, which was always suspended round his neck when the original was absent, and had hitherto, with a peculiar delicacy of feeling, been his own personal secret, he spoke of it with an interest which show that although the surpassing beauty delineated in the picture might have first charmed the imagination, more enduring qualities had left the impress of affection on his heart.*

He rested well through the night, and breakfasted as usual with the family on the morning of the 23d, and although he spoke of some vague indications of disease, he did not consider them sufficient to prevent his taking his seat in the senate, at the hour to which that body was adjourned. The carriage coming to carry him to the capital rather earlier than usual, he directed the coachman to stop on his way there at the office of the registry of the treasury, at which he had some business that required his attention. This being arranged he returned to his carriage, and had proceeded but a short distance, when a sudden extravasation of blood took place upon the lungs and terminated his life within twenty min-

* On the decease of the vice-president this miniature could not be found. Several months afterwards it was accidentally discovered by one of his family, stripped of its plain gold setting, and exposed for sale in one of the shops of the district, as a fancy piece of exquisite design. How it came there was never ascertained.

utes, almost without a struggle and apparently without pain.

On the news of his death congress appointed a committee " to report measures proper to manifes. the public respect for the memory of the deceased, and expressive of the deep regret of the congress of the United States for the loss of a citizen so highly respected and revered."

Under the charge of this committee his remains, attended the next day by the members of the executive government and both branches of the legislature, were deposited in the burying ground of the city of Washington, by the side of those illustrious men, who had died there in the service of their country.

A widow, three sons and six daughters survived him.

Like most of his eminent compatriots, Mr. Gerry left to his family his example only and his fame.

A political opponent and former rival for the chair of Massachusetts, then member of the senate from that state, with a nobleness of soul, which buries with the ashes of its enemy all feelings of animosity or revenge, recognising as a patriot the services of the departed statesman, and sympathizing as a man in the distress of an agonized family, introduced a bill " for paying to the widow of the late vice-president the salary, which would have become due, had he lived to complete his term of office."

This bill passed the senate, but was lost in the house. An objection was there taken, in which many friends of the late vice-president felt themselves reluctantly bound to concur, that it would become a precedent for the granting of pensions in the civil departments of the country.

One individual, however, was found to take other ground. Neither the services of patriotism, nor the claims of widowhood and orphanage could disarm his ancient animosity, or prevent him, over the green grave of his opponent, from assailing his memory in the same terms of vituperation, which had marked the past period of political warfare.*

But what was then wanting in kindness to the family of the vice-president was aftewards made up to them in consolation, by the respect which congress paid to his memory.

* Although the government of the United States could not directly aid the destitute family of the vice-president, they were disposed to consider their claims with great attention; and the eminent citizen, who was then the chief executive magistrate, appointed the eldest son of the deceased to a place in the collection of the revenue, that it should enable him to support the family thus unexpectedly thrown upon his charge; a duty which it is proper to say is still performed with filial assiduity, while the office bestowed for so worthy a purpose has been filled to general acceptation, and with unimpeached fidelity. The two other sons were soon after appointed to the navy of the United States, in which they continue honoured and esteemed as ornaments of their profession.

On the 3d March 1823, a law was passed to erect a monument over his tomb; an appropriation was at the same time made to defray the expense, and in the course of the summer this honourable testimonial to his character was placed over his remains.

The monument thus erected by order of congress is of pure white marble, from the native state of the eminent citizen whose ashes it protects. The pedestal is pyramidal. On the corners is a fillet, which lies in a scotia cut out of the angle. A rich and massy leaf covers each extremity of the fillet, a second leaf falls off at the bottom, spreading itself over the angle of the base mouldings. The ornaments of the frieze under the cornice, are made up of foliage modelled from nature, consisting of parsley, tulips, and amaranthus. Upon the parapet stand eight ballusters enriched with foliage supporting the soffit and blocks. The urn resembles in form a Grecian vase with a bold and elegant outline, and is enriched with various leaves, among which the oak and acanthus are most prominent. A towering flame crowns the whole.

The monument bears the following inscription :

The Tomb

OF

ELBRIDGE GERRY,

VICE-PRESIDENT

OF THE

UNITED STATES,

WHO DIED SUDDENLY IN THIS CITY,

NOVEMBER 23, 1814,

ON HIS WAY TO THE CAPITOL

AS

President of the Senate.

AGED 70 YEARS.

THUS FULFILLING

HIS OWN MEMORABLE INJUNCTION,

IT IS THE DUTY OF EVERY MAN

THOUGH HE MAY HAVE BUT ONE DAY TO LIVE

TO DEVOTE THAT DAY

TO THE GOOD OF HIS COUNTRY.

On the reverse is inscribed :

ERECTED BY ORDER

OF THE

CONGRESS

OF THE

UNITED STATES.

It has thus happened that the first, and as yet the only monument, which by virtue of a law of the United States, has been erected for a native citizen at the national expense, is placed over the earthly remains of the patriot statesman and christian, whose life is now traced to its close.

APPENDIX A.

(Page 326.)

SPEECH OF GOVERNOUR GERRY.

REIPUBLICÆ literariæ, per totam orbem, artium et scientia-
rum luminari magno, vos-ipsos amicos et fautores manifesti ;
amicissime vice-gubernator, vir honoratissime et clarissime,
consiliarii, spectatissimi fidissimique, curatores et senatores
academici, celeberrimi et generosissimi. Vir illustrissime,
nuper præses reipublicæ Americanæ, Elogio omni dignissime,
professores, tutores, et alii, functionibus academicis eruditis-
simi, pastores religiosi, semper venerandi, juventutes academiæ
carissimi, nunc spes, mox patriæ laureati, cujusque ordinis audi-
tores, literati et honorandi. Vos omnes, pariter amicus, saluto.

Hujusce diei munus est, hanc sedem consecratam supplere.
Nos monet viri præstantissimi et pii cujus mors vacuum fecit.
Amicula sua feralia lachrymis abundanter roravimus, et exe-
quias reverentiâ celebravimus. Valedecimus. Sua fama elogi-
um alte volat, et pectoribus nostris semper recordabitur.

Te, domine reverende, universitatis summi gubernatores liber-
issime supplere hanc sedem elegerunt. Virum quæsiverunt
religione, probitate, literis et honore ornatum ; atque benevo-
lentia, humanitate, affectionibusque generosissimis abundantem ;
confidenter credunt, quod hujus electionis sapientiam evinces.
Tu quasi sol coruscans, hacce systemate literata, radiis geniali-
bus suas plantas florentes fovebis, et illis novas vires præbebis,
donec fructus copiosos edent, civitates Dei Adorabilis, alere, de-
lectare et ornare.

Et nunc auctoritate munitus, trado tibi domine, et munus
est mihi jucundissimum, has vestes officiales, coronis victorum
potentium, honorabiliores, chartam, tabulas publicas, sigillum
et claves; symbola æquè ac officii testimonia. Omnibus juri-
bus, auctoritatibus, potestatibus et previligiis Præsidis Universitatis te munio. Hac sede consecrata te stabilio, et Collegii
Harvardiani Præsidem te annuncio ; quo nomine primò te ex
animo saluto. In te omnium oculi conjiciuntur. Tu eris, quasi
civitas in monte sita, conspicuus : et sic luceat vestra lux
apud hosce juvenes, ut vestra facta videntes nostrum patrem qui
est in cœlo adorent.

RESPONSUM PRÆSIDIS.

Illustrissime Domine, Gubernator.

Quantâ solicitudine meipsum hujus sellæ Academicæ dignitate ornatum sentio, verbis exsequi non possum, neque dicere oportet. Tu, domine, qui onus muneris jam suscepti recte perpendisti, bene intelligis, atque omnes qui secum cogitant quo loco sum, intellecturi, quæ curæ animum meum exercent.

Inter omnes constat quo affectu, quanto studio, quibus precibus et lachrymis hujusce societatis fundamenta posuerunt nostri majores; et quam multi, olim et nuper, opes, consilia, labores ei liberè impenderunt.

Mihi imperito, imparatoque curationem institutionis tam curæ, tam antiquæ mandatam esse video. Ita numini divino placuet.

Recte mihi indicasti domine, quod homines a me juste expectent, et verbis benignis mihi profecto animum addidisti. Dubitare non possum quin tu, Harvardiæ alumnus et semper amicus; tu, publicis, privatisque virtutibus præstans, et viros inter claros, qui libertatem Americanam ancipitem feliciter asserere cœperunt, semper nominandus; quin tu, vir excellentissime, in rebus agendis diu versatus, et nunc in summo dignitatis gradu constitutus, mihi pro merito lubenter sublevare præsto fueris; etiamque confido, cæteros in collegii rebus occupatos, quod ad illos attinet, adjumento mihi semper adfuturos.

Quod superest, deum optimum maximum domini nostri Jesu Christi Deum et Patrem veneremur, et precemur ut nobis cursum rectum ostendat, atque hunc diem tam serium quam festum, nostræ Academicæ totique reipublicæ et ecclesiæ pro benevolentiæ sua faustum atque felicem evadere sinat.

REPLICATIO GUBERNATORIS.

Restat Domine, hac solemnitate summa, nomine Gubernatorum Universitatis summorum tibi gratulari, benedictionem et gratiam divinam tibi obsecrare. In vestra æmulatione, sedulitate, et fidelitate officiali suam confidentiam exprimere; te juvare et sustinere in hoc munere honorabili, suam mentem et decisionem declarare; denique, quod juventutes harvardiani, obedientiam, affectionem, et reverentiam tibi semper manifestabunt, fide confirmare.

APPENDIX B.

(Page 343.)

BOSTON, COUNCIL CHAMBER, DECEMBER 17, 1811.

THE governour having on the 14th of August last, requested
the opinion of the council on the following points, viz. " who of
the sheriffs and clerks of the judicial courts ought to be superseded as a measure requisite to promote the public welfare ;" and
the council on the 16th of the same month, having expressed their
opinion, that the sheriffs of twelve, and the clerks of fifteen counties, named by the council should be superseded, have been silent, in regard to the sheriff and clerk of the county of Suffolk,
excepting some remarks, relative to the postponement of the
nomination of the latter. The sheriff of Suffolk, being a gentleman of amiable manners, correct morals, and in what relates to
himself of good conduct in his office, and being approved in other
respects by many persons in that county friendly to the national
and state governments, but being at the same time very obnoxious to a number of others, equally friendly to government, is
under circumstances very embarrassing to the governour. The
unpopularity of this sheriff, it is conceived arises from the same
cause as that of the sheriff of Essex ; a cause, which rendered
indispensable the preference to him of another candidate. The
governour alludes to the misconduct of some deputies of both
sheriffs ; and in particular to a deputy of Suffolk, against whom
Henry Warren, Esq. of Plymouth has exhibited the complaint,
contained in the document No. 1. In the nomination of officers,
the candidate who has appeared to unite in the greatest degree,
the approbation of the people, and who in every other respect,
has had equal pretensions, has had the preference. If in this
instance, the incumbent should be nominated, it is manifest, that
the measure would produce great uneasiness on the part of many
firm friends of government. The proceedings of these are contained in the document No. 2. Thus circumstanced the governour requests the opinion of the council, whether the nomination
and appointment of Col. Samuel Bradford, to the office of sheriff
for Suffolk, will promote the public welfare, in an equal degree
with one of the other candidates for this office ? Major Gibbs,

whose pretensions are contained in two papers, numbered 3, and Capt. Amos Binney, mentioned in the document No. 2, are candidates. The opinions on this subject of the members of the council respectively, are requested in writing.

E. GERRY.

COUNCIL CHAMBER, JANUARY 15, 1812.

His excellency the governour in a communication of the 17th of December last having requested the opinion of the council respecting the sheriff of the county of Suffolk, and in that communication having referred to a former one made the 14th of August last, in which he requested the opinion of the council, " who of the sheriffs and clerks of the judicial courts, ought to be superseded as a measure requisite to promote the public welfare :" The council in a communication made to his excellency the 16th of the same month of August, expressed their opinion that the sheriffs of twelve counties therein named ought to be superseded, and as the council understood the governour to request their opinion respecting all the sheriffs, and as it had become the duty of the executive to appoint sheriffs in all the counties, the council did intend to express their opinion respecting all of them, and to be understood to be in favour of a reappointment of all those whom they had not designated as proper to be superseded as a measure requisite to promote the public welfare. On a revision of the subject as it respects the several sheriffs the council see no sufficient cause to reverse their opinion, and agreeing with his excellency that "the sheriff of Suffolk" is "a gentleman of amiable manners, correct morals, and in what relates to himself of good conduct in his office, and being approved in other respects by many persons in that county friendly to government" are (as on the former occasion) unanimously of opinion that the public welfare does not require that he should be superseded.

WM. GRAY,	SAMUEL FOWLER,
MARSHALL SPRING,	AA. HILL,
M. KINSLEY,	THOMAS B. ADAMS.

THE END.